KB116486

TEPS

서울대 텝스 관리위원회 텝스 최신기출 1200제 2

문제집

서울대 텝스 관리위원회 텝스 최신기출 1200제 문제집 VOL. 2

문제제공 서울대학교 TEPS관리위원회
펴낸이 임상진
펴낸곳 (주)넥서스

초판 1쇄 발행 2016년 2월 10일
초판 25쇄 발행 2024년 11월 1일

출판신고 1992년 4월 3일 제311-2002-2호
10880 경기도 파주시 지목로 5
Tel (02)330-5500 Fax (02)330-5555

ISBN 979-11-5752-685-7 14740
979-11-5752-684-0 14740 (SET)

www.nexusbook.com

TEPS

서울대 텝스 관리위원회 텝스 최신기출 1200제

문제집

서울대학교 TEPS관리위원회 기출문제 제공

VOL. 2

넥서스

PREFACE

넥서스에서 정기 텝스 시험의 공식 출제 기관인 서울대 텝스 관리위원회가 제공하는 기출 문제를 독점 출간하게 되었다. 이미 최초로 TEPS 기출문제집 〈TEPS 기출 문제집〉, 〈유형별로 분석한 NEXUS 기출 800〉 등을 출간한 이후 〈서울대 텝스 관리위원회 최신기출 1000〉, 〈서울대 텝스 관리위원회 제공 최신기출 시크릿〉, 〈서울대 텝스 관리위원회 최신기출 1200 / SEASON 2, 3〉, 〈서울대 텝스 관리위원회 최신기출 Listening / Reading〉, 〈서울대 최신기출 TEPS VOCA〉, 〈서울대 텝스 관리위원회 공식 기출 1000 시리즈〉에 이르기까지 연이어 대표적인 TEPS 기출 교재로 자리매김할 수 있도록 많은 사랑과 관심을 보여준 TEPS 수험생들과 학교 및 학원에서 강의하시는 선생님들께 다시 한번 감사의 마음을 전한다. 다른 영어 능력 검정시험과 달리 많은 기출문제가 공식적으로 오픈된 TEPS 시험은 그만큼 과학적인 측정 도구와 신뢰할 수 있는 콘텐츠, 뛰어난 변별력 등 공인 영어 능력 시험으로서의 자격을 충분히 인정받았다.

TEPS 수험생들로부터 이 시험이 참으로 어렵다는 얘기를 많이 듣는다. 벼락치기가 가능할 만큼 단순한 실용 영어의 측정에 그치는 것이 아니라 그야말로 기초부터 고급까지 모든 수준의 영어를 심도 있게 측정하는 것이 바로 TEPS 시험의 목표이므로 TEPS 시험 준비에도 제대로 된 전략과 교재와 필요함은 두말할 나위가 없다. 따라서 지금까지의 출제 원리와 경향 분석을 위해서는 가장 확실한 기출 문제집을 하나 골라 반복해서 풀면서 정리하는 것이 무엇보다 중요할 것이다.

이번에 출간하는 서울대 텝스 관리위원회 최신기출 시리즈는 출제 기관이 지금까지 공개한 것 중 가장 최신의 공식 기출문제 6회분으로 구성했고, 학습자 편의를 위해 문제집과 해설집을 각각 별도로 제작했다. 또한 실제 TEPS 시험장에서 접했던 문제지와 동일한 페이지로 구성했고, 청해 방송에서 듣던 MP3 음원을 고스란히 그대로 실었다. 또한 별도의 해설집에는 마치 실제 해설 강의를 듣는 것 같이 정확하게 핵심을 짚어 주는 문제 해설로 수험생들의 만족을 높이고자 했다.

새로운 TEPS 기출문제집 출간을 위해 넥서스 TEPS연구소에서 참으로 많이도 성가시게 해 드렸는데도 그간 늘 한결같이 적극적으로 도움을 주신 서울대학교 TEPS관리위원회 관계자분들께 이 자리를 통해 감사의 마음을 전한다. 본 교재를 통해 수험생 각자의 목표가 제대로 실현되기를 진심으로 바란다.

목차

CONTENTS

서문 5

특징 8

TEPS에 대하여 10

TEPS 만점 전략 12

서울대 최신기출 • 1

Listening Comprehension 39

Grammar 43

Vocabulary 51

Reading Comprehension 59

서울대 최신기출 • 2

Listening Comprehension 77

Grammar 81

Vocabulary 89

Reading Comprehension 97

서울대 최신기출 • 3

Listening Comprehension 115

Grammar 119

Vocabulary 127

Reading Comprehension 135

서울대 최신기출 • 4
Listening Comprehension 153
Grammar 157
Vocabulary 165
Reading Comprehension 173

서울대 최신기출 • 5
Listening Comprehension 191
Grammar 195
Vocabulary 203
Reading Comprehension 211

서울대 최신기출 • 6
Listening Comprehension 229
Grammar 233
Vocabulary 241
Reading Comprehension 249

Listening Comprehension **Scripts** 266
Answer Keys 334

TEPS 등급표 340

특징

FEATURES

1 가장 최근에 공개된 공식 기출 1,200문항 독점 수록

서울대학교 TEPS관리위원회가 가장 최근에 공개한 현존 가장 최신 기출문제
1,200문항을 실제 TEPS 시험지와 동일한 페이지 구성으로 제공

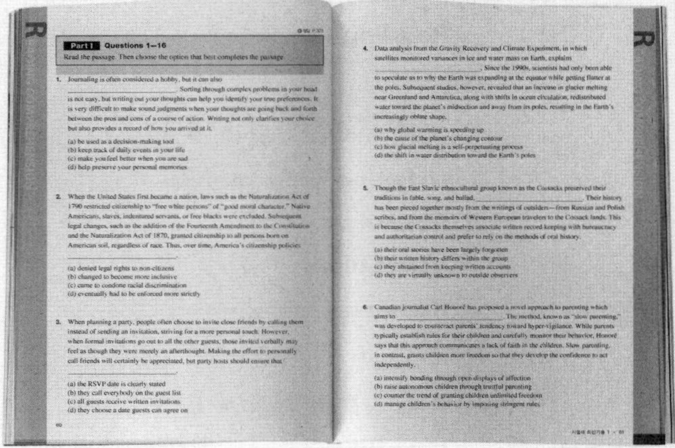

Part I Questions 1–16

Read the passage. Then choose the option that best completes the passage.

1. Journaling is often considered a hobby, but it can also ____________. Sorting through complex problems in your head is not easy, but writing out your thoughts can help you identify your true preferences. It is very difficult to make sound judgments when your thoughts are going back and forth between the pros and cons of a course of action. Writing not only clarifies your choice but also provides a record of how you arrived at it.

(a) be used as a decision-making tool
(b) keep track of daily events in your life
(c) make you feel better when you are sad
(d) help preserve your personal memories

2. When the United States first became a nation, laws such as the Naturalization Act of 1790 restricted citizenship to "free white persons" of "good moral character." Native Americans, slaves, indentured servants, or free blacks were excluded. Subsequent legal changes, such as the addition of the Fourteenth Amendment to the Constitution and the Naturalization Act of 1870, granted citizenship to all persons born on American soil, regardless of race. Thus, over time, America's citizenship policies ____________.

(a) denied legal rights to non-citizens
(b) changed to become more inclusive
(c) came to condone racial discrimination
(d) eventually had to be enforced more strictly

3. When planning a party, people often choose to invite close friends by calling them instead of sending an invitation, striving for a more personal touch. However, when formal invitations go out to all the other guests, those invited verbally may feel as though they were merely an afterthought. Making the effort to personally call friends will certainly be appreciated, but party hosts should ensure that ____________.

(a) the RSVP date is clearly stated
(b) they call everybody on the guest list
(c) all guests receive written invitations
(d) they choose a date guests can agree on

80

4. Data analysis from the Gravity Recovery and Climate Experiment, in which satellites monitored variances in ice and water mass on Earth, explains ____________. Since the 1990s, scientists had only been able to speculate as to why the Earth was expanding at the equator while getting flatter at the poles. Subsequent studies, however, revealed that an increase in glacier melting near Greenland and Antarctica, along with shifts in ocean circulation, redistributed water toward the planet's midsection and away from its poles, resulting in the Earth's increasingly oblate shape.

(a) why global warming is speeding up
(b) the cause of the planet's changing contour
(c) how glacial melting is a self-perpetuating process
(d) the shift in water distribution toward the Earth's poles

5. Though the East Slavic ethnocultural group known as the Cossacks preserved their traditions in fable, song, and ballad, ____________. Their history has been pieced together mostly from the writings of outsiders—from Russian and Polish scribes, and from the memoirs of Western European travelers to the Cossack lands. This is because the Cossacks themselves associate written record keeping with bureaucracy and authoritarian control and prefer to rely on the methods of oral history.

(a) their oral stories have been largely forgotten
(b) their written history differs within the group
(c) they abstained from keeping written accounts
(d) they are virtually unknown to outside observers

6. Canadian journalist Carl Honoré has proposed a novel approach to parenting which aims to ____________. The method, known as "slow parenting," was developed to counteract parents' tendency toward hyper-vigilance. While parents typically establish rules for their children and carefully monitor their behavior, Honoré says that this approach communicates a lack of faith in the children. Slow parenting, in contrast, grants children more freedom so that they develop the confidence to act independently.

(a) intensify bonding through open displays of affection
(b) raise autonomous children through trustful parenting
(c) counter the trend of granting children unlimited freedom
(d) manage children's behavior by imposing stringent rules

2 수험생들의 필살기 TEPS 만점 전략

청해-문법-어휘-독해 4영역 13개 파트에 대한 TEPS 출제 경향 및 고득점 대비
전략을 통합적으로 분석한 출제 비밀 노트 공개

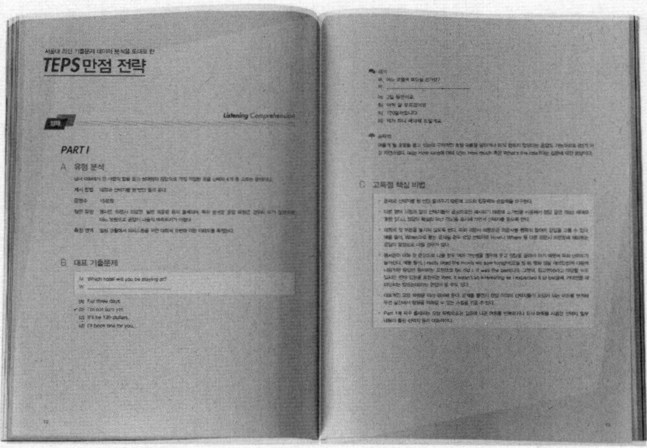

TEPS 만점 전략

Listening Comprehension

PART I

A 유형 분석

B 대표 기출문제

C 고득점 핵심 비법

실제 강의를 듣는 것 같은 완전 해설

넥서스 TEPS연구소의 오랜 노하우가 살아 있는 정확한 해설로 오답과 문제 경향에 대한 속시원한 해결책 제시

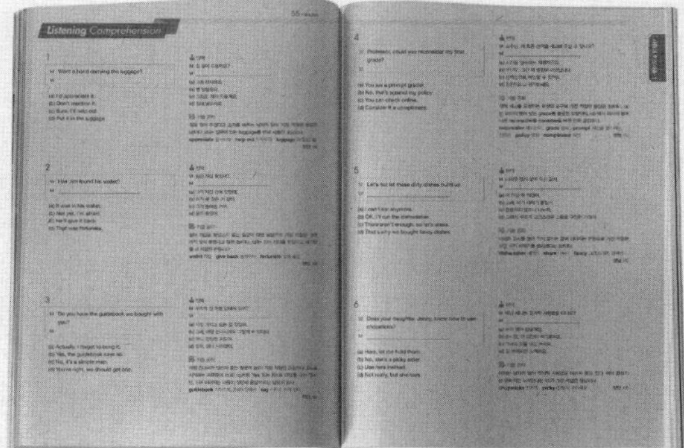

문제집과 해설집 별도 제작

학습자 편의를 위해 방대한 분량을 문제집과 해설집으로 별도 제작, 휴대하기 편할 뿐 아니라 학습 목적에 맞게 구매 가능

실제 고사장에서 듣던 청해 음성

정기 TEPS 고사장에서 청해 시험 시간에 사용했던 MP3 음원을 그대로 수록, 생생한 시험장 분위기 체험

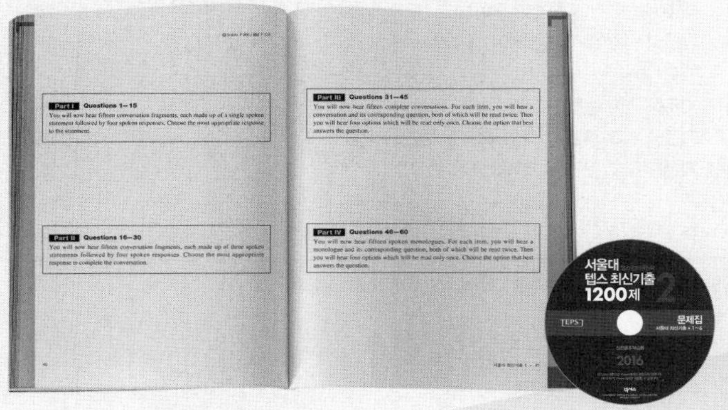

1 TEPS란?

❶ Test of English Proficiency developed by Seoul National University의 약자로 서울대학교 언어교육원에서 개발하고, TEPS관리위원회에서 주관하는 국가공인 영어시험
❷ 1999년 1월 처음 시행 이후 연 12~16회 실시
❸ 정부기관 및 기업의 직원 채용, 인사고과, 해외 파견 근무자 선발과 더불어 대학과 특목고 입학 및 졸업 자격 요건, 국가고시 및 자격 시험의 영어 대체 시험으로 활용
❹ 100여 명의 국내외 유수 대학의 최고 수준 영어 전문가들이 출제하고, 언어 테스팅 분야의 세계적인 권위자인 Bachman 교수(미국 UCLA)와 Oller 교수(미국 뉴멕시코대)로부터 타당성을 검증받음
❺ 말하기 – 쓰기 시험인 TEPS Speaking & Writing도 별도 실시 중이며, 2009년 10월부터 이를 통합한 *i*-TEPS 실시

2 TEPS 시험 구성

영역	Part별 내용	문항수	시간/배점
청해 Listening Comprehension	**Part I**: 문장 하나를 듣고 이어질 대화 고르기 **Part II**: 3문장의 대화를 듣고 이어질 대화 고르기 **Part III**: 6~8 문장의 대화를 듣고 질문에 해당하는 답 고르기 **Part IV**: 담화문의 내용을 듣고 질문에 해당하는 답 고르기	15 15 15 15	55분 400점
문법 Grammar	**Part I**: 대화문의 빈칸에 적절한 표현 고르기 **Part II**: 문장의 빈칸에 적절한 표현 고르기 **Part III**: 대화에서 어법상 틀리거나 어색한 부분 고르기 **Part IV**: 단문에서 문법상 틀리거나 어색한 부분 고르기	20 20 5 5	25분 100점
어휘 Vocabulary	**Part I**: 대화문의 빈칸에 적절한 단어 고르기 **Part II**: 단문의 빈칸에 적절한 단어 고르기	25 25	15분 100점
독해 Reading Comprehension	**Part I**: 지문을 읽고 빈칸에 들어갈 내용 고르기 **Part II**: 지문을 읽고 질문에 가장 적절한 내용 고르기 **Part III**: 지문을 읽고 문맥상 어색한 내용 고르기	16 21 3	45분 400점
총계	13개 Parts	200	140분 990점

☆ **IRT** (Item Response Theory)에 의하여 최고점이 990점, 최저점이 10점으로 조정됨.

3

TEPS 시험 응시 정보

현장 접수

❶ www.teps.or.kr에서 인근 접수처 확인

❷ 준비물: 응시료 39,000원(현금만 가능), 증명사진 1매(3×4 cm)

❸ 접수처 방문: 해당 접수기간 평일 12시~5시

인터넷 접수

❶ 서울대학교 TEPS관리위원회 홈페이지 접속 www.teps.or.kr

❷ 준비물: 스캔한 사진 파일, 응시료 결제를 위한 신용 카드 및 은행 계좌

❸ 응시료: 39,000원(일반) / 19,500원(군인) / 42,000원(추가 접수)

TEPS 시험 당일 정보

❶ 고사장 입실 완료: 9시 30분(일요일) / 2시 30분(토요일)

❷ 준비물: 신분증, 컴퓨터용 사인펜, 수정테이프, 수험표, 시계

❸ 유효한 신분증
성인: 주민등록증, 운전면허증, 여권, 공무원증, 현역간부 신분증, 군무원증, 주민등록증 발급 신청 확인서, 외국인 등록증
초·중고생: 학생증, 여권, 청소년증, 주민등록증(발급 신청 확인서), TEPS 신분확인 증명서

❹ 시험 시간: 2시간 20분 (중간에 쉬는 시간 없음, 각 영역별 제한시간 엄수)

❺ 성적 확인: 약 2주 후 인터넷에서 조회 가능

서울대 공식 기출문제 누적 데이터 분석에 기반한

TEPS 만점 전략

청해 **Listening** Comprehension

PART I

A 유형 분석

남녀 대화에서 한 사람의 말을 듣고 상대방의 응답으로 가장 적절한 것을 선택지 4개 중 고르는 문제이다.

제시 방법 대화와 선택지를 한 번만 들려준다.

문항수 15문항

질문 유형 평서문, 의문사 의문문, 일반 의문문 등이 출제되며, 특히 평서문 응답 유형은 경우의 수가 많으므로 어느 방향으로 응답이 나올지 예측하기가 어렵다.

측정 영역 일상 생활에서 의사소통을 위한 대화체 표현에 대한 이해도를 측정한다.

B 대표 기출문제

M Which hotel will you be staying at?
W ______________________________

(a) For three days
✔ (b) I'm not sure yet.
(c) It'll be 120 dollars.
(d) I'll book one for you.

해석

M 어느 호텔에 묵으실 건가요?
W ______________________________

(a) 3일 동안이요.
(b) 아직 잘 모르겠어요.
(c) 120달러입니다.
(d) 제가 하나 예약해 드릴게요.

공략법

머물게 될 호텔을 묻고 있는데 구체적인 호텔 이름을 말하거나 아직 정하지 않았다는 응답도 가능하므로 (b)가 가장 자연스럽다. (a)는 How long에 대해, (c)는 How much 혹은 What's the rate?라는 질문에 대한 응답이다.

C 고득점 핵심 비법

- 예전보다 Part 1도 많이 까다로워졌으며 문제와 선택지를 한 번만 들려주기 때문에 고도의 집중력과 순발력이 요구된다.
- 다른 영어 시험과 달리 선택지들이 음성으로만 제시되기 때문에 소거법을 사용해서 정답 같은 것(o), 애매모호한 것(△), 정답이 확실히 아닌 것(x)을 표시해 가면서 선택지를 듣도록 한다.
- 대화의 첫 부분을 놓치지 않도록 한다. 특히 의문사 의문문은 의문사를 정확히 들어야 정답을 고를 수 있다. 예를 들어, When으로 묻는 문제일 경우 오답 선택지로 How나 Where 등 다른 의문사 의문문에 해당하는 응답이 함정으로 나올 경우가 많다.
- 평서문이 대화 첫 문장으로 나올 경우 여러 가능성을 염두에 두고 정답을 골라야 하기 때문에 특히 난도가 높아진다. 예를 들어, I really liked the movie we saw tonight(오늘 밤 본 영화 정말 재미있었어) 다음에 동의하는 표현으로 So did I. It was the best(나도 그랬어. 최고였어)라고 대답할 수도 있지만, 반대 입장을 표현하는 Well, it wasn't so interesting as I expected it to be(글쎄, 기대만큼 재미있지는 않았는데)라는 응답이 올 수도 있다.
- 대표적인 오답 유형을 미리 정리해 둔다. 문제를 풀면서 정답 이외의 선택지들이 오답이 되는 이유를 분석해 두면 실전에서 함정을 피해갈 수 있는 스킬을 키울 수 있다.
- Part 1에 자주 출제되는 오답 유형으로는 질문에 나온 어휘를 반복하거나 유사 어휘를 사용한 선택지, 일부 내용이 틀린 선택지 등이 대표적이다.

PART II

A 유형 분석

남녀 대화에서 세 번째 대화까지 듣고 그 다음 이어질 응답으로 가장 자연스러운 것을 4개의 선택지 중에서 고르는 문제이다.

제시 방법 대화와 선택지를 한 번만 들려준다.

문항수 15문항

질문 유형 평서문, 의문사 의문문, 일반 의문문 등이 출제되며, 이 중 특히 평서문인 경우 어느 방향으로 응답이 나올지 예측하기 어렵다.

측정 영역 일상 대화 속 표현에 대한 이해도 측정이라는 점에서 Part 1과 동일한데, 이와 더불어 전반적인 대화 흐름의 이해도를 측정하기도 한다.

B 대표 기출문제

M Nice car, Mia. It looks pretty new.
W Really? It's actually a 2008 model.
M It's certainly in good condition.
W ______________________________

(a) In that case, I'll buy it.
(b) I appreciate your advice.
✔ (c) Well, I take good care of it.
(d) True, but yours is no better.

해석

M 미아, 차 좋다. 꽤 새 차 같은데.
W 정말? 실은 2008년 식이야.
M 상태가 아주 좋구나.
W ______________________________

(a) 그렇다면 내가 살게.
(b) 네 충고 고마워.
(c) 음, 내가 관리를 많이 하거든.
(d) 맞아, 하지만 네 차라고 더 나을 것도 없어.

공략법

여자가 연식에 비해서 차의 상태가 좋다고 칭찬을 했으므로 그만큼 많은 관리를 한다는 (c)가 남자의 응답으로 가장 적절하다. 충고가 아니라 칭찬이므로 (b)는 advice가 아닌 compliment가 되면 자연스러운 응답이 될 수 있다.

C 고득점 핵심 비법

- 한 번만 들려주는 세 줄의 대화를 정확하게 잘 듣도록 한다. 첫 문장을 잘 들어야 그 다음에 이어지는 두 줄의 대화를 잘 이해할 수 있기 때문에 Part 2 역시 고도의 집중력을 요한다.
- 만일 첫 줄을 놓쳤다면 당황하지 말고 그 다음 이어지는 두 줄의 대화를 잘 듣도록 한다. 가장 이상적인 청취는 세 줄을 다 알아듣는 것이지만, 혹시 그렇지 못하더라도 선택지가 나오기 직전의 말을 잘 들으면 자연스럽게 이어지는 응답을 고르는 데 도움이 된다.
- 소거법을 활용해서 정답을 고르는 것도 들려주기만 하는 선택지에 대처할 수 있는 한 방법이다.
- 남녀 각각 어떤 말을 했는지 구분해서 들어야 오답을 피해갈 수 있다.
- 풀어본 문제의 오답을 매번 분석해서 실전에서 신속하고 정확하게 오답을 피하도록 한다.
- Part 2의 대표적인 오답 유형으로는 대화의 앞부분을 일부 놓치고 착각해서 선택할 만한 선택지, 대화에 언급된 어휘로 만든 선택지, 대화에 등장한 어휘의 또 다른 의미를 가지고 만든 선택지, 질문한 사람이 이어서 할 만한 말로 만든 선택지 등이 있다.

PART III

A 유형 분석

남녀가 세 번씩 주고받는 대화를 듣고 4개의 선택지 중 질문에 가장 적절한 답을 고르는 문제이다.

제시 방법 대화 → 질문 → 대화 → 질문 → 선택지 순으로 들려준다.

문항수 15문항

질문 유형 대의 파악(7문항) → 세부 내용 파악(6문항) → 추론(3문항) 순으로 나온다.

측정 영역 일상 대화에 등장하는 다양한 표현에 대한 이해도를 바탕으로 전체 대의 파악, 세부 내용 파악, 추론 능력을 측정한다.

B 대표 기출문제

M Any special plans for your two-week vacation?
W I think I'll visit my family and relax somewhere.
M Where do you plan on relaxing?
W Oh, I don't know, maybe go somewhere warm.
M What about Jeju island?
W Actually, that sounds good. I'll put it on my list.

Q What is the main topic of the conversation?
(a) The best way to spend a vacation
✔ (b) The woman's vacation plans
(c) Popular holiday destinations
(d) Setting aside time to visit family

해석

M 2주 휴가 동안 특별한 계획이 있나요?
W 집에 들렀다가 어디 가서 좀 쉴 생각이에요.
M 어디서 쉬려고 하는데요?
W 글쎄요. 모르겠어요. 아마 따뜻한 곳으로 가겠죠.
M 제주도는 어때요?
W 좋은 생각이네요. 그곳도 고려해 봐야겠어요.

Q 대화의 중심 소재는?
(a) 휴가를 보낼 가장 좋은 방법
(b) 여자의 휴가 계획
(c) 인기 있는 휴양지
(d) 가족을 방문하기 위한 시간을 남겨 놓기

공략법

대화의 중심 소재는 여자가 휴가 동안 무엇을 하는지이다. 가족을 방문하고 나서 어디로 가서 좀 쉴 거라는 말에 제주도를 권하고 있으므로 (b)가 가장 적절한 답이다. 따뜻한 곳이나 제주도라는 특정 지명을 언급하긴 했지만 인기 있는 휴양지 자체가 대화의 소재는 아니므로 (c)는 오답이다.

C 고득점 핵심 비법

- 처음 대화를 들을 때 전체 대화 내용을 파악한 뒤, 질문에 따라 집중할 부분에 더 집중하는 두 번째 듣기를 한다. 대화의 흐름을 파악해야 대의 파악 문제뿐 아니라 세부 내용 파악이나 추론 문제도 더 쉽게 풀 수 있다.
- 질문에 따라서 메모를 해야 하는 경우도 있다. 특히 세부 내용 파악 문제의 경우 숫자, 연도, 물건의 종류 등을 명확하게 기억하는 것이 유리하고, 남녀 각각 어떤 말을 했는지 구분해서 알아 두는 것이 오답을 피하는 데 많은 도움이 된다. 추론 능력은 대의 또는 세부 내용을 바탕으로 하기 때문에 세부 내용도 간과할 수 없다.
- 선택지를 한 번밖에 들려주지 않기 때문에 대화 내용을 다 이해하고도 선택지를 놓쳐서 정답을 고르지 못하는 경우가 있다. 이를 방지하기 위해 소거법을 적용해서 선택지를 차례대로 표시하면서 최종 정답을 고르도록 한다.
- 질문 종류별로 오답 확률이 높은 유형을 알아 두는 것도 도움이 된다.
  - 대의 파악 오답 유형: 대화 중 일부 세부 사항만 포함한 선택지, 너무 일반적인 내용의 선택지, 대화 중 특정 키워드를 조합한 전혀 엉뚱한 내용의 선택지 등이다.
  - 세부 내용 파악 오답 유형: 대화에서 언급된 어휘를 반복한 선택지, 대화와 전혀 무관한 선택지, 일부 내용만 사실인 선택지, 남녀의 역할이 뒤바뀐 선택지, 시제가 대화 내용과 일치하지 않는 선택지 등이 있다.
  - 추론 오답 유형: 상식적으로는 맞는 진술이지만 대화 내용과는 무관한 선택지, 대화에서 언급된 어휘로 만들었지만 대화 내용과 무관한 선택지, 추론 가능한 내용과 정반대인 선택지 등이 있다.
- 대의 파악이나 세부 내용 파악 유형에 대비해 패러프레이징(paraphrasing) 연습을 하는 것이 좋다. 대화에서 언급된 어휘가 그대로 사용된 경우는 오답일 확률이 높은 반면, 언급된 어휘를 비슷한 말로 바꾸어 만든 선택지는 정답일 확률이 높으므로 paraphrasing 연습이 많은 도움이 된다.

PART IV

A 유형 분석

담화문을 듣고 4개의 선택지 중 질문에 가장 적절한 정답을 고르는 문제이다.

제시 방법 담화문 → 질문 → 담화문 → 질문 → 선택지 순으로 들려준다.

문항수 15문항

질문 유형 대의 파악(7문항) → 세부 내용 파악(5문항) → 추론(3문항) 순으로 나온다.

측정 영역 연설, 강의, 라디오 방송 등에 나오는 다양한 표현에 대한 이해도 측정을 바탕으로 전체 대의 파악, 세부 내용 파악, 추론 능력을 측정한다.

B 대표 기출문제

Wildlife officials announced today that a tiny snail that could harm American river trout populations is spreading throughout the country. The New Zealand mud snail was first discovered in Idaho's Snake River in 1987. Since then, it has shown up in eight more rivers. The snails reproduce rapidly and destroy the habitat of trout and other aquatic life. Fishermen are being asked to clean their boots, fishing equipment and boats to prevent the snails from spreading from one river to another.

Q Which is correct according to the news report?
(a) American river trout are damaging waterways.
(b) Snails from the U.S. have been found in New Zealand.
✔ (c) It was in Snake River that the mud snail was first found.
(d) Fishermen have been asked to collect the snails they find.

해석

야생 생물 관계자는 오늘 미국 민물송어 개체군에 해를 끼칠 수 있는 작은 달팽이가 전국적으로 확산되고 있다고 발표했습니다. 뉴질랜드 진흙 달팽이는 1987년 아이다호 주 스네이크 강에서 처음으로 발견됐습니다. 그 이후 이 달팽이는 8개 강에 추가로 나타났습니다. 이 달팽이는 번식이 빠르고 송어 및 다른 수생 생물의 서식처를 파괴합니다. 이들 달팽이가 하나의 강에서 다른 강으로 확산되는 것을 막기 위해 어부에게 장화와 낚시 장비, 배를 청소하도록 요청하는 바입니다.

Q 뉴스 보도에 따르면 옳은 것은?
(a) 미국 민물송어는 수로를 손상시킨다.
(b) 미국산 달팽이가 뉴질랜드에서 발견되었다.
(c) 진흙 달팽이가 최초로 발견된 곳은 스네이크 강이었다.
(d) 발견한 진흙 달팽이를 어부들에게 채집하도록 요청했다.

공략법

외래종의 확산으로 발생하는 문제에 대한 내용이다. 두 번째 문장에서 진흙 달팽이가 스네이크 강에서 처음 발견되었다고 했으므로 (c)가 정답임을 쉽게 알 수 있다. (a)는 언급되지 않은 내용이며, (b)는 정반대 진술이다. 또한 어부들에게 달팽이의 확산을 막기 위해 노력해 달라고 했으므로 (d) 역시 오답이다.

C 고득점 핵심 비법

- 먼저 담화문의 전체 흐름을 파악한 뒤, 두 번째 듣기에서 질문과 연계된 부분에 집중하여 정확하게 듣는다.
- 질문 유형에 따라 맞춤식 메모를 한다. 특히 세부 사항 파악 유형 문제에 대비해서는 숫자, 연도, 물품 종류 등을 세세하게 메모해야 하고, 추론 능력은 대의 또는 세부 내용을 바탕으로 하기 때문에 세부 내용도 간과할 수 없다는 것을 기억한다.
- 질문 종류별로 오답일 확률이 높은 경우를 알아 두면 도움이 된다.
  - 대의 파악 오답 유형: 담화문 내용의 일부에 해당하는 세부 사항으로 만든 선택지, 주제와 관련은 있으나 너무 범위가 넓은 일반적인 내용의 선택지, 언급된 어휘로 구성된 점 외에는 내용과 전혀 관련이 없는 선택지 등이 오답일 확률이 높다.
  - 세부 내용 파악 오답 유형: 담화문에 언급된 어휘로 만들어진 선택지나 내용과 전혀 무관한 선택지, 일부만 사실인 선택지 등이 오답으로 제시될 가능성이 크다.
  - 추론 오답 유형: 상식적으로는 맞지만 내용과는 무관한 선택지, 담화문에서 언급된 어휘로 만들었지만 내용과는 무관한 선택지, 추론 가능한 내용과 정반대의 선택지 등이 종종 사용되는 오답 유형이다.
- 대의 파악이나 세부 내용 파악 유형의 문제를 대비하려면 paraphrasing 연습을 하는 것이 좋다. 언급된 어휘를 그대로 사용하면 오답일 확률이 높은 반면, 정답의 경우 언급된 어휘를 paraphrasing해서 만드는 경우가 많다.

PART I

A 유형 분석

두 줄의 대화문을 읽고 빈칸에 문법적으로 적절한 표현을 4개의 선택지 중에서 고르는 문제이다.

제시 방법 두 줄의 대화문이 주어진다.

문항수 20문항

측정 영역 실시간과 비슷한 시간 제약 속에서 문법적으로 정확한 영어를 대화 속에서 구사할 수 있는지 측정한다.

빈출 토픽 일상 생활 대화 중에 흔히 접할 수 있는 주제가 많이 사용되므로 청해나 어휘 영역의 대화 부분과 비슷한 내용이 나온다.

B 대표 기출문제

A Don't take that last cookie. It's for Dan.
B But he ____________ all the cookies last time.

✔ (a) ate
(b) eats
(c) has eaten
(d) had been eating

해석

A 마지막 쿠키 먹지 마. 댄 줄 거니까.
B 하지만 댄은 지난번에 쿠키를 다 먹었잖아요.

공략법

시제 문제는 함께 쓰이는 시간의 부사에서 힌트를 찾아야 한다. 이 문장에서는 last time이 시간의 부사 역할을 하고 있다. last는 지난 일을 나타내므로 항상 과거 시제와 함께 쓰인다. 따라서 (a)가 정답이다.

C 고득점 핵심 비법

- 정확한 영어를 적재적소에 사용하는 능력이 중요하므로 눈으로만 익히는 문법 지식을 배제한다. 대화체를 소리 내어 읽는 연습을 해서 문법이 내재화되어 상황에 맞게 즉각적으로 사용할 수 있는 수준까지 끌어올리도록 한다.
- 문법 네 가지 Part 중 비교적 평이한 수준이기 때문에 시간 안배 차원에서 신속하게 풀고 다음 Part로 넘어가도록 한다. 단, 첫 줄은 빈칸에 올 적절한 답을 찾는 데 단서가 되므로 생략하고 넘어가면 함정에 빠지는 경우가 종종 있다. 신속하게 문제를 읽어나가되 읽지 않고 건너뛰는 일은 없어야 한다.
- 문법 문제의 빈칸은 주로 두 번째 줄에 오지만 일부 문제는 첫 번째 줄에 빈칸이 오기도 한다. 이런 유형에서는 두 번째 줄을 제대로 읽어야 출제자의 함정에 걸려들지 않는다. 즉, 빈칸 위치에 상관없이 문제에 나오는 대화는 모두 다 읽고 정확한 내용을 파악해야 오답 함정을 피해 정답을 찾을 수 있다.
- 문법 문제라고 해서 대화의 문법적인 요소만 신경 쓰면 안 된다. 상황에 적절한 어법을 고른다는 자세로 문제를 풀도록 한다. 예를 들어 대화 내용에 현재 시제가 여러 개 나온다고 무조건 현재 시제를 답으로 고르면 오히려 오답일 경우가 많다.
- 일상 대화 구문의 어법을 묻는 Part이므로 대화체의 정확한 표현을 익히는 것이 도움이 된다. 즉, 문법책의 모든 문법 요소를 처음부터 공부하는 것보다는 일상 대화 구문 표현 위주로 외울 수 있는 수준까지 익혀 두면 짧은 시간 내에 정확하게 구사할 수 있는 표현들이 많아지고 이렇게 되면 문법 Part 1도 쉽게 정복할 수 있다.

PART II

A 유형 분석

하나의 문장을 읽고 빈칸에 문법적으로 가장 적절한 표현을 4개의 선택지 중에서 고른다.

제시 방법 하나의 문어체 문장이 주어진다.

문항수 20문항

측정 영역 문어체 영어의 정확한 어법 구사력을 측정한다.

빈출 토픽 학술문과 실용문 등 일상에서 접하는 문어체 문장에 언급되는 주제가 주로 사용된다.

B 대표 기출문제

____________________ the movie twice, Bob did not want to see it again.

(a) He had seen
(b) Had he seen
✔ (c) Having seen
(d) To have seen

해석

그 영화를 두 번 봤기 때문에 밥은 그것을 또 보고 싶지 않았다.

공략법

접속사가 없으므로 (a)와 같은 완전한 절은 올 수 없다. (d)와 같은 to부정사는 문두에 오면 보통 목적의 의미를 가지므로 문맥상 어울리지 않는다. 따라서 빈칸에는 분사구문이 나와야 하는데 주절의 주어 Bob이 영화를 직접 본 것이므로 능동의 현재분사 (c)가 정답이다. 영화를 본 것이 먼저 일어난 일이므로 완료분사 Having seen을 썼다.

C 고득점 핵심 비법

- 구어체 문장보다 문어체 문장의 의미 파악이 까다로울 수 있으므로 평상시 문어체 문장의 직독직해 연습을 충분히 한다. 특히 관계사들로 연결된 문장, 절 안에 또 다른 절이 있는 문장 등 복잡한 문장을 평상시에 많이 접해 보도록 하자. 난해한 문장을 만났을 때 바로 의미를 파악할 수 있어야 문법 Part 2 문제를 신속하게 해결할 수 있다.
- 주어와 동사가 여러 개 나오는 긴 문장은 주절의 주어와 동사를 파악한 후, 다른 문법 사항들을 따져 보도록 한다. 특히 대표 빈출 유형이자 기본이 되는 주어-동사 수 일치 문제는 주절의 주어와 동사를 파악해야만 풀 수 있는 문제이다.
- TEPS 시험에서는 한국인이 특히 취약한 관사와 문장 구조 등에 대해 묻는 문제가 다수 출제된다. 이를 대비하기 위해서는 문장 내 쓰임새를 익혀 두는 것이 낱낱의 문법 지식을 알고 있는 것보다 신속하고 정확하게 문제를 푸는 데 많은 도움을 줄 것이다. 영어 활용 능력 수준 측정을 위해 TEPS가 고안된 점을 염두에 두고, 평소에 정확한 영어 구사 능력 함양에 집중하도록 한다.
- 문법 Part 1과 마찬가지로 정확한 어법을 익히려면 청해 Part 4 긴 담화문 속에 나오는 문장이나 어휘 Part 2 문장을 익혀 두는 것도 좋다. 각 분야별 어휘와 구문에 익숙해질수록 읽고 이해하는 속도가 자연히 빨라지게 되고, 아울러 문장 안에서 정확한 쓰임새도 익힐 수 있기 때문이다.

PART III

A 유형 분석

네 줄의 대화문을 읽고 문법적으로 이상한 부분이 있는 문장을 고르는 유형의 문제이다.

제시 방법 네 줄의 대화문이 주어진다.

문항수 5문항

측정 영역 길어진 대화에서 비문법적 요소를 가려내는 능력을 측정한다.

빈출 토픽 일상 생활에서 접하는 대화에 나오는 주제가 주로 사용된다.

B 대표 기출문제

(a) A Let's go to an amusement park this weekend.
✔ (b) B Well, that's not what I had planned during the weekend.
(c) A Oh, are you going to do anything special?
(d) B Actually, I just want to stay home and relax.

해석

(a) **A** 이번 주말에 놀이공원에 가자.
(b) **B** 음, 그건 내가 주말에 계획한 게 아닌데.
(c) **A** 아, 뭐 특별한 거라도 하게?
(d) **B** 실은 그냥 집에서 쉬고 싶어서.

공략법

과거완료 had p.p.는 과거보다 더 앞선 시제를 나타낼 때 쓰므로 (b)에서처럼 현재 시제와 함께 쓸 수 없다. 다른 계획을 세운 것은 과거의 일이므로 had planned가 아니라 단순과거인 planned가 되어야 한다.

C 고득점 핵심 비법

- 주어진 선택지가 따로 없어서 어떤 문법에 관한 문제인지 전혀 알 수 없고 주어진 대화 내용을 읽으면서 틀린 부분을 골라야 하기 때문에 보다 적극적인 태도로 문제에 임해야 한다. 즉, 각 대화에서 어느 문법 요소가 틀렸는지 모르는 상태에서 틀린 부분을 찾아야 하기 때문에 대화 내용을 파악함과 동시에 모든 품사와 구문 요소가 정확한지도 일일이 확인하는 습관을 평소에 들여야 당황하지 않고 실전에서 실력 발휘를 할 수 있다.
- 주어진 시간 내에 틀린 문법 사항을 골라야 하기 때문에 즉각적으로 비문법적인 부분을 찾아내는 훈련이 평상시에 필요하다. 이렇게 하기 위해서는 다른 문법 Part의 문제 대비와 마찬가지로 일상 대화 및 학술문과 실용문을 많이 접해서 다양한 문장에 익숙해져야 한다.
- 모든 문법 학습 요소들이 다 출제되는 것이 아니라 단골로 출제되는 문법 사항이 있음을 알자. 문장 구조, 시제, 수 일치, 관사 등에 해당하는 문법 요소들을 집중해서 훈련하는 것도 단기간에 Part 3을 정복할 수 있는 길이다. 물론, Part 3 역시 제한된 문법 사항에만 국한해 다른 문법 요소를 무시했다가 낭패를 볼 수 있다는 것을 유의하자.
- Part 4에 비해 짧은 대화체라 약간 수월하게 보일 수 있겠지만 선택지가 주어진 Part 1과 2보다는 고난도인 경우가 많다. 특히 재빨리 읽으면서 틀린 문법 사항도 찾아내야 하므로 평상시 대화문의 정확도를 분석하는 것도 실전에서 틀린 부분을 파악하는 데 도움이 될 것이다. 즉, 정답을 찾는 데에만 급급하지 말고 한 문제를 풀더라도 문법적으로 옳고 그른 부분들에 대한 분석을 자세히 하다 보면 실전에서 당황하지 않고 틀린 부분을 찾아낼 수 있다는 것이다.

PART IV

A 유형 분석

4개의 문어체 문장을 읽고 문법적으로 어색한 부분이 있는 문장을 고르는 유형의 문제이다.

제시 방법 4개의 문어체 문장이 하나의 지문으로 주어진다.

문항수 5문항

측정 영역 문어체 문장으로 구성된 지문에서 비문법적인 요소를 가려내는 능력을 측정한다.

빈출 토픽 신문, 잡지, 교재 등 일상 생활에서 문어체로 접하게 되는 주제가 등장한다.

B 대표 기출문제

✔ (a) In a study, separate groups of men was asked to run as hard and as long as possible on a treadmill. (b) Each group was cheered and encouraged, but at different intervals—either every 20, 60 or 180 seconds. (c) Researchers perceived no gains among those who were given verbal cues every 180 seconds. (d) It was found, however, that performance did improve for men cheered every 20 or 60 seconds.

해석

(a) 한 연구에서 서로 다른 남성 집단에게 러닝머신 위에서 최대한 빨리 그리고 최대한 오래 달리도록 요구했다. (b) 각 집단은 각각 20초, 60초, 180초 간격으로 응원과 격려를 받았다. (c) 연구자들은 180초마다 응원을 받은 사람들에게는 이득이 없다는 것을 발견했다. (d) 그러나 20초, 혹은 60초마다 응원을 받은 남성들의 경우는 성과가 실제로 향상되었음이 밝혀졌다.

공략법

A of B 형태에서 동사는 A와 일치시킨다. (a)에서 주어 separate groups of men의 동사는 groups와 일치시켜 복수 동사를 취해야 하므로 was를 were로 고친다.

C 고득점 핵심 비법

- Part 3 대화체에 비해 Part 4는 지문 길이도 더 길고 문어체라서 내용 파악이 훨씬 더 어렵고 시간도 가장 많이 걸린다. 그렇기 때문에 비문법적인 요소를 찾기가 특히 더 어려울 수 있으므로 신속하게 문어체 문장들을 읽고 직독직해를 통해 내용을 즉시 파악할 수 있는 능력을 평상시에 훈련하도록 한다.

- 지문 내용은 물론 문제에서 요구하는 문법 사항 예측이 어렵기 때문에 더욱 적극적인 문제 풀이 전략이 필요하다. 4개의 문장을 읽으면서 내용 파악을 하는 동시에 모든 가능성을 열어 두고 비문법적으로 보이는 부분을 찾아 나가야 하는데 이때 가능성이 있는 부분을 일단 밑줄 그어 놓은 뒤 신속하게 다시 그 부분들을 재확인하는 것도 정확도를 높이는 한 방법이 될 수 있다.

- 주어진 시간 내에 틀린 문법 사항을 골라야 하기 때문에 즉각적으로 비문법적인 부분을 찾아내는 훈련이 필요하다. 이를 위해서는 정확한 표현을 즉각적으로 사용할 수 있을 정도로 알고 있어야 한다. 즉, Part 3 대비를 위해서 대화체를 많이 익혀 둠으로써 신속하게 비문법적인 대화 부분을 알아차리는 훈련을 하듯이, Part 4 대비책으로 학술문과 실용문을 접하면서 거의 암기할 정도로 정독하는 것도 문법 내재화를 도울 것이며, 이런 훈련 과정을 거치고 나면 자연스럽게 틀린 부분이 눈에 잘 띌 것이다.

- Part 2에 나오는 문장 네 개가 한꺼번에 출제된다고 생각하면 좀 부담이 덜어질 것이고 Part 2 문장들에서 문법적 오류를 찾는다고 생각하면 이제 마음도 편해질 것이다.

  – 시제 문제: 각 문장마다 여러 시제가 혼합되어 있는 경우가 대부분이기 때문에 시제의 형태만 참고해서 틀린 시제를 찾는 것은 거의 불가능하다고 봐야 한다. 내용 파악이 선행되어야만 시제가 잘못 쓰인 곳을 찾을 수 있다.

  – 관사 문제: a와 the의 쓰임 여부는 4개 문장에서 어떤 명사가 이미 앞서 언급된 것이고 아닌지를 이해한 후에 결정되므로 내용 파악이 우선되어야 한다.

PART I

A 유형 분석

두 줄의 대화문을 읽고 빈칸에 가장 잘 어울리는 어휘를 고르는 문제이다.

제시 방법 두 줄의 대화문이 주어진다.

문항수 25문항

측정 영역 대화에서 사용하는 구어체 표현을 적절하게 활용할 수 있는지 측정한다.

빈출 토픽 일상 생활과 관련 있는 주제가 많이 출제된다.

B 대표 기출문제

A What took you so long to get here?
B Sorry, I was ________________ a meeting.

✔ (a) attending
(b) including
(c) reducing
(d) skipping

해석

A 여기 오는 데 왜 이렇게 오래 걸렸니?
B 미안, 회의에 참석했었어.

(a) 참석하다
(b) 포함하다
(c) 줄이다
(d) 건너뛰다

공략법

시간이 오래 걸린 이유를 묻고 있으므로 회의에 '참석했다'는 문장이 되어야 한다. '참석하다'는 의미의 동사 (a) attend는 다음에 전치사를 쓰지 않는 타동사이므로 attend a meeting이 된다.

C 고득점 핵심 비법

- 짧은 시간 내에 문맥에 어울리는 어휘를 골라야 하기 때문에 많은 어휘를 알고 있는 것뿐만 아니라 문맥(context)에 적절한 어휘를 사용할 수 있는 능력을 키우는 것도 중요하다. 따라서 어휘를 처음 접할 때엔 참고 자료를 동원해서 문장 내에서 쓰이는 다양한 예문을 동시에 익혀 두어야 한다. 시간 내에 모든 어휘 문제를 잘 풀기 위해서는 특히 문맥 속에서 각 어휘의 쓰임을 거의 외우다시피 알고 있어야 시간 낭비 없이 즉각적으로 빈칸에 올 정답을 고를 수 있을 것이다.
- 해당 어휘의 우리말을 단순하게 암기하는 것은 별 도움이 안 된다. 우리말로는 그럴듯해도 쓰임이 어색한 어휘의 뉘앙스 차이를 구분할 줄 알아야 하므로 문장 전체로 어휘를 이해하는 것이 장기적으로 유리하다.
- 청해의 대화 파트뿐만 아니라 문법 Part 1과 3에 언급된 대화들도 어휘 실력 향상을 위해 활용될 수 있음을 기억하고 어휘 영역 이외의 빈출 표현도 문맥 속에서 익혀 두도록 한다.
- 대화를 신속히 읽고 즉각적으로 빈칸을 채워 넣어야 하기 때문에 실제 대화를 하면서 적절한 어휘를 사용할 수 있을 정도의 실력이 되도록 많은 표현을 통째로 익혀 두어야 한다.
- 일상적인 대화 속에서 자주 등장하는 어휘뿐만 아니라 이어동사, 이디엄 등도 출제되므로 숙지해 두도록 한다.
- 형태상 · 의미상 혼동되는 어휘, 의미 덩어리로 사용되는 연어 등의 정확한 활용법도 아울러 알아 둔다.

PART II

A 유형 분석

한 개의 문어체 문장을 읽고 빈칸에 가장 잘 어울리는 어휘를 고르는 문제이다.

제시 방법 한 개의 문어체 문장이 주어진다.

문항수 25문항

측정 영역 일상 생활에서 접할 수 있는 문어체 표현을 문맥에 맞게 사용할 수 있는지 측정한다.

빈출 토픽 학술문뿐만 아니라 실용문에 이르기까지 매우 다양한 주제를 다룬다.

B 대표 기출문제

To ________________ military messages over radio, a secret code based on a Native American language was used by the US in World War II.

(a) infuse
(b) conflict
✔ (c) transmit
(d) intercept

해석

무선으로 군사 메시지를 전송하기 위해, 제2차 세계대전 당시 미국은 인디언 언어를 기반으로 한 비밀 코드를 사용했다.

(a) 불어넣다
(b) 상충하다
(c) 전송하다
(d) 가로막다

공략법

목적어가 메시지이기 때문에 '보내다, 전송하다'는 의미의 동사가 필요하다. 따라서 답은 (c)이다. 접두어 trans-에는 이동의 의미가 있다.

C 고득점 핵심 비법

- 학술문과 실용문의 주제별 빈출 어휘를 익혀 둔다. 빈출 어휘는 정답 선택지뿐만 아니라 오답 선택지에 나오는 어휘도 포함한다. 주제별로 자주 출제되는 어휘는 한정되어 있기 때문에 기출 어휘가 다시 출제될 확률이 높다.
- Part1과 마찬가지로 각 어휘의 쓰임새를 알아야 하기 때문에 전체 문장을 익히도록 한다. 그래야만 문법적으로도 정확한 어휘 활용 능력을 키울 수 있기 때문이다.
- 미묘한 뉘앙스 차이가 있는 쉬운 어휘의 용례 예문을 적극적으로 활용해야 한다. 의미가 비슷해 보이는 어휘들끼리 묶어서 따로 정리하면 도움이 될 것이다.
- 신문 기사, 잡지, 광고, 학술지, 비평 등의 실용문과 전문적인 학술문에서 다양하게 출제되므로 평상시 이런 종류의 글을 많이 접하는 것이 도움이 된다. 15분이라는 짧은 시간 내에 50문항이나 되는 문제를 무리 없이 풀기 위한 대비법 중 하나가 주제별로 다양한 문장을 평소에 자주 읽는 것이다. 이렇게 함으로써 필수 어휘를 자주 접할 수 있을 뿐만 아니라 문장 이해 속도도 향상될 수 있다.
- 대화체 문제와 마찬가지로 주제별 어휘뿐만 아니라 연어 및 형태상 · 의미상 혼동되는 어휘도 잘 알아 두도록 한다.

PART I

A 유형 분석

100단어 내외의 단일 지문을 읽고 빈칸에 들어갈 적절한 선택지를 고르는 문제이다. 14문항은 구나 절을 고르는 문제이고, 나머지 2문항은 문장과 문장 사이를 이어주는 연결어를 찾는 문제이다.

제시 방법 지문의 처음 문장이나 마지막 문장, 드물게 중간 문장에 빈칸이 있는 한 개의 글이 주어진다.

문항수 16문항

측정 영역 글의 전반적인 이해 능력 및 논리적인 흐름 파악 능력을 평가한다.

빈출 토픽 학술문과 실용문에서 골고루 출제된다.

B 대표 기출문제

Deerbar's annual sale is now on! To make way for next year's new models, Deerbar is selling off its entire remaining inventory at wholesale prices! This week only, get heavily discounted refrigerators, washer-dryer combos, freezers and microwaves. We will even include free delivery anywhere within the city limits! Don't delay. If you want ________________, come to Deerbar!

(a) this year's latest kitchen gear
(b) fashionable home furnishings
✔ (c) deals on major home appliances
(d) affordable equipment for the office

해석

디어바 연례 세일 중입니다! 내년도 신형 모델 입고를 위해 디어바에서는 남아 있는 전 재고 물량을 도매가에 처분하고 있습니다. 이번 주 단 한 주, 폭탄 세일가로 냉장고, 세탁기-건조기 콤보, 냉동고와 전자레인지를 들여가십시오. 시 경계 내라면 어디든 무료 배달까지 해 드립니다! 미루지 마십시오. 저렴한 가격의 주요 가전제품을 원하시면 디어바로 오십시오!

(a) 올해의 최신 부엌용품을
(b) 유행하는 가구를
(c) 저렴한 가격의 주요 가전제품을
(d) 적정한 가격의 사무용 장비를

공략법

디어바의 연례 세일 광고이다. 이 가게에서 취급하는 물건은 냉장고, 세탁기, 전자레인지 등이므로 가전제품을 구매하려고 하는 사람을 대상으로 하는 광고임을 알 수 있다. 가전제품은 home appliances라고 하며 정답은 (c)이다.

C 고득점 핵심 비법

- 모든 지문을 자세히 읽겠다는 생각을 접는다. 1분에 한 문제씩 풀어야 하기 때문에 정독을 하기에는 절대적으로 시간이 부족하므로 주요 어휘 위주로 대의 파악 및 흐름 파악에 주력해야 시간 내에 문제를 다 풀 수 있다.
- 주제별 어휘를 평소 많이 알아 둔다. 청해, 문법, 어휘 등 TEPS의 다른 영역과 마찬가지로 방대한 어휘 지식을 갖추고 있어야 독해 속도도 빨라지고 정확한 이해가 가능하다.
- 빈칸의 위치에 따라 독해의 목적이 달라져야 한다. 빈칸이 첫 문장에 있는 경우 대의 파악만 해도 되지만 마지막 문장에 올 때에는 대의 파악뿐만 아니라 논리적 흐름도 염두에 두면서 독해를 해야 한다.
- 오답 함정 선택지 유형을 연습해 둔다.
  - 지문에 나오는 어휘로 만들었지만 문맥과 전혀 상관없는 선택지
  - 너무 일반적인 내용으로 만든 선택지
  - 상식적으로는 괜찮아 보이지만 내용과는 무관한 선택지
  - 지문 내용의 일부처럼 보이기는 하지만 논리적인 흐름 면에서는 어울리지 않는 선택지

PART II

A 유형 분석

100단어 내외의 단일 지문을 읽고 주어진 질문에 적절한 답을 4개의 선택지에서 고르는 유형이다.

제시 방법 한 개의 지문에 한 개의 질문이 주어진다.

문항수 21문항

측정 영역 단일 지문에 대한 전체 및 세부 내용 이해 및 추론 능력을 측정한다.
대의 파악(6문항) → 세부 내용 파악(10문항) → 추론(5문항) 순으로 나온다.

빈출 토픽 학술문과 실용문에서 모두 골고루 출제된다.

B 대표 기출문제

Sam Cantwell and Jack Hansen are two of America's best-loved motivational speakers. They have each delighted thousands of listeners with their wit and wisdom, and now—in a never-before-held event—they have teamed up to create a unique, doubly rewarding experience. Join them as they tell their favorite tales of inspiration at Chancellor Hall this Friday and Saturday only, from 8:00 pm. Tickets are available at the door, or you may purchase tickets in advance through www.ticketsite.com.

Q What can be inferred about Cantwell and Hansen from the passage?
(a) They will stay together for a national tour.
(b) They are not likely to attract high ticket sales.
✔ (c) They are appearing together for the first time.
(d) They will give talks advocating a religious doctrine.

해석

샘 캔트웰과 잭 핸슨은 미국 내에서 가장 사랑받는 두 명의 동기부여 연사입니다. 이들은 각각 재치와 지혜로 수천 명의 청중들에게 기쁨을 주었으며, 이제 과거에 유례없던 한 행사를 통해 이들이 의기투합하여 독특하며 두 배로 보람 있는 경험을 만들고자 합니다. 이번 주 금요일과 토요일 단 이틀, 오후 8시부터 챈슬러 홀에서 이들이 가장 좋아하는 감동의 이야기를 들려주는 자리에 함께하십시오. 입장권은 행사장에서 구매 가능하며, www.ticketsite.com 을 통해 예매를 하실 수도 있습니다.

Q 캔트웰과 핸슨에 대해 유추할 수 있는 것은?
(a) 전국 투어를 함께 다닐 것이다.
(b) 높은 입장권 판매를 유치할 것 같지 않다.
(c) 처음으로 함께 출연한다.
(d) 종교적 교의를 옹호하는 이야기를 할 것이다.

공략법

두 번째 문장에서 언급한 과거에 유례없는 행사(a never-before-held event)라는 표현으로 보아 두 사람의 연사가 함께 출연하는 것이 처음임을 추론할 수 있다. 따라서 정답은 (c)이다. (a)와 (b)는 지문의 내용만으로는 알 수 없으며, 사람들에게 영감을 주고 동기를 부여해 주는 내용의 연설을 할 것으로 예상되므로 (d)도 오답이다.

C 고득점 핵심 비법

- 직독직해하는 습관을 들인다. 우리말로 해석부터 하려고 덤벼들지 말고 신속하게 영어 지문을 읽으면서 내용을 이해하는 습관을 들여야 한다.
- 지문을 다 읽겠다는 생각을 버려라. 대의 파악 문제의 경우 주요 내용어 중심으로 읽고, 세부 내용 파악 문제는 질문에 따라 선택지의 진위 여부를 한 개씩 확인해 가며 읽거나 육하원칙 문제는 질문 내용을 제대로 파악하고 해당 부분을 신속히 찾아서 그 부분을 자세히 읽는다. 추론 문제는 대의 파악 및 세부 내용 파악이 선행되어야 하기 때문에 좀 더 시간을 할애해야 할 것이다.
- 오답 함정을 각 문제 유형마다 미리 알아 두고 잘 피하도록 한다.
  - 대의 파악 오답 유형 : 세부 사실을 대의로 혼동하게 하는 오답이 자주 출제된다.
  - 세부 내용 파악 오답 유형 : 일부 내용만 사실인 경우, 지문에서 언급된 어휘로 만들었지만 내용과는 상관없는 선택지를 주의하자.
  - 추론 오답 유형 : 그럴듯해 보이지만 지문 내용과는 상관없는 오답, 정답과 정반대 진술이 선택지로 제시되기도 한다.

PART III

A 유형 분석

5개의 문장으로 구성된 100단어 내외의 단일 지문을 읽고 글의 흐름상 어색한 문장을 찾는 유형의 문제이다.

제시 방법 주제문에 이어 4개의 문장이 제시된다.

문항수 3문항

측정 영역 지문의 응집력 파악 능력을 측정한다.

빈출 지문 토픽 학술문과 실용문 모두 골고루 출제된다.

B 대표 기출문제

See the memorable sights of London with Black Taxi Tours! (a) Our tour is the only one where you can enjoy seeing the sites of London in genuine London taxi cabs. (b) A detailed commentary from a trained London cabbie is included in your comprehensive two-hour tour. ✔ (c) To become a cabbie in London, you must have an extensive knowledge of the city's roads. (d) You won't find a better guide than our cabbies, so call our office now to book your tour.

해석

블랙 택시 관광으로 기억에 남을 런던 명승지를 돌아보세요! (a) 저희 관광은 진짜 런던 택시를 타고 런던의 관광지를 즐길 수 있는 유일한 관광 상품입니다. (b) 숙련된 런던 택시 기사의 자세한 해설이 전체 2시간 관광에 포함되어 있습니다. (c) 런던에서 택시 기사가 되려면 런던의 도로에 대한 해박한 지식이 있어야 합니다. (d) 저희 기사들보다 더 나은 가이드는 찾을 수 없을 것입니다. 그러니 지금 저희 사무실로 전화하셔서 블랙 택시 관광을 예약하십시오.

공략법

런던 택시를 이용한 관광을 홍보하는 광고문으로, 택시 관광에 대한 간단한 안내와 함께 빨리 예약을 하라는 광고 문구가 나와 있는 글이다. 그러나 (c)에는 관광과는 관련없는, 택시 기사가 되기 위해 필요한 조건이 나와 있으므로 전체 문맥과 어울리지 않는다.

C 고득점 핵심 비법

- 처음 제시되는 주제문에서 벗어난 문장을 찾는 것이므로 4개의 선택지 문장을 읽을 때에 항상 주제문과의 연관성을 염두에 두고 읽도록 한다. 문법 Part 4의 경우 각 문장 간의 연관성까지 염두에 두고 내용을 파악할 필요는 없으나 독해 Part 3에서는 주제문과의 연관성이 문제 풀이의 핵심이다.
- 주제문과 연관성은 있으나 문장의 위치가 잘못되어 흐름을 깨는 유형도 있으니 흐름상 잘 어울리는지도 살피도록 한다.
- 글의 어조가 갑자기 바뀌는 경우도 어색한 문장에 해당하므로 어조의 변화도 주의하도록 한다.
- 주어진 주제문에 대한 문장이 3개 나온 뒤 새로운 주제문이 4번째 문장으로 나오게 되면 어색한 문장이 된다는 것도 기억한다.

서울대 최신기출 1

Listening *Comprehension*

Grammar

Vocabulary

Reading *Comprehension*

Listening Comprehension

Directions

1. In the Listening Comprehension section, all content will be presented orally rather than in written form.
2. This section contains four parts, each with fifteen individual items. For each part, you will receive separate instructions. Listen to the instructions carefully, and choose the best answer from the options for each item.

Scripts P 268 / 정답 P 334

Part I **Questions 1–15**

You will now hear fifteen individual spoken questions or statements, each followed by four spoken responses. Choose the most appropriate response for each item.

Part II **Questions 16–30**

You will now hear fifteen short conversation fragments, followed by four spoken responses. Choose the most appropriate response to complete each conversation.

Part III **Questions 31—45**

You will now hear fifteen complete conversations. For each conversation, you will be asked to answer a question. Each conversation and its corresponding question will be read twice. Then you will hear four options which will be read only once. Based on the given information, choose the option that best answers the question.

Part IV **Questions 46—60**

You will now hear fifteen short talks. After each talk, you will be asked to answer a question. Each talk and its corresponding question will be read twice. Then you will hear four options which will be read only once. Based on the given information, choose the option that best answers the question.

GRAMMAR

DIRECTIONS

This section tests your grammar skills. You will have 25 minutes to complete the 50 questions. Be sure to follow the directions given by the proctor.

정답 P 334

Part I Questions 1—20

Choose the option that best completes each gap.

1. A: Can I return the library books late?
   B: No, they really should be returned ___________ their due date.
   (a) in
   (b) to
   (c) by
   (d) until

2. A: Did you have a good weekend?
   B: I sure did. I got ___________ shopping done at the Grove Outlets.
   (a) few
   (b) any
   (c) some
   (d) many

3. A: Have you called the apartment manager about vacancies?
   B: Yes. I inquired as to ___________ there were any available units.
   (a) because
   (b) as far as
   (c) whether
   (d) as long as

4. A: I don't know how to pick a partner for the research project.
   B: Choose a person ___________ working style you believe will be most compatible with yours.
   (a) whoever
   (b) whose
   (c) whom
   (d) who

5. A: Do you like living in Thailand?
   B: Yes, I love ___________ here. It's such a nice change from home.
   (a) climate
   (b) a climate
   (c) the climate
   (d) another climate

6. A: My knee has been bothering me ever since I started running frequently.
   B: Maybe you should exercise ___________. You may be overdoing it.
   (a) too
   (b) less
   (c) little
   (d) either

7. A: Jackie, why didn't you stop when I called you?
   B: Sorry. I ___________ to my MP3 player.
   (a) listened
   (b) had listened
   (c) was listening
   (d) have listened

8. A: You didn't wear your new jeans.
   B: I was worried some people might ___________ to wear something so casual.
   (a) deem it inappropriate
   (b) inappropriately deem it
   (c) inappropriate deem about it
   (d) deem about it inappropriately

9. A: Are you excited about moving?
B: Yes. As we ___________ in Hunstown for a long time, it's time for a change.

(a) will have lived
(b) have lived
(c) will live
(d) live

10. A: I want to take a sick day, but I don't want to fall behind on my work.
B: Stay home. Your work won't ___________.

(a) for a day suffer much losing
(b) suffer much from losing a day
(c) lose much of a day for suffering
(d) suffer losing much of from a day

11. A: Where did the cat go?
B: I looked for her everywhere, but she was nowhere ___________ found.

(a) was
(b) to be
(c) being
(d) to have been

12. A: Did you know that our neighbor is listed in the biographical dictionary?
B: You mean Mr. Halls? Wow, I didn't know he was ___________ famous.

(a) far
(b) that
(c) such
(d) much

13. A: It turns out that Mike Evan's estate was worth millions of dollars.
B: That's surprising, considering most people knew ___________ a modest life.

(a) he has led to
(b) he has to lead
(c) to have him led
(d) him to have led

14. A: Are you ever going to travel abroad?
B: Maybe. But I don't see it ___________ any time soon.

(a) happens
(b) to happen
(c) happened
(d) happening

15. A: Are you still saving up your money?
B: Not at all. If I ___________, I wouldn't be taking this vacation.

(a) am
(b) were
(c) will be
(d) would be

16. A: Your son is really getting into those educational comic books.
B: I know. Every day after school he's in his room ___________ in one.

(a) engrosses
(b) engrossed
(c) to engross
(d) engrossing

GRAMMAR

17. A: What did you think of the last interviewee?

B: I think she has ___________ needed for the job, but she lacks experience.

(a) knowledges
(b) a knowledge
(c) the knowledge
(d) the knowledges

18. A: Where can I go sightseeing?

B: Downtown. It ___________ with tourist sites.

(a) abounds
(b) is abounded
(c) has abounded
(d) will be abounded

19. A: Is your mother feeling better?

B: She's still coping ___________ recurring pneumonia.

(a) for
(b) with
(c) from
(d) about

20. A: Will you take your kids to visit your family in Moscow next month?

B: No, it would be ___________ to our kids' education, so they won't go.

(a) a too great interruption
(b) interrupting too greatly
(c) too greatly interrupting
(d) too great an interruption

Part II Questions 21–40

Choose the option that best completes each gap.

21. Whenever she met new people, Gina felt shy and avoided ___________ conversation.

(a) to have made
(b) having made
(c) to make
(d) making

22. The government was shocked by the news of the uprising, as ___________ the citizens.

(a) is
(b) are
(c) was
(d) were

23. Having started out as a part-time helper, Jason never imagined that one day he ___________ director.

(a) became
(b) is becoming
(c) had become
(d) would become

24. The majority of federal programs are managed efficiently; however, ___________ there is no room for improvement.

(a) to say not that
(b) not saying that
(c) that is not to say
(d) to say is not that

GRAMMAR

25. Tom finally secured a job at a firm ___________ he does not have to work late every night.

(a) that
(b) what
(c) which
(d) where

26. As a basic human right, freedom of expression ___________ be upheld at all costs, and nothing should be permitted to jeopardize it.

(a) may
(b) must
(c) might
(d) would

27. Roger always chose chocolate ice cream as his treat because ___________.

(a) of it all he liked best
(b) best of all it he liked
(c) he liked it best of all
(d) he liked best of it all

28. Since his assistant had not informed him of the agenda, John was unsure about ___________ was scheduled for the evening.

(a) what
(b) when
(c) which
(d) whom

29. When multiple patients arrive at the emergency room at once, the hospital's policy is to treat ___________ with the most urgent health problems first.

(a) this
(b) their
(c) them
(d) those

30. Anna was proud that she had finished most of her math homework on her own with ___________ assistance from her tutor.

(a) few
(b) any
(c) little
(d) either

31. Some infants wake up multiple times during the night, ___________ other babies sleep soundly through the night without waking up.

(a) since
(b) unless
(c) whereas
(d) whenever

32. Pleasant working conditions result in lower levels of stress and, in turn, ___________ absenteeism and turnover among employees.

(a) reduce
(b) reduces
(c) has reduced
(d) have reduced

33. It is often the case that artists ___________ to flourish in an academic environment feel repressed and frustrated.

(a) attempt
(b) attempted
(c) attempting
(d) are attempting

34. The boy apologized for forgetting to take out the trash, saying that he had not ___________.

(a) meant
(b) meant to
(c) meant to do
(d) meant to take

35. The roll call ___________ as the latecomers arrived at the auditorium.

(a) has conducted
(b) was conducting
(c) has been conducted
(d) was being conducted

36. Professor Miller announced that students could request extensions, but ___________ that there would be no penalty for late submissions.

(a) at no time did he state
(b) he did state at no time
(c) at no time he did state
(d) did not state at no time

37. Despite ___________, businesses remained open as usual.

(a) the area was in a blizzard
(b) a blizzard in the area being
(c) there was a blizzard in the area
(d) there being a blizzard in the area

38. The reclusive author now lives alone in a remote town, with not many locals ___________ who he is.

(a) realize
(b) realized
(c) realizing
(d) have realized

39. Some experts feel it is imperative that cell phones and accompanying electromagnetic fields ___________ identified as possibly carcinogenic.

(a) be
(b) are
(c) were
(d) would be

40. Innovations move society forward, and ___________ than the Internet.

(a) an example of this is no truer exists
(b) this exists no truer an example
(c) no truer example of this exists
(d) this example exists is no truer

GRAMMAR

Part III **Questions 41—45**

Read each sentence carefully and identify the option that contains a grammatical error.

41. (a) A: Jacob told me you're running in the marathon this weekend, too. Good for you!

(b) B: Yeah, I'm hoping to complete it in less than six hours. What's your best time?

(c) A: Somewhere around the three-hour mark.

(d) B: Wow. By the time I'll pass the halfway point, you'll probably already have crossed the finish line!

42. (a) A: What has you in a such good mood? You're beaming.

(b) B: I opened the door to my office and out jumped an old college friend.

(c) A: How long had it been since you last saw each other?

(d) B: We last met at graduation, which was ten years ago.

43. (a) A: So you're looking to rent a compact car?

(b) B: Yes, for about seven days. I'm going on a cross-country road trip.

(c) A: Can you tell me from what exactly day you need the car?

(d) B: From the first day of next month. That's when I plan to depart.

44. (a) A: If I may ask, how much was your season pass to Funland Amusement Park?

(b) B: Well, there was a special promotion, so I only had to pay $300.

(c) A: How should you afford that with all of your other expenses?

(d) B: Well, with the payment plan, it only comes out to about $25 a month.

45. (a) A: I really need to get to this message to Bill from the client.

(b) B: Why don't you just call his cell phone? He always has it with him.

(c) A: I tried that a few times, but to no avail. It seems to be turned off.

(d) B: Then why don't you give the message to me? I'll be seeing him this afternoon.

Part IV **Questions 46–50**

Read each sentence carefully and identify the option that contains a grammatical error.

46. (a) The early twentieth century saw gospel music enjoying widespread popularity in the US. (b) The genre started gaining a wider audience with the introduction of the radio in the 1920s. (c) In addition, numerous new gospel groups formed and began performing across the nation. (d) The greater exposure through touring and radio attracted an audience greater to gospel music.

47. (a) Administering four times a year, the Test of Proficiency in Korean (TOPIK) is in strong demand. (b) The number of test takers at the test's first administration in 1997 totaled slightly under 2,500. (c) Now people are taking the TOPIK in increasing numbers, not only in Korea but also in 49 other countries. (d) That more people are taking the TOPIK signifies that Korean is quickly becoming a global language.

48. (a) George Orwell's *Animal Farm* is an allegorical tale of a well-intentioned society gone bad. (b) The novel opens as the farm's anthropomorphized animals, victorious after a revolution against human oppression, begins to organize. (c) However, not much time passes before the pigs, who have assumed command, actually adopt many of the very practices they despised. (d) As such, *Animal Farm* shows how quickly leaders can become corrupted by greed and power.

49. (a) For most Europeans living during the Renaissance, the exploration of new lands was of little interest. (b) Rather, their focus was on delving into their own past and rediscovering the classics. (c) However, contact with other parts of the world has a profound impact on some Europeans during this time. (d) Being enlightened to the fact that many of the world's peoples had different behaviors and beliefs was earth shattering for them.

50. (a) The human nose is an especially sensitive organ that allows us to distinguish innumerable odors. (b) However, the nose is also vulnerable, easily irritated anything from pollen to animal fur. (c) Some people have even reported that sudden exposure to bright light can make them sneeze. (d) This shows just how easily the nose can become overstimulated.

This is the end of the Grammar section. Do NOT move on to the next section until instructed to do so. You are NOT allowed to turn to any other section of the test.

VOCABULARY

DIRECTIONS

This section tests your vocabulary skills. You will have 15 minutes to complete the 50 questions. Be sure to follow the directions given by the proctor.

정답 P 334

Part I **Questions 1—25**

Choose the option that best completes each gap.

1. A: Nice meeting you. Let's keep in touch.
B: Sure. I'll ___________ you my e-mail address so you can contact me.

(a) ask
(b) dial
(c) give
(d) loan

2. A: Stanley is on the phone for you. Can you talk?
B: Of course, I'll ___________ his call.

(a) like
(b) pick
(c) take
(d) click

3. A: I can't concentrate because of the noise from the construction site.
B: It won't ___________ your studies much longer. It'll be done soon.

(a) reveal
(b) disturb
(c) decline
(d) remove

4. A: Do I need much money to start investing in stocks?
B: No. In the ___________ stages, a small investment is fine.

(a) prior
(b) initial
(c) prompt
(d) surplus

5. A: Can you show me where Main Street is on this map?
B: Sure. I'll ___________ its location for you.

(a) solve
(b) classify
(c) pinpoint
(d) recognize

6. A: Why does Andy always keep to himself?
B: He doesn't like to ___________ much.

(a) pack
(b) bunch
(c) socialize
(d) combine

7. A: Marcus loves old classic cars.
B: Yes, he says the ___________ ones are superior to modern cars.

(a) daring
(b) vintage
(c) dubious
(d) vehicular

8. A: Excuse me, is this the only line for immigration?
B: If you're a European Union citizen, you may go to the ___________ on the left.

(a) series
(b) locale
(c) queue
(d) interim

9. A: Do I need to see a specialist after my operation?

B: No. Seeing your family physician will be ___________.

(a) mitigating
(b) complicit
(c) adequate
(d) fulfilling

10. A: I'm afraid to tally up all the extra expenses on our hotel bill.

B: I know. We've ___________ a lot of added charges.

(a) imparted
(b) increased
(c) auctioned
(d) accumulated

11. A: It's taking me a long time to adjust to my new job.

B: Hang in there. Those kinds of transitions are usually ___________.

(a) stale
(b) final
(c) affixed
(d) gradual

12. A: Have you started studying for your exams?

B: Not yet, but I really should ___________ soon.

(a) hold tight
(b) get cracking
(c) drop the ball
(d) pass the buck

13. A: We saw so many fish on our dive today!

B: Yes, the reef was positively ___________ with different species.

(a) instilling
(b) strewing
(c) teeming
(d) pouring

14. A: Your hair and makeup look great!

B: Thanks. All the time I spent ___________ paid off.

(a) draping
(b) clinging
(c) gleaming
(d) grooming

15. A: My allergies are getting worse.

B: Mine, too. They really ___________ in the spring.

(a) put on
(b) rub off
(c) flare up
(d) spread out

16. A: Skiing down such a dangerous mountain must have been terrifying.

B: It was ___________, but the challenge made it exciting.

(a) daunting
(b) repellent
(c) cathartic
(d) scoffing

17. A: Looking back on your life, do you sometimes have regrets?

B: Yes. In ___________, I wish I had pursued a singing career.

(a) backlash
(b) hindsight
(c) refraction
(d) viewpoint

18. A: Your little girl seems very curious about the world.

B: Yes, children at that age are ___________ by nature.

(a) salient
(b) apparent
(c) noticeable
(d) inquisitive

19. A: Should I keep the summary short?

B: Yes, please be as ___________ as possible.

(a) deficient
(b) sporadic
(c) succinct
(d) elusive

20. A: You've been too tough on Sally lately.

B: You're right. I will ___________ from now on.

(a) cut her some slack
(b) foam at the mouth
(c) add fuel to the fire
(d) drive her up the wall

21. A: Janine must have been very disappointed after losing the debate.

B: Yes. She was absolutely ___________ over it.

(a) dissuaded
(b) crestfallen
(c) parsimonious
(d) magnanimous

22. A: You don't seem sure about your decision to go to France.

B: I do have some ___________, but I've already committed to going.

(a) vagaries
(b) segments
(c) intrusions
(d) misgivings

23. A: This article raises questions but doesn't make any authoritative assertions.

B: I agree, but the author never ___________ to be an expert on the subject.

(a) emulated
(b) connoted
(c) purported
(d) implicated

24. A: What are some of the teachings espoused by Buddha?

B: Well, he ___________ the virtue of self-reliance, for one.

(a) adjudicated
(b) apportioned
(c) consolidated
(d) promulgated

25. A: Dinner won't be ready for another hour.

B: OK, then I may need a snack to ___________ my hunger.

(a) assuage
(b) infiltrate
(c) augment
(d) intercede

VOCABULARY

Part II Questions 26–50

Choose the option that best completes each gap.

26. The kitchen was a ___________ because Jack had not cleaned it in weeks.

(a) cluster
(b) mess
(c) stain
(d) pile

27. Known for their indiscriminate appetites, tiger sharks will ___________ anything from seabirds to other sharks.

(a) oblige
(b) devour
(c) partake
(d) contend

28. In her weight-loss book, Mimi Delaware ___________ healthy eating by listing its positive impacts on health.

(a) protects
(b) deduces
(c) appeases
(d) encourages

29. Private parties who wish to ___________ a boat for their exclusive use should contact Party Boat Company for booking details.

(a) lend
(b) span
(c) pledge
(d) charter

30. The Jones's impressive Christmas display is ___________ by some 30,000 colored light bulbs.

(a) emitted
(b) radiated
(c) glittered
(d) illuminated

31. The Bible is the text which lays forth Christian ___________, the teachings at the foundation of the religion.

(a) warrants
(b) doctrines
(c) sanctions
(d) credentials

32. In the interest of transparency, all city departments must ___________ their financial records to the public.

(a) disclose
(b) endorse
(c) accredit
(d) promote

33. Wireless networks ___________ data between electronic devices by sending signals over radio waves.

(a) allay
(b) excel
(c) attend
(d) convey

34. All Priza Motors contracts are ___________ and thus cannot be dissolved for any reason.

(a) joining
(b) binding
(c) heralding
(d) confining

35. Jeremy had not meant to break his mother's vase—it was the result of an unfortunate ___________.

(a) hazard
(b) mishap
(c) interlude
(d) adversity

36. The manager ___________ his security guards for falling asleep, showing his frustration with a torrent of angry words.

(a) defaced
(b) inveigled
(c) upbraided
(d) trumpeted

37. Oak Farm Bread is ___________ with nine different vitamins essential for good health.

(a) rectified
(b) enriched
(c) amplified
(d) compounded

38. Important announcements should be sent over the instant messaging system to ensure the quick ___________ of information.

(a) dilation
(b) diffusion
(c) dissolution
(d) dissimulation

39. Watching too much television can ___________ a child's development of literacy, leading to below-average reading scores.

(a) stunt
(b) numb
(c) wince
(d) dodge

40. The deal was considered ___________, since all parties had not yet agreed on it.

(a) aversive
(b) tentative
(c) skeptical
(d) implacable

41. A facility with maps and 3-D puzzles can be a(n) ___________ of good spatial intelligence in a person.

(a) indication
(b) exposition
(c) collocation
(d) predilection

42. The rapidly falling birth rate is ___________ serious problems for the Korean government.

(a) posing
(b) ascribing
(c) expending
(d) witnessing

43. Jane Austen's *Pride and Prejudice* is ___________ with examples of irony, it being one of the book's most striking characteristics.

(a) astray
(b) replete
(c) satiated
(d) forgone

44. After receiving excellent training, Roberta was so ___________ a writer that she could write competently in several styles and genres.

(a) deft
(b) livid
(c) captive
(d) vacuous

45. The students asked the professor to ___________ on the topic and explain it more fully.

(a) prostrate
(b) elaborate
(c) proliferate
(d) exacerbate

46. In the mid-1920s, Argentina's politicians were split into two hostile ___________ that were divided over the role of former President Yrigoyen.

(a) factions
(b) partitions
(c) allegations
(d) conflations

47. Bisphenol-A, or BPA, is such a(n) ___________ chemical that virtually all humans have been exposed to it.

(a) effervescent
(b) voracious
(c) pervasive
(d) effusive

48. Many people have a(n) ___________ attitude about technological development, but this kind of optimism can blind one to its potential pitfalls.

(a) discursive
(b) sanguine
(c) ornate
(d) florid

49. The public must accept that doctors are not ___________ and will make mistakes from time to time.

(a) indelible
(b) ineffable
(c) infallible
(d) intangible

50. In contrast to the bright feathers of the male peacock, the plumage of female peacocks is more ___________.

(a) prolix
(b) muted
(c) strident
(d) onerous

This is the end of the Vocabulary section. Do NOT move on to the Reading Comprehension section until instructed to do so. You are NOT allowed to turn to any other section of the test.

READING COMPREHENSION

DIRECTIONS

This section tests your ability to comprehend reading passages. You will have 45 minutes to complete the 40 questions. Be sure to follow the directions given by the proctor.

정답 P 334

Part I **Questions 1–16**

Read the passage and choose the option that best completes the passage.

1. Journaling is often considered a hobby, but it can also ______________________. Sorting through complex problems in your head is not easy, but writing out your thoughts can help you identify your true preferences. It is very difficult to make sound judgments when your thoughts are going back and forth between the pros and cons of a course of action. Writing not only clarifies your choice but also provides a record of how you arrived at it.

(a) be used as a decision-making tool
(b) keep track of daily events in your life
(c) make you feel better when you are sad
(d) help preserve your personal memories

2. When the United States first became a nation, laws such as the Naturalization Act of 1790 restricted citizenship to "free white persons" of "good moral character." Native Americans, slaves, indentured servants, or free blacks were excluded. Subsequent legal changes, such as the addition of the Fourteenth Amendment to the Constitution and the Naturalization Act of 1870, granted citizenship to all persons born on American soil, regardless of race. Thus, over time, America's citizenship policies ______________________.

(a) denied legal rights to non-citizens
(b) changed to become more inclusive
(c) came to condone racial discrimination
(d) eventually had to be enforced more strictly

3. When planning a party, people often choose to invite close friends by calling them instead of sending an invitation, striving for a more personal touch. However, when formal invitations go out to all the other guests, those invited verbally may feel as though they were merely an afterthought. Making the effort to personally call friends will certainly be appreciated, but party hosts should ensure that ______________________.

(a) the RSVP date is clearly stated
(b) they call everybody on the guest list
(c) all guests receive written invitations
(d) they choose a date guests can agree on

READING COMPREHENSION

4. Data analysis from the Gravity Recovery and Climate Experiment, in which satellites monitored variances in ice and water mass on Earth, explains ______________________________. Since the 1990s, scientists had only been able to speculate as to why the Earth was expanding at the equator while getting flatter at the poles. Subsequent studies, however, revealed that an increase in glacier melting near Greenland and Antarctica, along with shifts in ocean circulation, redistributed water toward the planet's midsection and away from its poles, resulting in the Earth's increasingly oblate shape.

(a) why global warming is speeding up
(b) the cause of the planet's changing contour
(c) how glacial melting is a self-perpetuating process
(d) the shift in water distribution toward the Earth's poles

5. Though the East Slavic ethnocultural group known as the Cossacks preserved their traditions in fable, song, and ballad, ______________________________. Their history has been pieced together mostly from the writings of outsiders—from Russian and Polish scribes, and from the memoirs of Western European travelers to the Cossack lands. This is because the Cossacks themselves associate written record-keeping with bureaucracy and authoritarian control and prefer to rely on the methods of oral history.

(a) their oral stories have been largely forgotten
(b) their written history differs within the group
(c) they abstained from keeping written accounts
(d) they are virtually unknown to outside observers

6. Canadian journalist Carl Honoré has proposed a novel approach to parenting which aims to ______________________________. The method, known as "slow parenting," was developed to counteract parents' tendency toward hyper-vigilance. While parents typically establish rules for their children and carefully monitor their behavior, Honoré says that this approach communicates a lack of faith in the children. Slow parenting, in contrast, grants children more freedom so that they develop the confidence to act independently.

(a) intensify bonding through open displays of affection
(b) raise autonomous children through trustful parenting
(c) counter the trend of granting children unlimited freedom
(d) manage children's behavior by imposing stringent rules

7. Plumpy'Nut, a peanut-based foodstuff used to fight severe acute malnutrition, has been highly successful because ______________________. In the past, when famine struck an area, the traditional course of treatment for malnutrition involved therapeutic milk, which requires a supervising nutritionist. What makes Plumpy'Nut more convenient and therefore more effective is that it can be prepared and eaten at home, with no need for formal medical attention. Children can even feed themselves Plumpy'Nut since it is a soft paste that is easy to consume.

(a) it boosts the absorption of the nutrients in therapeutic milk
(b) its efficacy means it can prevent malnutrition from reoccurring
(c) its taste and texture are more appealing to children than milk's
(d) it is easier to administer than other treatments for malnutrition

8. When living in a foreign country, a person is likely to find both positive and difficult experiences lying in wait. For me, my first six months as a Canadian expatriate in France were a honeymoon period; everything about the culture was fascinating. Of course, after some months, ______________________. What at first were minor frustrations—the language barrier, for example—became a source of constant stress and embarrassment. Though leaving France never crossed my mind, I had to struggle with the fact that the charm of expatriate life was wearing off.

(a) I began to consider going back home
(b) my awe ultimately gave way to angst
(c) the homesickness mercifully subsided
(d) I became enamored with expatriate life

9. With the number of nurses rapidly shrinking, the health care sector is ______________________. Signing bonuses, cash prizes, and even vacations are becoming common incentives for new hires. But if the sector is serious about recruiting more nurses, prizes are not the answer. Improvements in working conditions, status, and base pay are. In a national survey of registered nurses, 49% reported that if they were starting out today, they would pursue a different career. These results make it clear that a fundamental rethinking of health care recruitment is necessary, not game-show tactics.

(a) desperate to keep experienced nurses from retiring
(b) admitting too many inexperienced workers into its ranks
(c) taking the wrong tack with frivolous recruitment gimmicks
(d) implementing measures to address current staff dissatisfaction

10. Edward Jenner's development of the smallpox vaccine in 1796 was important not only because it was the first step toward modern vaccination, but also because it ______________________________. Before Jenner's innovation, doctors practiced variolation, a procedure imported to England by Lady Mary Wortley Montagu. Variolation involved purposely infecting a person with smallpox to build up immunity through a controlled infection. But variolation, though effective, was unpredictable and risky; many of its recipients became fatally ill. Jenner's method of inoculation against smallpox was far safer, so it quickly replaced variolation in medical circles.

(a) eliminated the use of a more dangerous preventive measure
(b) improved upon variolation by means of a controlled infection
(c) set a precedent for importing medical procedures from abroad
(d) showed how safer but less powerful treatments gain popularity

11. Digital artist Cory Arcangel makes artworks that exemplify that making meaningful digital art ______________________________. Perhaps because digital art is a relatively young field, digital artists have felt pressure to stay on the cutting edge. But Arcangel is the exception. For instance, in his most famous work, "Super Mario Clouds," he hacked into an old Nintendo Super Mario Brothers cartridge and stripped away everything but the cloud graphics, essentially making digital art using media that is twenty years out of date. Arcangel's creation proves that in order to do interesting work, the most up-to-date version of software is not always necessary.

(a) is best done by those with extensive experience
(b) depends on ensuring it will not become obsolete
(c) often involves collaborating with younger artists
(d) is not contingent on having the latest technology

12. At its core, Shakespeare's *Hamlet* is a revenge tragedy that centers on Hamlet's father's murder and the onus on Hamlet to avenge it. One major critical controversy regarding this plot is ______________________________. Some critics explain this by deeming Hamlet a coward and therefore incapable of swift action. But this is contradicted by his decisive, but mistaken, slaying of Polonius. Other analyses have surmised that Hamlet was simply too sensitive and philosophical a character to engage in brutality and that accounts for his procrastination.

(a) Hamlet's ostensible lack of morality
(b) the brutality of how the revenge is enacted
(c) Hamlet's delay in carrying out the revenge
(d) the emotional plausibility of the play's characters

13.

To the Editor:

Thank you for highlighting the state's poverty problem in "Virginia's Poverty Up." It is incredible that our state has four out of the ten wealthiest counties in the nation, yet 9% of the state's children live in poverty. Statistics show that more people are becoming poorer and, even with the majority having jobs, cannot support their families. Meanwhile, the rich are getting richer—a trend occurring nationwide yet being ignored by policymakers. In fact, the state of things in Virginia reflects this country's ______________________________.

Janet Brighton

(a) growing problem of inequitable wealth distribution
(b) inability to fill the increasing number of job vacancies
(c) tendency to offer handouts before they are even requested
(d) persistent refusal to acknowledge that employment is a privilege

14. When compared with the moral philosophy of Immanuel Kant, Danish philosopher Søren Kierkegaard emphasized the ______________________________. For Kant, the moral agent can either behave morally autonomously, by imposing obligations on himself, or heteronomously, by obeying externally imposed rules or laws; the latter he considered slavish insofar as the person does not feel truly committed to the moral actions. For Kierkegaard, in contrast, man cannot comprehend what is truly right or wrong and so has to submit to a faith in a higher power. Thus, Kierkegaard exalted the biblical figure of Abraham, who obeyed God's command to sacrifice his son, Isaac.

(a) capacity to act morally based solely on reason
(b) primacy of autonomy in moral agents' actions
(c) necessity of yielding to belief in a higher being
(d) progress made in defining ethical responsibilities

15. Examples of self-regulating systems can be found in everything from nature to human learning processes. A corporation ensuring its survival through its staffing and operational processes, for instance, can be considered a self-regulating system. Earth's ecosystem is another example: the biosphere and all the life on Earth contribute to maintaining things like the global temperature and general habitability of the planet. ________________________, the human body is a self-regulating system, since it maintains a constant temperature and pH level.

(a) Likewise
(b) All in all
(c) Nonetheless
(d) In other words

16. The Bedouins are a nomadic ethnic group in the Middle East who, as shepherds, have traditionally organized their lives around the seasons of the desert. Beginning in the 1950s, however, keeping up a nomadic lifestyle became less and less feasible for the Bedouins as space became scarce and populations boomed. On top of that, many of the countries they traversed, including Egypt and Israel, enacted policies to urge Bedouins to leave behind their nomadic wanderings and settle in towns. ________________________, many Bedouins have now transitioned to a semi-nomadic or stationary lifestyle.

(a) Even so
(b) After all
(c) Accordingly
(d) On the other hand

Part II **Questions 17—37**

Read the passage, question, and options. Then, based on the given information, choose the option that best answers the question.

17. Are you an American living abroad who misses your favorite US-made products? Then get a membership with USAddy. Some retailers don't ship globally or charge excessive fees to do so. What USAddy does is provide you with a US street address—one of our warehouses—that you can use when placing online orders. Once your package arrives at our warehouse, it'll be forwarded to your international address. Shop online with any US merchant, using your USAddy address at check-out, and get your products delivered for reasonable shipping fees.

Q: What is mainly being stated about USAddy in the advertisement?
(a) It arranges package exchanges between countries.
(b) It ships American products abroad at affordable rates.
(c) It makes products especially for American expatriates.
(d) It has several warehouses where Americans may shop.

18. When friends in distress come to you seeking consolation, do you say "It's going to be OK," or advise them to just forget about their worries? Though well-intentioned, such responses are dismissive and don't acknowledge the real pain a person is in. When people are struggling, what they need most is for you to listen and empathize with them. While reassuring platitudes may seem helpful, it's really better to just pay attention and let your friends know you're there for them.

Q: What is the writer's main point?
(a) Listening is the best help to give a person in distress.
(b) Failing to listen to reason will leave you friendless.
(c) Concrete advice is better than a sympathetic ear.
(d) It is often easier to give advice than to take it.

19. In France, it is widely believed to be the height of rude manners to cut the "nose"—or the point—off a triangular block of cheese. This action is ill-mannered because the nose represents the choicest part of the cheese wheel. To take the whole nose would be considered extremely selfish. Therefore, when presented with a triangle of cheese, it is best to take slices from the side of the block.

Q: What is the main topic of the passage?
(a) French etiquette for slicing triangular cheese
(b) The difference between parts of a cheese wheel
(c) How the French present cheese to dinner guests
(d) The impropriety of taking the last slice of cheese

20. With its violent and exploitative lyrics, current rap music has come a long way from its roots, mostly in the wrong direction. Rap originally evolved as a form of protest music, with politically conscious messages forming the backbone of the lyrics. However, as the profitability of rap music was recognized, it was appropriated by the mainstream media and its political power was deflated. Once a powerful outlet for social commentary, mainstream rap music now represents little more than empty commercialism.

Q: What is the passage mainly about?
(a) Criticisms of rap as an exploitative genre of music
(b) How rap has evolved to respond to current social issues
(c) How rap music is no longer a vehicle for social commentary
(d) The attempts rap artists have made to gain musical credibility

21. Having trouble selling your product or getting people to use your service? Looking for a way to get your message out in a variety of channels? Turn to McKinley Public Relations Agency! With experience in print, radio, online, and viral marketing, our consultants can help you diversify your advertising strategies across several platforms to reach the widest audience. Taking advantage of diverse media, we'll help you effectively execute your message to ensure your target audience is reached and your sales grow.

Q: What is mainly being advertised about McKinley Public Relations Agency?
(a) It helps clients advertise across a variety of media platforms.
(b) Its consultants give advice on managing sales revenues.
(c) Its work centers on the visual design of advertisements.
(d) It focuses its advertising efforts on the youth market.

22. Virtually no industry has escaped the impact of the Internet, and newspapers are among the hardest hit. But the newspapers themselves have to shoulder much of the blame for their current predicament. For an industry that prides itself on having its finger on the pulse of society, newspapers were shockingly oblivious to the sea change the Internet was about to bring. And once newspapers did recognize the Internet's ascendancy, they were too slow in moving online. This failure to see the coming change—and the opportunity it represented—is why newspapers have to admit their own role in their obsolescence.

Q: What is the passage mainly about?
(a) How the Internet forced newspapers to move online
(b) How newspapers are responsible for their own demise
(c) The greater range of news sources the Internet provides
(d) The changing role of newspapers in contemporary society

23. The Roman emperor Diocletian provides an example of the ultimate futility of attempting to restrict religious freedom. In an empire that was hostile to Christians, Diocletian was content to simply exclude them from society. But others in his court called for more violent persecution, and he eventually acceded to their demands. His attempts garnered him censure, though; even pagans were unsympathetic to the brutal executions Diocletian enacted. Far from its intended effect, the martyring of Christians strengthened their fellow believers' resolve. The large number of ascetics who absconded to the desert during this period formed the basis of Christian monasticism.

Q: Which of the following is correct according to the passage?
(a) Diocletian ultimately flouted his court's demands to oppress Christians.
(b) Pagans mostly supported Diocletian's decision to persecute Christians.
(c) Martyring succeeded in spurring Christians to abandon their faith.
(d) Christian monasticism arose from a group of ascetics who fled to the desert.

24. Tramadol is a drug that is often prescribed to provide pain relief after surgery and for chronic conditions such as arthritis. It comes in immediate-release tablets and extended-release tablets, which can be taken with or without food. However, be advised that the extended-release tablets must be taken whole. Do not split, chew, or crush them, as doing so can result in faster absorption and possible overdose. Recommended dosages can range from 50 to 100 milligrams every four to six hours, and no more than eight tablets or 400 milligrams daily.

Q: Which of the following is correct about Tramadol according to the document?
(a) It cannot be used to treat chronic pain.
(b) It is available in immediate-release tablets.
(c) It is recommended that it be taken with a meal.
(d) Its extended-release tablets may be split in half.

25. One of the most eccentric and devout believers in environmentalism is John Francis. After a devastating 1971 oil spill in California, Francis joked about never riding in a vehicle again. But the joke turned into a vow that he would keep for 22 years. During his early years of traveling on foot, Francis often found himself arguing with people about his decision. So in 1973, on his 27th birthday, he started an experiment wherein he stopped speaking, simply listening instead. And once again, the experiment became a lifestyle, as he continued his silence until Earth Day in 1990.

Q: Which of the following is correct about John Francis according to the passage?
(a) A 1971 oil spill made him break his vow of silence.
(b) He refused to ride in vehicles until the age of 22.
(c) He stopped speaking because no one disagreed with him.
(d) He remained silent between the years 1973 and 1990.

26. Skulls have a long history as a motif in both gallery and decorative arts. Although their association with death is obvious, they are not always used to conjure a sense of mortal pessimism. In medieval Europe, skulls decorated drinking glasses to remind beer-drinkers to enjoy their earthly existence. The skull-and-crossbones motif of pirate ships symbolized a free-wheeling refusal to avow allegiance to any one country. And in Mexico, images of skulls are prominently featured in Day of the Dead celebrations, which honor those who have passed away.

Q: Which of the following is correct according to the passage?
(a) The skull motif's exclusive use in art has been to inspire fear.
(b) The skull motif appeared on drinking vessels in medieval Europe.
(c) Pirates flew skull flags to prove their loyalty to their homeland.
(d) Mexicans avoid displaying skull images when honoring the dead.

27. The Battle of Bull Run in 1861 was the first major engagement of the American Civil War. Both sides, the Union forces in the North and the Confederate forces in the South, believed it would decide the outcome of the war. Civilians from Washington, cheering for the Union, came with picnic lunches to watch the battle. Anxious that the war would end before they had their chance at glory, volunteer soldiers signed up in droves. Though romanticized at first, Bull Run was a tragically bloody battle, and far from ending the war, it preceded a further four years of conflict.

Q: Which of the following is correct about the Battle of Bull Run according to the passage?

(a) It was thought it would determine the war's winner.
(b) Washingtonians watching it supported the South.
(c) Volunteer soldiers were reluctant to participate in it.
(d) It was a minor battle that definitively ended the war.

28.

Dear Mrs. Adams,

Our records show an outstanding balance of $2,240 for our catering service for your corporate event. Despite the complaint you lodged regarding the missing menu items, you have already been advised that the service provided was in accordance with the contract you signed. I therefore regret to inform you that if payment is not forthcoming within the next 21 days, we will proceed with litigation.

Sincerely,
Paul Tomkins
Coach Catering

Q: Which of the following is correct about Mrs. Adams according to the letter?

(a) Her event was not catered because she did not pay the $2,240.
(b) Her complaint against the caterer regarded the food's freshness.
(c) She neglected to sign the agreed-upon contract for the catering.
(d) She must pay her balance within three weeks to avoid legal action.

29. The tap water advisory issued last week for Brick County will remain in effect until further notice. The Department of Public Works has fixed the last of the main water and sewage lines damaged in last week's storms, but until microbial test results come back negative, officials recommend that residents continue to boil their water as a precaution before drinking or cooking with it. Residents will be notified as soon as the city's Water Management Bureau approves the safety of tap water.

Q: Which of the following is correct according to the announcement?
(a) Last week's tap water advisory has been canceled by Brick County.
(b) Repair work on the main water and sewage lines has been completed.
(c) Negative test results mean residents must continue to boil their water.
(d) Residents are advised to refrain from using tap water for cooking.

30. When oranges first came to France, they were a prized delicacy. So scarce were they that cookbooks offered guidelines for exactly how many orange slices each rank of nobility was entitled to. King Louis XIV, wanting to have this delicacy year-round, had an orangerie built at Versailles in 1686. These gardens featured orange trees in movable boxes that could be brought indoors for safekeeping during winter. And the orangerie's gardeners used gardening techniques to get the trees to bloom year-round, making oranges available at any time of the year for royals.

Q: Which of the following is correct according to the passage?
(a) The first oranges served in France were not sought after by the nobility.
(b) The Versailles orangerie had orange trees planted in movable containers.
(c) The orangerie's trees were left outdoors and covered during winter.
(d) The orangerie failed to produce a constant supply for the royal court.

31. This report presents a meta-analysis of studies conducted between 1970 and 2005 on the health effects of meditation. After a comprehensive search of the literature, 400 studies that met the criteria for this review—clinical trials with more than ten adult participants—were assessed. While most studies found that meditation had some positive effect on conditions including hypertension and cardiovascular disease, nearly all lacked a common theoretical perspective and suffered from methodological shortcomings. Until a more concrete body of research is developed, the authors of this report assert that meditation's benefits remain unsupported.

Q: Which of the following is correct according to the report?
(a) Studies with no more than ten participants were the only ones considered.
(b) Few studies reported meditation having any beneficial health effects.
(c) All of the studies that were assessed shared the same theoretical perspective.
(d) Its authors find that the health effects of meditation are not substantiated.

32. Welcome to the Vatican website! We invite all guests to be part of a general audience with the Pope, held every Wednesday beginning at 10:30 a.m. in the Pope Paul IV Hall. All are welcome, but note that free tickets must be requested from the Prefecture of the Papal Household at least 10 days in advance. Seating is not assigned, so the best way to guarantee good seats is to arrive at least an hour early. The venue opens at 8:00 a.m. to accommodate early arrival.

Q: Which of the following is correct according to the announcement?
(a) Papal audiences take place once a week.
(b) Tickets must be purchased in advance.
(c) Ticket holders must sit in their designated seats.
(d) Admission to the Pope Paul IV Hall closes at 8 a.m.

33. Southern Coast Airlines is happy to announce that work on the first of our Bellcraft King F20 planes is finished. Our designers have substantially improved on this very successful model. We've completely refurbished the interior of economy class, with more leg room, larger overhead luggage storage bins, and individual in-seat entertainment. And first class now includes private lay-flat beds and showers for long-haul flights. Fly Southern Coast on your next trip, and see the difference!

Q: What can be inferred about Southern Coast Airlines from the advertisement?
(a) Its refurbishments were made to increase passenger comfort.
(b) Its planes have always had individual in-seat entertainment.
(c) It is a new airline that is targeted at travelers on a budget.
(d) It is reducing the number of destinations it flies to.

34. The first baseball cards were marketed to grown men and were included in cigarette packs. In 1909, the American Tobacco Company (ATC) released a card featuring Baseball Hall of Famer Honus Wagner. But Wagner recognized that the cards appealed to young boys and did not want his image to be used in influencing children to smoke. After he threatened legal action, the ATC stopped production of his card. Just 57 of them remain in existence today, making them among the most sought after and expensive baseball cards.

Q: What can be inferred from the passage?
(a) Wagner claimed his card image was altered to depict him smoking.
(b) Children had no interest in the cards since they could not buy them.
(c) The ATC destroyed all Wagner cards in existence to prevent a lawsuit.
(d) Wagner's insistence on discontinuing his cards ultimately raised their price.

35. Although scientific research is not the primary goal of amateur astronomers, many have made major discoveries. For instance, one of the brightest comets in recent history was discovered in 1965 by a pair of Japanese amateurs, Kaoru Ikeya and Tsutomu Seki. So how do amateurs beat professionals to these discoveries? It has to do with equipment. The shorter focal lengths on amateurs' smaller telescopes give them an advantage over professionals, whose huge telescopes are built to scan for large, distant galaxies, not smaller nearby objects.

Q: What can be inferred from the passage?
(a) Ikeya and Seki used a large professional telescope to detect the comet.
(b) The comet spotted by Ikeya and Seki was traveling in a distant galaxy.
(c) Professional-grade telescopes are superior to amateur ones in every way.
(d) Telescopes with shorter focal lengths can see nearby objects in space better.

36.

> To the Editor:
>
> The new bill that proposes mandatory community service in order for citizens to receive unemployment benefits is preposterous. I am employed full-time myself, but I believe forcing the unemployed to devote 24 hours of their time every week to volunteering is unfair. They have little money as it is, and this bill will increase their transportation costs. Also, if they do three days of service in a week, they would only have two days for job searching. Community service is usually reserved for people that commit crimes. Don't treat the unemployed like criminals.
>
> Russell Douglas

Q: Which statement would the writer most likely agree with?
(a) More volunteers are needed to provide services to the unemployed.
(b) Employers should prioritize community service as a hiring criterion.
(c) Mandating community service is tantamount to punishing the unemployed.
(d) The unemployed should be required to give back to the community for their benefits.

37. A study of humans' primate cousins, capuchin monkeys, has shed light on the question of whether our aversion to unfair treatment is an instinctual behavior or a social construct. Thirteen capuchin monkeys were taught to swap stones for food, with some receiving cucumber slices while others received grapes, a more desirable reward. When the monkeys that received cucumbers became aware of the unfair treatment, they refused to eat the cucumbers or stopped participating in exchanges. This showed that the monkeys' sense of fairness was based on instinct.

Q: What can be inferred from the passage?
(a) The monkeys preferred no reward over an unfair reward.
(b) The monkeys were taught the concept of fairness prior to trading.
(c) Capuchins that benefited from the exchange sided with those that did not.
(d) Scientists were circumspect because of the experiment's inconclusive results.

Part III Questions 38 – 40

Read the passage and identify the option that does NOT belong.

38. Like many exceptionally gifted musicians, Frederic Chopin had music teachers who could not keep up with him. (a) His first piano teacher was his elder sister Ludwika, but his talent quickly surpassed hers. (b) At age six, Chopin began studying with Czech teacher Wojciech Zywny, whom he also outgrew. (c) Chopin became conversant with music early on, influenced by his mother, a piano teacher herself. (d) Even when Chopin was under the tutelage of composer Jozef Elsner, the latter realized he was outmatched and could merely observe Chopin's genius.

39. A black bear got more than it bargained for after wandering into Springfield resident Alan Smith's backyard. (a) Ostensibly in search of food, the bear had no idea it would have to confront Mitzy, Smith's fiercely territorial dog. (b) Upon encountering the bear, Mitzy chased him up into a tree and barked incessantly at him. (c) Feeding bears is not only illegal but also dangerous, as it leads to bears viewing humans as sources of food. (d) No doubt the black bear had not expected such a small dog to defend her owner's home so vociferously.

40. Despite starting out the fiscal year 2011 with financial difficulties, Cycom Telecommunications has ended the year on a positive note. (a) We partly attribute this to the decision to expand our broadband service in rural areas, widening our customer base. (b) For example, the telecommunications industry reached record levels of profitability in 2011. (c) Also, as shareholders are aware, we experienced a change in leadership midway through the year. (d) New CEO Donna Rogers has re-focused Cycom's operations on our core capabilities, with positive effects.

This is the end of the Reading Comprehension section. Please remain seated until the proctor has instructed otherwise. You are NOT allowed to turn to any other section of the test.

서울대 최신기출 2

Listening Comprehension
Grammar
Vocabulary
Reading Comprehension

LISTENING COMPREHENSION

DIRECTIONS

1. In the Listening Comprehension section, all content will be presented orally rather than in written form.
2. This section contains four parts, each with fifteen individual items. For each part, you will receive separate instructions. Listen to the instructions carefully, and choose the best answer from the options for each item.

Scripts P 279 / 정답 P 335

Part I **Questions 1–15**

You will now hear fifteen individual spoken questions or statements, each followed by four spoken responses. Choose the most appropriate response for each item.

Part II **Questions 16–30**

You will now hear fifteen short conversation fragments, followed by four spoken responses. Choose the most appropriate response to complete each conversation.

Part III **Questions 31—45**

You will now hear fifteen complete conversations. For each conversation, you will be asked to answer a question. Each conversation and its corresponding question will be read twice. Then you will hear four options which will be read only once. Based on the given information, choose the option that best answers the question.

Part IV **Questions 46—60**

You will now hear fifteen short talks. After each talk, you will be asked to answer a question. Each talk and its corresponding question will be read twice. Then you will hear four options which will be read only once. Based on the given information, choose the option that best answers the question.

GRAMMAR

DIRECTIONS

This section tests your grammar skills. You will have 25 minutes to complete the 50 questions. Be sure to follow the directions given by the proctor.

정답 P 335

Part I **Questions 1—20**

Choose the option that best completes each gap.

1. A: Let's play a game of chess.
B: Well, you'll have to teach me, ___________ I've never played before.

(a) if
(b) but
(c) since
(d) while

2. A: I feel a headache coming on.
B: Have some aspirin and you ___________ better.

(a) feel
(b) will feel
(c) are feeling
(d) will have felt

3. A: Where did you learn how to make curry from scratch?
B: I had an Indian roommate in college ___________ mother taught me.

(a) that
(b) who
(c) which
(d) whose

4. A: Politicians spend so much time on campaign fundraising!
B: I know. Among the many duties of legislators ___________ meeting with donors.

(a) were
(b) was
(c) are
(d) is

5. A: Are you satisfied with the smartphone you got?
B: Yes! I never thought ___________ one would transform my life so much.

(a) own
(b) owned
(c) owning
(d) to be owning

6. A: Your chicken parmesan is phenomenal.
B: Thanks! Feel free ___________ seconds.

(a) have
(b) having
(c) to have
(d) having had

7. A: My son wants to get a pet tarantula.
B: I find the idea ___________ keeping a spider as a pet revolting.

(a) of
(b) to
(c) for
(d) with

8. A: I'm getting behind in my work these days.
B: Me, too. It's really hard to get ___________ work done in this hot weather.

(a) few
(b) little
(c) many
(d) much

GRAMMAR

9. A: I don't think my stomach's handling the food ___________

B: In that case, you'd better go get some medicine for indigestion.

(a) that I just well had all
(b) I had that just all well
(c) that had I just well all
(d) I just had all that well

10. A: Our competitors at the tournament seem really weak.

B: Yes, our chances of winning are ___________ better this year than last.

(a) far
(b) too
(c) such
(d) very

11. A: Do you like to listen to jazz in the morning?

B: Yes, it's ___________.

(a) best waking up the music
(b) to wake up the best music
(c) the best music to wake up to
(d) the best music to be waking up

12. A: Who's in charge of expense reports?

B: I'm not sure ___________.

(a) whose responsibility for it
(b) whose responsibility it is
(c) who it is responsible for
(d) who is it responsible

13. A: Should I take an umbrella? It's cloudy, but the weather forecast says it's not going to rain.

B: I'd take one. I don't think the forecast can ___________.

(a) be trusted
(b) be trusting
(c) have trusted
(d) have been trusted

14. A: What are you and your wife doing for your summer vacation?

B: What with ___________ our first child, nothing too extravagant.

(a) her being pregnant
(b) she is pregnant with
(c) she is being pregnant
(d) her being pregnant with

15. A: Robin's finally coming to town tomorrow! Aren't you excited?

B: Yes, but I wish he'd told me earlier that he ___________ to visit us.

(a) has come
(b) will come
(c) was coming
(d) will be coming

16. A: Which papers would you like me to look at first?

B: The documents ___________ immediate attention are on top.

(a) required
(b) requiring
(c) to require
(d) will require

17. A: How long will you live here in Rome?
B: I'll be here for a while, ___________ I get a better job elsewhere.

(a) as long as
(b) in case
(c) unless
(d) once

18. A: I heard you barely caught your flight.
B: Yeah. Only by running straight to my gate ___________ my connection.

(a) I made
(b) made I
(c) I did make
(d) did I make

19. A: Can you still fit into your wedding gown?
B: No way! I'm not as thin as I ___________.

(a) used to
(b) used to be
(c) used to do
(d) used to be thin

20. A: When is the deadline for our rent payment?
B: We have ___________ it.

(a) a week we are until paying
(b) until a week ending to pay
(c) the week ending until paying
(d) until the end of the week to pay

Part II Questions 21–40

Choose the option that best completes each gap.

21. Ray prided himself on having ___________ collection of records.

(a) diverse
(b) a diverse
(c) much diverse
(d) many diverse

22. Camptrail stores sell their own brand of ___________ for hiking, as well as several other well-known brands.

(a) gear
(b) gears
(c) the gear
(d) the gears

23. For many older people, their house is their only asset, ___________ some financial security but no income.

(a) being offered
(b) offering
(c) offered
(d) offer

24. The city's smoking ban will apply to all bars and restaurants, ___________ outdoor seating areas.

(a) excepting of
(b) with excepting
(c) of the exception with
(d) with the exception of

25. After running a marathon on Saturday morning, Elizabeth still somehow had ___________ energy to go out with friends later that evening.

(a) an
(b) the
(c) any
(d) every

26. Bill will be promoted once he ___________ his master's degree.

(a) will have earned
(b) will be earning
(c) earns
(d) earned

27. The number of anthropology classes to be offered next year ___________ yet to be decided.

(a) has
(b) have
(c) has been
(d) have been

28. University rules state that all students ___________ hand in immunization records in order to be eligible to live in dormitories.

(a) can
(b) may
(c) must
(d) could

29. Following the company's fiscal crisis, massive layoffs left hundreds of workers ___________ jobs.

(a) without
(b) against
(c) beside
(d) under

30. TV and magazines show famous people leading perfect lives, but celebrities actually have more problems than they ___________.

(a) portray to have
(b) are portrayed as
(c) have them portrayed as
(d) are portrayed as having

31. Lamar was upset that he ___________ about the proposed staff changes before they went into effect.

(a) has not told
(b) was not telling
(c) has not been told
(d) had not been told

32. Had he known that his comment about politics would create such controversy, James never ___________ the topic.

(a) would have brought up
(b) will have brought up
(c) would bring up
(d) had brought up

33. When Carol retires next spring, she ___________ as a teacher for 40 years.

(a) has worked
(b) will be working
(c) has been working
(d) will have worked

34. Ever since the manager resigned, there ___________ a lot of confusion about the chain of command among employees.

(a) has been
(b) was being
(c) have been
(d) were being

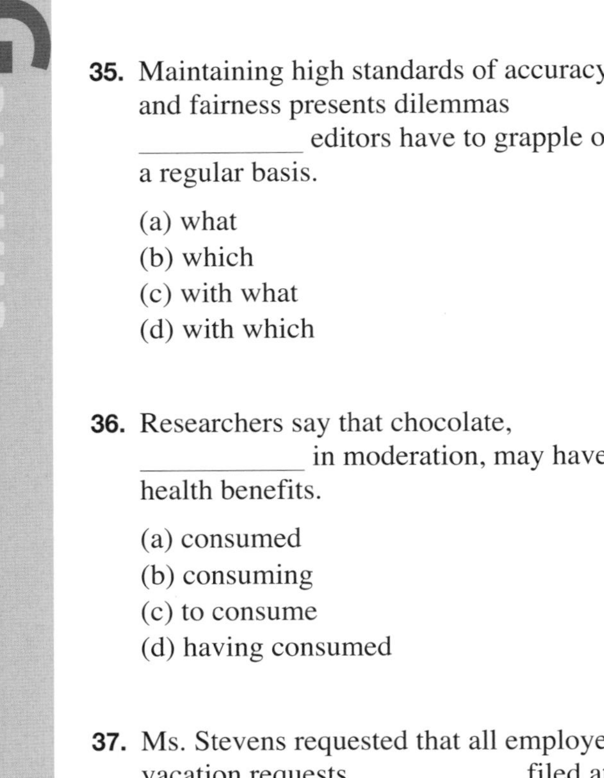

35. Maintaining high standards of accuracy and fairness presents dilemmas __________ editors have to grapple on a regular basis.

(a) what
(b) which
(c) with what
(d) with which

36. Researchers say that chocolate, __________ in moderation, may have health benefits.

(a) consumed
(b) consuming
(c) to consume
(d) having consumed

37. Ms. Stevens requested that all employee vacation requests __________ filed at least a week in advance.

(a) be
(b) are
(c) were
(d) would be

38. Those who observed Catherine and Patrick said that __________ seemed to be a marriage filled with affection.

(a) theirs
(b) those
(c) them
(d) they

39. __________ that his sons were falling behind in math, Mr. Phillips sought a tutor who could work with them individually.

(a) Concerned
(b) Concerning
(c) To be concerned
(d) Having concerned

40. At the start of his contract negotiations, the coach clearly expressed __________ him working for the team.

(a) what it would take to keep
(b) it would take what to keep
(c) what to keep it would take
(d) it would keep what to take

Part III **Questions 41–45**

Read each sentence carefully and identify the option that contains a grammatical error.

41. (a) A: Sam, I need all the applications for the sales position immediately.
(b) B: Sure, but why? I thought you decided to hire that woman from Texas.
(c) A: I did. But she backed out, and now I'm in urgently need of a replacement.
(d) B: I'll email you the information right away. I'm sure you can find someone suitable for the position.

42. (a) A: What were you and Michelle debating during that phone call?
(b) B: She wants me to sign up for a dating website, that I have no intention of doing.
(c) A: Well, a lot of people are meeting their partners that way nowadays.
(d) B: I'm sure they are, but I'd still prefer to meet someone the old-fashioned way.

43. (a) A: I wonder if the hiking trails are any good now after the rain.
(b) B: As long as we wear some sturdy hiking boots, we'll be fine.
(c) A: It must be best if we packed ponchos, too, just in case.
(d) B: Well, all right. But I don't think it'll rain any more today.

44. (a) A: I hear you and your wife aren't coming to the office party this Christmas.
(b) B: Right, we're leaving a trip just the day before. We're going to visit her parents.
(c) A: Oh, that sounds nice. But the party won't be as much fun if you two aren't there.
(d) B: Thanks, that's kind of you to say. Hopefully we'll be able to make it next year.

45. (a) A: How has your job search been going lately? Do you have any leads?
(b) B: Not really, so I'm looking into going to abroad as an English teacher. What about you?
(c) A: I've been thinking about entering a graduate program somewhere.
(d) B: Yeah, I hear a lot of people are doing that to wait out this recession.

Part IV Questions 46–50

Read each sentence carefully and identify the option that contains a grammatical error.

46. (a) Most people have a reverent attitude toward the symbols of their nation. (b) One such patriotic symbol that every country has a national flag. (c) Evoking feelings of allegiance, flags adorn both private and public spaces. (d) Accordingly, many countries have protocols for the respectful display of flags.

47. (a) The human retina contains cone cells which can detect red, blue, and green light. (b) Stimuli activate these cells in different combinations, producing the colors we see. (c) However, genetic factors may cause one or more of the types of cone cells to be missing or faulty. (d) This results either total color blindness or an inability to see certain colors.

48. (a) Customers do not look kindly on inadequate service, which is why service failures must be rectified promptly. (b) The procedures needing in service recovery situations differ according to the type of problem that needs to be addressed. (c) Sometimes a sincere apology is the best way to effect a recovery, while in other cases, tangible compensation is necessary. (d) Addressing service failures properly can actually improve customer loyalty and encourage repeat business.

49. (a) Prions are a type of infectious agent which operates different from other types of pathogens. (b) They are composed of misfolded proteins, and unlike viruses or bacteria, they contain neither DNA nor RNA. (c) When prions infect a host, they induce the organism's properly folded proteins to mutate into an abnormal form. (d) This disrupts the structure of otherwise healthy tissue and causes irreversible tissue damage.

50. (a) Born to a peasant family in 1935, the present Dalai Lama is the spiritual leader of the Tibetan people. (b) He has also been the political leader of Tibet until 2011, when he ceded power to an elected government. (c) The Dalai Lama explained that his aim was not to shirk his duties but to promote democracy in his country. (d) His decision was lauded by the international community and earned him respect among fellow Tibetans.

This is the end of the Grammar section. Do NOT move on to the next section until instructed to do so. You are NOT allowed to turn to any other section of the test.

TEPS

VOCABULARY

DIRECTIONS

This section tests your vocabulary skills. You will have 15 minutes to complete the 50 questions. Be sure to follow the directions given by the proctor.

정답 P 335

Part I **Questions 1–25**

Choose the option that best completes each gap.

1. A: This plant has tripled in size in just two weeks!
   B: Yes, this species usually grows very ___________.
   (a) firmly
   (b) rapidly
   (c) accurately
   (d) identically

2. A: How much does it cost to get downtown?
   B: The ___________ for the bus is $10, and the train costs $15.
   (a) fine
   (b) fare
   (c) check
   (d) change

3. A: I just found out I got an A on the test!
   B: You must be ___________ that your studying paid off.
   (a) indulged
   (b) balanced
   (c) pleased
   (d) settled

4. A: I've heard this restaurant is famous for its ice cream.
   B: Yes, hand-churned ice cream is its ___________.
   (a) honor
   (b) tribute
   (c) gratuity
   (d) specialty

5. A: Did giving a blood sample hurt?
   B: No, they just ___________ my finger with a needle.
   (a) spliced
   (b) pricked
   (c) pinched
   (d) splintered

6. A: There aren't many taxis in this city.
   B: I know. They're pretty ___________ here, compared with back home.
   (a) distinct
   (b) scarce
   (c) amiss
   (d) naive

7. A: Who takes care of Alastair's house when he's away?
   B: His gardener handles the ___________ of the lawn, and I manage the bills.
   (a) grant
   (b) output
   (c) upkeep
   (d) proceeds

8. A: When will the workshop finish?
   B: It's scheduled to ___________ around three o'clock.
   (a) tune out
   (b) wrap up
   (c) stop over
   (d) break down

9. A: Did you give your children traditional names?

B: No, my wife wanted them to have ___________ names.

(a) unconventional
(b) harmonious
(c) prospective
(d) erroneous

10. A: I'm worried my essay didn't explain my topic completely.

B: Why? It seemed very ___________ to me.

(a) sheer
(b) integral
(c) thorough
(d) conditional

11. A: I hope you're not too upset about losing that art contest.

B: No, I knew it'd be ___________ since my painting wasn't that great.

(a) in the bag
(b) a long shot
(c) out of the blue
(d) the bottom line

12. A: Do I turn left at this next intersection?

B: Don't make a full turn—just ________ left slightly at the fork in the road.

(a) tilt
(b) veer
(c) slant
(d) swap

13. A: This job includes housing support and paid leave.

B: Wow. Those sound like great ___________.

(a) coups
(b) perks
(c) alms
(d) dibs

14. A: How much is it to have this letter ___________?

B: Sending it the quickest way possible costs $10.

(a) postdated
(b) expedited
(c) reiterated
(d) imparted

15. A: We're spending too much on this vacation.

B: But we work hard! We deserve to spend ___________ on a nice trip.

(a) lavishly
(b) stealthily
(c) languidly
(d) equivocally

16. A: We're out of tea in the break room.

B: It's a good thing I ___________ some away for an occasion like this.

(a) cached
(b) flocked
(c) hurtled
(d) revered

17. A: Did you see how Ted parked in the boss's spot this morning?

B: Yeah, I can't believe he had the ___________ to do that.

(a) prudence
(b) vibrancy
(c) temerity
(d) remorse

18. A: How did the brownie baking go?

B: Great! They ___________ even better than last time!

(a) came to
(b) carried on
(c) turned out
(d) showed off

19. A: Has Katrina really turned down Zach's proposals twice?

B: Yes, she has been ___________ in her refusal to marry him.

(a) steadfast
(b) inanimate
(c) intermittent
(d) spontaneous

20. A: I couldn't see how Ed's criticisms related to Laura's central argument.

B: Me, neither. Everything he mentioned was ___________ to the main issue.

(a) nomadic
(b) reclusive
(c) alienated
(d) tangential

21. A: Professor Adams is amazing. He has published ten books in three years!

B: I know. He's a tremendously ___________ writer.

(a) strenuous
(b) usurious
(c) teeming
(d) prolific

22. A: What caused that big road accident yesterday?

B: A truck ___________ suddenly to avoid a fallen branch and flipped over.

(a) vaulted
(b) collided
(c) swerved
(d) deflected

23. A: I'm intimidated by how ___________ Sharon is.

B: Don't be. She's very knowledgeable but also quite down-to-earth.

(a) erudite
(b) intrinsic
(c) insidious
(d) exorbitant

24. A: Lana's speech was absolutely captivating!

B: I know. The entire audience was ___________ with attention.

(a) awry
(b) staid
(c) terse
(d) rapt

25. A: Dave's so shy at work—he never talks about his home life.

B: Yes, he's quite ___________ when it comes to general conversation.

(a) diffident
(b) fallacious
(c) unabashed
(d) mendacious

VOCABULARY

Part II Questions 26–50

Choose the option that best completes each gap.

26. Many companies encourage applicants to ___________ their résumés in person rather than by e-mail.

(a) submit
(b) replace
(c) arrange
(d) indicate

27. When investing in a new company, the first ___________ is to gather information about its history and dealings.

(a) drop
(b) post
(c) step
(d) hint

28. In terms of size, the blue whale is absolutely ___________, stretching over 30 meters long.

(a) distant
(b) remote
(c) mature
(d) gigantic

29. Many people ___________ money with happiness, even though wealth does not always translate into personal fulfillment.

(a) inflate
(b) equate
(c) immerse
(d) expound

30. On the basis of the available evidence, some scientists believe that life first developed around deep-sea vents, but others reject this ___________.

(a) scrutiny
(b) regulation
(c) hypothesis
(d) formulation

31. The debate became so ___________ that the mediator called a break to allow everyone to regain his composure.

(a) suave
(b) singed
(c) heated
(d) content

32. To prevent ___________ by harmful bacteria, raw meat should be prepared separately from vegetables.

(a) distortion
(b) exposition
(c) deprivation
(d) contamination

33. Most countries use security measures such as watermarks and holographic images to make it difficult for forgers to produce ___________ passports.

(a) irrational
(b) vapid
(c) hasty
(d) fake

34. When a foreign loan word enters a language, its pronunciation is often ___________ so that it fits native pronunciation.

(a) lifted
(b) revolved
(c) modified
(d) transferred

35. Rabbits can reproduce very quickly, some having dozens of ___________ in just one season.

(a) heredity
(b) offspring
(c) seedlings
(d) pedigrees

36. Some viewers found the controversial sculpture attractive, but an equal number disagreed, saying it was completely ___________.

(a) repulsive
(b) delectable
(c) contrasted
(d) inequitable

37. Management checks to be sure that interview questions do not include ___________ topics that could bias interviewers, such as place of birth or marital status.

(a) irritable
(b) irascible
(c) demonstrable
(d) discriminatory

38. Finding no internal reason for the computer system's failure, investigators said it was a deliberate act of ___________ by hackers.

(a) hostage
(b) sabotage
(c) exemption
(d) exoneration

39. Population growth and income distribution are two of the ___________ trends that social scientists study.

(a) sectarian
(b) provident
(c) geological
(d) demographic

40. The principal was accused of being ___________ for not properly addressing disruptive behavior at school events.

(a) stifling
(b) negligent
(c) engrossed
(d) impetuous

41. Scientists are developing the first drug capable of reversing the effects of Alzheimer's, which could be a major ___________ in treating the disease.

(a) breakthrough
(b) contrivance
(c) projection
(d) overdose

42. Consumers should purchase electronics only from ___________ retailers, who have the manufacturer's exclusive permission to sell the products.

(a) specious
(b) officious
(c) authorized
(d) susceptible

43. What started as a civilized lecture degenerated into an angry ___________ filled with abusive statements.

(a) crevice
(b) surge
(c) diatribe
(d) conclave

44. Patients suffering from anosognosia cannot ___________ that one side of their body is paralyzed and so think that they can move it.

(a) redeem
(b) perceive
(c) condone
(d) assimilate

45. Following the team's initial victory, its ___________ in the tournament worsened as it lost one match after another.

(a) facing
(b) holding
(c) handling
(d) standing

46. The ___________ views among the moderate and radical members of the Conservative Party have nearly split it apart.

(a) resplendent
(b) compliant
(c) disparate
(d) judicious

47. Accused of embezzling company funds, the executive ___________ to Mexico and eluded capture for years.

(a) pillaged
(b) desisted
(c) forfeited
(d) absconded

48. After ___________ unsuccessful campaigns in the early 1960s, Richard Nixon finally won the presidency in 1968.

(a) waging
(b) filching
(c) contouring
(d) underpinning

49. Visit our website to read the ___________ of hundreds of customers satisfied with the Hercules Exercise System.

(a) remissions
(b) testimonials
(c) convocations
(d) procurements

50. The toy store was ___________ with many excited holiday shoppers scrambling to make last-minute gift purchases.

(a) bustling
(b) fluttering
(c) scurrying
(d) quivering

This is the end of the Vocabulary section. Do NOT move on to the Reading Comprehension section until instructed to do so. You are NOT allowed to turn to any other section of the test.

Reading comprehension

Directions

This section tests your ability to comprehend reading passages. You will have 45 minutes to complete the 40 questions. Be sure to follow the directions given by the proctor.

정답 P 335

Part I **Questions 1–16**

Read the passage and choose the option that best completes the passage.

1. In ancient Sparta, the reign of a king ______________________________. The king was required to undergo an evaluation by designated officials every eight years. Whether he was still fit to lead was determined by telling signs in the night sky, such as unusual meteor activity, rather than by his past performance as a king. If officials observed any signs, they would know the king had sinned and might need to be replaced. For further confirmation, the officials also consulted the Delphic Oracle for instructions from the gods.

(a) would last until he abdicated in old age
(b) influenced the religious beliefs of the time
(c) was determined by his competence as a leader
(d) could be ended by cosmic omens and divine signs

2. Average life expectancy is generally lower for men than for women, but it also varies according to region, which suggests that life expectancy is influenced by factors other than biology. The shorter average lifespan of men could be influenced by many social and economic factors. For instance, men generally have higher rates of consumption of alcohol and tobacco. Also, more men are employed in harmful or dangerous occupations, such as construction or the military. Thus, viewing male life expectancy from the point of view of biology alone ______________________________.

(a) ignores crucial differences in men and women's physiology
(b) overlooks significant variables that influence life expectancy
(c) produces a more plausible explanation for women's longevity
(d) undermines sociologists' beliefs in regional differences in lifespans

3. "Spam" refers to mass emails that are generally unwanted, and a new related term, "bacn," has come to describe emails that ______________________________. They typically comprise newsletter-style advertisements and sale announcements from businesses such as banks or stores. Since email users often have a generally beneficial consumer relationship with the sender and provided their email addresses in the first place, bacn is harder to ignore or block than spam. However, it can be just as annoying as spam and can clutter up email inboxes quickly if not managed properly.

(a) are erroneously sent to junk mailboxes by spam filters
(b) circulate information about events currently in the news
(c) users opted to receive but may not find immediately useful
(d) contain personal information pertaining to financial transactions

4. Certain essays expressing strong personal convictions ______________________________. For example, Thoreau's influential essay "Civil Disobedience," which explored the right of individuals to follow their conscience, inspired Martin Luther King Jr. to become an advocate for reform in American race relations. Likewise, William James's essay "The Moral Equivalent of War" is thought to have inspired President Jimmy Carter to argue that the US should lower its consumption of fossil fuels. These works demonstrate the essay's power to move people in a positive direction.

(a) have prompted people to initiate social change
(b) have been appropriated to justify the status quo
(c) were written to make peace with one's conscience
(d) were used to keep subversive political ideas in check

5. In his masterpiece, *Madam Bovary*, Gustave Flaubert presents juxtaposing worldviews. The novel's central character, Emma Bovary, sees the world through a veil of dreamlike romance. She experiences passion, longing, and torment at the hands of her husband and her illicit lovers. The story's anonymous narrator, though, presents the plot's emotionally charged events in a tone of clinical detachment; the narrator does little to exhort readers to sympathize with the main character's predicament. In this way, Flaubert offers a contrast between the ______________________________.

(a) heroine's emotional and intellectual passions
(b) detachment of Emma and the passion of her lovers
(c) narrator's sympathy for and censure of Emma's indiscretions
(d) romanticism of the heroine and the objectivity of the storytelling

6. It seems that in many scientific fields, more and more published articles are reflecting findings of diminishing significance. This could indicate stagnating creativity, with researchers failing to undertake imaginative projects. It could also suggest that we have reached the limits of scientific knowledge with current technology. Or, most worryingly, the published conclusions could have been skewed by researchers' subconscious drive to conform. In any case, the present state of published research seems to suggest that ______________________________.

(a) studies are failing to incorporate previous scholarship
(b) science is becoming increasingly inaccessible to the public
(c) controversies in science are multiplying at an alarming rate
(d) researchers are failing to move scientific knowledge forward

7. The increase in workplace productivity engendered by modern office technology has ________________. At the end of the twentieth century, companies were investing in communications technology to facilitate workplace planning, organization, and collaboration. Economists suggested that technological innovation would afford highly productive workers additional leisure time. What has actually transpired, though, is that electronic devices have allowed people to work from anywhere. This has left many employees feeling continuous pressure to perform for their employers whether they are in the office or not.

(a) enabled employees to maximize their leisure time
(b) resulted in workers' perception of constantly being at work
(c) been thwarted by the use of electronic gadgets for personal purposes
(d) been accompanied by the challenge of training workers to use new devices

8. A recent survey looked at the factors that make for a powerful speech. When asked to react to seasoned public speakers defending causes to which they were indifferent, audiences found the speeches unconvincing. The grandiose gestures and facial expressions employed by these trained speakers struck audiences as insincere and patronizing. By contrast, untrained speakers who were passionate about their topics were regarded as credible and compelling, despite their somewhat clumsy delivery. The survey indicated that ________________.

(a) effective public speakers can mislead audiences
(b) conviction trumps theatrics in the eyes of spectators
(c) certain aspects of speeches must be studied formally
(d) audiences unconsciously prefer grandiose gesticulation

9. The Westmont Professional Women's Network would like to announce that we are ________________. Having started out with a focus on networking for women in the corporate sector, we have received numerous requests from women in other fields such as education, health care, and technical fields to allow them to join our network. With that in mind, we'd like to invite all working women to our spring luncheon on Saturday, May 1 at the Marion Hotel, where we will introduce our current leadership and give new members a chance to meet one another.

(a) looking to partner with similar groups in other industries
(b) expanding the scope of our organization's membership
(c) offering corporate positions to women in other sectors
(d) starting a chapter for full-time stay-at-home moms

10. Published in 1755, the *Dictionary of the English Language* compiled by Samuel Johnson was more comprehensive than any of its predecessors. One interesting fact about this dictionary is that it ______________________________. For the most part, Johnson followed in the tradition of existing bilingual and technical dictionaries, which provided definitions and illustrative sentences. But he often injected his opinions into these sentences in humorous ways. In one of Johnson's most famous instances of wry self-deprecation, he defined "lexicographer" as "a writer of dictionaries; a harmless drudge that busies himself in tracing the original and detailing the signification of words."

(a) included personal commentary in definitions
(b) was the only one at the time to offer translations
(c) paid attention to both obscure and common words
(d) was the first such work to provide examples of usage

11. Komodo dragons are huge predatory lizards that inhabit islands in eastern Indonesia. Researchers studying them ______________________________. Reaching up to three meters in length, Komodo dragons were formerly considered an example of the Island Rule, whereby island species with abundant prey and few competitors evolve massive bodies. However, fossil evidence shows that their size has not changed much for the last 900,000 years. Also, ancient remains of similarly large lizards found across Australia suggest that rather than having evolved hulking bodies by living on isolated islands, Komodo dragons are survivors of a relict population of gigantic lizards that once populated Australia and Indonesia.

(a) have yet to find theories that can explain their evolution
(b) agree that they are a classic case that proves the Island Rule
(c) believe their size diminished considerably since they first evolved
(d) have found evidence to contradict the previous explanation for their size

12. After the death of American writer Edgar Allan Poe in 1849, Rufus Griswold published an obituary which ______________________________. Griswold was a fellow poet and rival of Poe, and the obituary was in fact largely fictitious. Up to that point, Poe had generally been accepted as a talented writer and literary critic, but Griswold's obituary started to disseminate the idea that Poe was deranged and degenerate. A subsequent biography of Poe by Griswold repeated his accusations, deepening the public's misconception of Poe.

(a) put to rest the longstanding rumors about Poe
(b) began a character assassination of the late author
(c) added undeserved accolades to Poe's poetic legacy
(d) revealed the author's secret depravity to the public

13. With sports-related head injuries in the media spotlight, some Canadian high schools are taking part in a program that ______________________________. The program administers a short online test to young hockey players prior to the season to establish baseline performance in the four key areas of cognitive function—working memory, attention, learning, and information processing—that can be affected by concussions. If a concussion is suspected during the season, follow-up tests can be administered, and any decline in an athlete's score will allow doctors to diagnose concussions that cannot be detected through imaging tools like MRI or CT scans.

(a) trains athletes to enhance their cognitive skills
(b) screens players to look for pre-season head injuries
(c) monitors players' mental acuity to detect concussions
(d) teaches players how to prevent concussions while playing

14.

Dear Editor,

Your paper published an article that commended the Rovers' recent performance and attributed their winning streak to "a wise managerial decision." As the article said, having acquired several veterans, the Rovers are now a genuine championship contender. But what you forgot to mention is that they have had to trade their up-and-coming younger players for these seasoned players. Over the next few seasons, these veterans are going to retire, and the team is not going to have any young talent to fill its roster. Obviously, the team's quest for victory this season ______________________________.

Steven Crew

(a) hurts their chances of recruiting more veterans
(b) has put the championship out of reach for them
(c) comes at the expense of their future performance
(d) has been disappointing due to their current lineup

15. Pygmy hippopotamuses live in several western African countries, where they dwell primarily in forests and swamps. Unfortunately, the need for farm land in western Africa has led to the destruction of their natural habitat, and conservationists have estimated that fewer than 3,000 pygmy hippos are left in the wild. ______________________, the species has been categorized as critically endangered. In 2007, it was designated as one of the top ten "focal species" of the Evolutionary Distinct and Globally Endangered project.

(a) To reiterate
(b) Regardless
(c) As a result
(d) Otherwise

16. Since ancient times, comets have been regarded as omens of wars, disease, and all manner of evil. Although these are superstitious beliefs, sometimes they seem to have coincided with actual events. ______________________, a comet is said to have appeared before Julius Caesar was assassinated. Also, before King Harold was defeated by William the Conqueror at the Battle of Hastings, he had seen a comet and believed it to be a sign of evil.

(a) In short
(b) Meanwhile
(c) For instance
(d) Nevertheless

Part II Questions 17—37

Read the passage, question, and options. Then, based on the given information, choose the option that best answers the question.

17. The Weston Community Center would like to announce a change to our fall tennis schedule. Due to resurfacing of the tennis courts, all group classes and individual lessons will be canceled from September 20-27. Participants may receive a refund for missed lessons or obtain credit for extra lessons in the spring session. Please talk to a registration representative for further information about receiving this credit. We thank you for your patience as we improve our facilities.

Q: What is the announcement mainly about?
(a) How to handle the canceled tennis lessons
(b) A change of venue for upcoming tennis classes
(c) The registration procedure for fall tennis programs
(d) How to apply for a refund for canceled tennis lessons

18. Thank you for buying the Jetline printer. The most common cause of printing problems is dirt on the roller. This buildup can cause paper to be fed into the printer unevenly. To prevent this, open the cover and gently brush the roller with a soft, lint-free cloth. If desired, add a little rubbing alcohol to the cloth to remove fine dust particles. These steps will allow you to get many years of reliable use out of your printer.

Q: What is the main purpose of the passage?
(a) To provide instructions for cleaning a printer
(b) To explain the various causes of printer failure
(c) To give advice on repairing broken printers
(d) To promote the sale of printer cleaning products

19. Falcon Airlines customers have an opportunity to earn 50% extra air miles on all online bookings to destinations in Australia for this winter travel season. Simply enter your air miles card number when booking your flight, and the extra miles will automatically be applied to your account. Enjoy your winter vacation and earn points toward your next flight with Falcon Airlines. Offer ends December 15.

Q: What is mainly being advertised?
(a) Changes to the booking procedure for flights to Australia
(b) An incentive for seasonal flights to Australia booked online
(c) A temporary 50% discount on certain Falcon Airlines flights
(d) Extra air miles for all tickets booked through Falcon Airlines

20. *Health Science Quarterly* has strict policies regarding the research it publishes. Work presented must be the author's own and must constitute an original contribution to the field. Authors bear full responsibility for ensuring that their work appropriately cites prior research and publications on the topic in question. Note also that we do not accept papers that have been sent simultaneously to other publications.

Q: What is the main purpose of the instructions?
(a) To offer guidelines for article formatting
(b) To explain a journal's submission policies
(c) To define the scope of a scholarly publication
(d) To describe a journal's criteria for research topics

21. A study has shown that ibuprofen, a common over-the-counter pain reliever, can reduce the symptoms of altitude sickness. And everyone has welcomed the news, from tourists on skiing trips to hard-core mountain climbers. Why the excitement? The drugs typically used to treat altitude sickness, dexamethasone and acetazolamide, require prescriptions and are expensive. They also come with unpleasant side effects, such as nausea, headaches, and sleeplessness. Ibuprofen, on the other hand, has few major side effects when used for short periods and is widely available and inexpensive.

Q: What is the writer's main point about ibuprofen?
(a) It is now available without a prescription.
(b) It has been improved to have fewer side effects.
(c) It has advantages over prescription drugs for altitude sickness.
(d) It relieves altitude sickness symptoms faster than other remedies.

22. In the 1960s and 70s, when science fiction writers wanted a character to speak an alien language, they would often draw on minority languages. For instance, in the *Star Wars* films, the character Greedo spoke Quechua, an indigenous language from South America. But these attempts at linguistic exoticism often came off as laughably simplistic, or worse, racist. Fortunately, more authentic custom-made languages have come into fashion in recent decades: the best-known example is probably Klingon, the language concocted for the *Star Trek* series. And a more recent famous example is Na'vi, from the film *Avatar*.

Q: What is the passage mainly about?
(a) How custom-made alien languages have been criticized as racist
(b) The science fiction community's rejection of custom-made languages
(c) The effect that the creation of Klingon had on the science fiction genre
(d) How the representation of alien languages has changed in science fiction

23. Come and join us at Monsieur Bagnon's—the newest French bistro in town. We serve a mouthwatering menu of French dishes and are currently offering a 10% discount on our entire wine list. Our head chef hails from Provence, the heartland of French food, and was trained under French celebrity chef Jean Roubel. We are conveniently located on Newmarket Street opposite the Magnolia Theater and are open every day from 11 a.m. to 10 p.m.

Q: Which of the following is correct according to the advertisement?
(a) Monsieur Bagnon's is a long-established French restaurant.
(b) A discount is currently available for all the bistro's wines.
(c) The head chef trained the famous French chef Jean Roubel.
(d) The restaurant is located inside of the Magnolia Theater.

24.

> Dear Susan,
>
> It's been a long time since we've been in touch, but I wanted to share some good news. My husband and I will be coming out to Denver in June to look for an apartment for my son, who has found a job there. His position starts in the beginning of July, almost immediately after graduation! Anyhow, I'm really looking forward to this trip, so if you're going to be in town, let me know. We'll be staying at the Sunnyvale Hotel and can meet up anytime!
>
> All the best,
> Lydia

Q: Which of the following is correct about Lydia according to the letter?
(a) She and Susan have recently communicated.
(b) She and her husband are relocating to Denver.
(c) Her son will be starting his new job in early July.
(d) Her plans are to stay with Susan while in Denver.

25. Frank Miller, an Australian software engineer and amateur mountain climber, passed away last week while climbing Mount Holbrook. Miller, who had reached the mountain's summit twice before, was a mere 310 meters short of the peak when he died of natural causes. During the climb, he was in the process of testing software he created, called IRC-OP, which was designed to provide mountain expeditions with more effective computer support. Miller's associates have already taken over development of IRC-OP and are determined to finish their late colleague's final project.

Q: Which of the following is correct about Frank Miller according to the article?
(a) He passed away on his first ascent of Mount Holbrook.
(b) His death was the result of a mountain climbing accident.
(c) He was testing mountaineering technology when he died.
(d) His death has halted development of his computer program.

26. Although urban sprawl in the US existed on a limited scale before the invention of the automobile, cars allowed cities to spread out as they never had before. After World War II, developers designed suburbs with the assumption that residents would forgo walking and use cars to get around instead. Midwestern and Western cities tended to spread more widely than older Eastern cities, and soon suburban areas exceeded the area within city limits. For example, by the end of the twentieth century, 94% of metropolitan Chicago was located outside the city limits.

Q: Which of the following is correct according to the passage?
(a) The invention of the automobile predates the start of urban sprawl.
(b) Developers assumed that suburban residents would both walk and drive.
(c) Western cities were generally more compact than older Eastern ones.
(d) Chicago's city limits contained a small fraction of its metropolitan area.

27. Digisecure invites applications for a customer care representative position. Primary responsibilities include responding to customer inquiries and compiling feedback reports for our development department. Prior knowledge of digital security technology is not required, as extensive technical training will be provided for the right candidate. However, applicants must have solid experience in customer relations and must be prepared to work on a fixed schedule under time pressure. If you are up for the challenge, apply now!

Q: Which of the following is correct according to the advertisement?
(a) The position's main duty is contacting potential clients.
(b) In-depth training is available for the newly hired staff.
(c) Prior experience in customer relations is not required.
(d) Applicants can opt for flexible working hours once hired.

28. Felix Savon is a Cuban boxing legend who won his third Olympic gold medal in the year 2000. This feat has only been accomplished by two other boxers, one being Savon's compatriot, Teofilo Stevenson. In fact, Savon might have won another medal, had the Cuban Olympic team not boycotted the 1988 Seoul Olympics. He retired as an amateur in 2004, passing up lucrative offers to go professional, and became a coach for the Cuban Olympic team.

Q: Which of the following is correct about Felix Savon according to the article?
(a) He had won three Olympic gold medals prior to the year 2000.
(b) He is the only Cuban boxer with three Olympic gold medals.
(c) He did not compete in the 1988 Seoul Olympics.
(d) He retired as a professional boxer in 2004.

29. The Lunashine is a powerful handheld spotlight perfect for outdoor enthusiasts. Its LED bulb can produce up to 600 lumens and has fully adjustable brightness settings. The 12-volt battery provides hours of energy and can be charged through a household electrical outlet or the lighter socket of a car or boat. The Lunashine is equipped with a molded rubber handle for a comfortable grip and rugged ABS plastic body for durability. And it comes with a lifetime warranty. Order your Lunashine today!

Q: Which of the following is correct about the Lunashine according to the advertisement?
(a) It can be adjusted to yield over 600 lumens of light.
(b) It can be plugged into a vehicle to recharge the battery.
(c) It has a durable metal body and comfortable handle.
(d) It is sold with a warranty that expires after five years.

30. In these times of recession, one local employer is making an interesting offer to workers who are being let go. The Bronson Plastics Company has proposed an arrangement whereby laid-off employees who work for a local nonprofit organization for one year can receive an amount that equals one-third of their salary. They also will be the first to return to work once economic conditions improve. This severance package, which was offered to 750 employees and accepted by 600, allows those who would be out of work to retain an income as well as a daily occupation.

Q: Which of the following is correct about the severance package according to the passage?
(a) It has been offered to workers retiring from Bronson.
(b) It requires voluntary work at the Bronson Plastics plant.
(c) It promises priority in rehiring to participating employees.
(d) It was universally accepted by staff who received the offer.

31. Polo, the ball sport played on horseback, was brought to Argentina by the British in the nineteenth century, and it quickly gained popularity among Argentinians. The country took the first of its two Olympic gold medals for polo in 1924, and it spearheaded the establishment of an international polo competition, hosting the first World Polo Championship in 1987. Polo remains popular in Argentina, with over 6,000 registered players and many top horse-breeding programs for the sport.

Q: Which of the following is correct about Argentina according to the passage?
(a) It introduced polo to Britain in the nineteenth century.
(b) It won two Olympic gold medals for polo in 1924.
(c) It hosted the inaugural World Polo Championship.
(d) It is witnessing a decline in the popularity of polo.

32. Researchers at MIT are collaborating to develop micro-computers that can duplicate shapes. Dubbed "Smart Sand," these tiny cubes contain a nano-processor, and four of the cube's six sides are studded with magnets that can be demagnetized. The cubes work by surrounding an object and sensing its shape, then communicating with each other to rearrange themselves into an exact replica of the object. When the replica is no longer needed, Smart Sand can disintegrate to be used for duplicating another object. At the moment, researchers are working to shrink Smart Sand particles down to less than their current size of ten millimeters per edge.

Q: Which of the following is correct about Smart Sand cubes according to the passage?
(a) Several universities are collaborating to develop them.
(b) Each of them is equipped with magnets on all six faces.
(c) Those that have been used to replicate an object can be reused.
(d) They have recently been shrunk to less than ten millimeters across.

33. Some historians believe that Dutch colonists in New York, called New Amsterdam before the city was purchased by the English, imported quality yellow bricks from Holland. They cite this as the reason for the Dutch character of the city's early architecture. The logistics behind such claims, though, clearly reveal why this is implausible. The journey across the Atlantic was very long, and there was other much more lucrative cargo to be transported. Besides, clays of excellent quality were found in abundance on the shores of New Amsterdam's Hudson River, which provides support for the view that New York's bricks were likely made domestically.

Q: What can be inferred from the passage?
(a) Bricks imported to New York were not from Holland but from England.
(b) Material imported from Holland was used to make bricks in New York.
(c) Bricks were made in New York to be exported to European countries.
(d) Importing bricks from Europe to New York was financially unsound.

34. A new finding in research on Salmonella, a type of bacteria that can cause severe food poisoning, may hold the key to a new vaccine. By altering the bacteria's metabolic processes, scientists engineered a strain of Salmonella bacteria that was unable to use glucose as energy. Lacking energy, the bacteria could not replicate and thus could not withstand the onslaught of a living host's immune system. This mutant Salmonella strain has been patented by researchers, who hope to turn it into a vaccine for more virulent forms of the bacteria.

Q: What can be inferred from the passage?
(a) Salmonella overcomes the immune system by replicating.
(b) Drugs that help metabolize glucose could fight Salmonella.
(c) The only current treatment for Salmonella is a preventive vaccination.
(d) The mutant Salmonella is attacked by normal Salmonella strains inside hosts.

35. The Chile earthquake of 1960 was the largest earthquake ever recorded. Originally measured to be 8.5 on the Richter scale, the earthquake was later assigned a more accurate magnitude of 9.5 after a new scale called the moment magnitude scale was introduced in 1979 to better measure larger earthquakes. In Chile, the quake resulted in massive structural damage, personal injury, and loss of life. And its aftereffects reached far: the resulting tsunami traveled across the Pacific Ocean to Japan, where it wrought significant property damage. This earthquake, along with the 1964 Alaska earthquake, induced Pacific countries to establish an international tsunami warning system.

Q: What can be inferred about the Chile earthquake of 1960 from the passage?
(a) Official warnings that it would strike mitigated its impact.
(b) The Richter scale turned out to be inadequate to measure its full magnitude.
(c) The extent of its damage was disproportionate to its magnitude.
(d) Most of the casualties it caused occurred outside Chile's borders.

36. The Pareto principle states that 80% of a phenomenon's effects can be attributed to 20% of its causes. This 80/20 rule has successfully been applied to many areas of business, such as customer relationships or time and resource management. However, a recent trend called "Superstar Management"—which applies this idea to personnel management and proposes that a company should focus its efforts on making the top 20% of its employees better—is a misappropriation of this rule. Great employees are already, by definition, great, and if a company worked on making average employees better, it would see larger overall gains.

Q: Which statement about the Pareto principle would the writer most likely agree with?
(a) It suggests that companies should reward all workers equally.
(b) It is too outdated to be applicable to any area of business.
(c) Applying it to personnel management can be counterproductive.
(d) Modern businesses tend to use it to justify terminating employees.

37.

To the Editor:

The article "What Infrastructure Crisis?" questions the Society of Civil Engineers for releasing a report that gave the nation's infrastructure poor grades. The writer assumes that the real motive behind the report is promoting public spending, not the health of the country. His argument—that since civil engineers would potentially profit from this report, they should not have been tasked with evaluating the infrastructure—is not only ungrounded but also impractical. Who should evaluate it, then? That's like saying doctors should not diagnose patients because they would profit from treating them.

Douglas Schofield

Q: Which statement would the writer most likely agree with?
(a) Infrastructure evaluations are too frequently undertaken.
(b) Government engineers are not to be trusted with infrastructure.
(c) Today's engineers are to blame for deficiencies in the infrastructure.
(d) Civil engineers' advice about the nation's infrastructure should be heeded.

Part III Questions 38 – 40

Read the passage and identify the option that does NOT belong.

38. Raymond was impressed with his contractor's efficient method for preparing for his home renovation. (a) At their first meeting, the contractor discussed Raymond's vision and took measurements. (b) After preparing an estimate of the project's costs, he visited once more to answer questions. (c) The contractor ran the company himself, though he worked with assistants during construction. (d) He even accompanied Raymond to showrooms to select fixtures and fittings before starting.

39. A new breed of business person, the serial entrepreneur, has been identified by business researchers. (a) These entrepreneurs start one new business after another, selling them off as they go. (b) Investing in new entrepreneurial ventures can be financially risky for first-time investors. (c) The advantage for serial entrepreneurs is that they constantly have new and interesting challenges. (d) However, as continually starting over can be psychologically draining, it often takes a toll on the entrepreneur.

40. In May of 1941, two German ships were deployed into the waters of the Atlantic. (a) The ships, *Bismarck* and *Prinz Eugen*, had the mission of targeting Allied shipping to Britain. (b) Allied convoy escorts reduced the effectiveness of German strikes toward the war's end. (c) Upon detection, however, the German ships drew engagements from the British Royal Navy. (d) After sustaining multiple blows, the *Bismarck* quickly went down in the Denmark Strait.

This is the end of the Reading Comprehension section. Please remain seated until the proctor has instructed otherwise. You are NOT allowed to turn to any other section of the test.

서울대 최신기출

3

Listening *Comprehension*

Grammar

Vocabulary

Reading *Comprehension*

LISTENING COMPREHENSION

DIRECTIONS

1. In the Listening Comprehension section, all content will be presented orally rather than in written form.
2. This section contains four parts, each with fifteen individual items. For each part, you will receive separate instructions. Listen to the instructions carefully, and choose the best answer from the options for each item.

Scripts P 290 / 정답 P 336

Part I **Questions 1—15**

You will now hear fifteen individual spoken questions or statements, each followed by four spoken responses. Choose the most appropriate response for each item.

Part II **Questions 16—30**

You will now hear fifteen short conversation fragments, followed by four spoken responses. Choose the most appropriate response to complete each conversation.

Part III **Questions 31–45**

You will now hear fifteen complete conversations. For each conversation, you will be asked to answer a question. Each conversation and its corresponding question will be read twice. Then you will hear four options which will be read only once. Based on the given information, choose the option that best answers the question.

Part IV **Questions 46–60**

You will now hear fifteen short talks. After each talk, you will be asked to answer a question. Each talk and its corresponding question will be read twice. Then you will hear four options which will be read only once. Based on the given information, choose the option that best answers the question.

TEPS

GRAMMAR

DIRECTIONS

This section tests your grammar skills. You will have 25 minutes to complete the 50 questions. Be sure to follow the directions given by the proctor.

정답 P 336

Part I **Questions 1–20**

Choose the option that best completes each gap.

1. A: Do you have any plans for tomorrow?

B: I ___________ John to play tennis.

(a) meet
(b) have met
(c) am meeting
(d) will have met

2. A: The guests will be here soon, but I'm not dressed yet!

B: Go get ready. I'll be the one ___________ greets them.

(a) who
(b) what
(c) which
(d) whose

3. A: I spent one hundred dollars on back-to-school supplies.

B: Really? Mine came out to much less. Twenty dollars ___________ enough for me this time.

(a) is
(b) are
(c) was
(d) were

4. A: Some people get really depressed during the winter.

B: I know. I always feel my mood ___________ when it gets colder.

(a) changed
(b) changing
(c) to change
(d) to be changing

5. A: Have you finished your Brookings College application?

B: No. ___________ is still weeks away.

(a) Any deadline
(b) The deadline
(c) A deadline
(d) Deadline

6. A: Those concert tickets are pretty expensive.

B: Well, I'm going, ___________ it costs a lot.

(a) or else
(b) in case
(c) so that
(d) even if

7. A: When are you leaving for your road trip tomorrow?

B: I'm going bright and early, ___________ the weather's nice.

(a) assumed
(b) assuming
(c) to assume
(d) to be assuming

8. A: Did you like that book I lent you?

B: I ___________ put it down! I read the whole thing in a day.

(a) shouldn't
(b) couldn't
(c) mustn't
(d) can't

9. A: Was the repair job done properly?
B: Yes. All replacement parts ___________ before the mechanic installed them.

(a) are inspected
(b) had inspected
(c) have inspected
(d) were inspected

10. A: Have you been following the news about the economic crisis?
B: Yeah, but I doubt it's really as bad as it's ___________.

(a) made out to be
(b) made to be out
(c) making to be out
(d) making out to be

11. A: My slide show is finally ready.
B: It'd be wise of you ___________ everything one last time.

(a) reviewed
(b) to review
(c) reviewing
(d) having reviewed

12. A: This diner is Alex's favorite place to get brunch.
B: I know. He ___________ here every Sunday for years.

(a) comes
(b) is coming
(c) will have come
(d) has been coming

13. A: Why don't you like Professor Cho?
B: It's not ___________. I just don't like her teaching style.

(a) that I dislike as her a person
(b) a person that I dislike as her
(c) as her a person that I dislike
(d) that I dislike her as a person

14. A: Rob is upset about his essay grade.
B: Well, if he ___________ his essay in on time, he might have done better.

(a) has turned
(b) had turned
(c) would turn
(d) was turning

15. A: Are you still debating between those two movies?
B: Yeah, I can't decide ___________ I'd prefer to see.

(a) any
(b) one
(c) that
(d) which

16. A: Peggy seems stressed these days.
B: I know ___________ the thing to cheer her up.

(a) just
(b) such
(c) right
(d) much

17. A: Let's turn the air conditioner on.
B: How about the fan? I'd rather ___________ air conditioning.

(a) not to use
(b) us not to use
(c) we didn't use
(d) we're not to use

18. A: The authorities do nothing when companies pollute the river.
B: I know. Companies damage the environment ___________ impunity.

(a) at
(b) by
(c) for
(d) with

19. A: Does the teacher make comments on our assignments?
B: Yes. He gives ___________ on all our work.

(a) feedback
(b) feedbacks
(c) the feedback
(d) the feedbacks

20. A: We can't finish this project tonight, so let's just go home.
B: You're right. It's not ___________.

(a) worth losing sleep over
(b) worth to lose over sleep
(c) worthy of lost sleep over
(d) worthy of losing over sleep

Part II Questions 21–40

Choose the option that best completes each gap.

21. Rio de Janeiro is one of the most ___________ cities in South America.

(a) visit
(b) visited
(c) visiting
(d) being visited

22. The difficulty of growing up in multicultural households ___________ an important theme in this coming semester's modern fiction course.

(a) is
(b) are
(c) was
(d) were

23. When Thomas arrived at the airport, he realized he had ___________ but also his passport.

(a) only not forgotten his ticket
(b) forgotten his ticket not only
(c) only his ticket not forgotten
(d) forgotten not only his ticket

24. Near the end of the intermission, the theater lights were dimmed briefly to signal that the play ___________ in two minutes.

(a) is resuming
(b) has resumed
(c) had resumed
(d) was resuming

25. In their novels, authors sometimes make references to cities ___________ they have lived.

(a) that
(b) what
(c) in which
(d) in where

26. Michael ___________ have missed his flight, or he would have arrived in San Francisco already.

(a) must
(b) could
(c) would
(d) should

27. Stephanie insisted on her children ___________ a vegetarian diet, so she never cooked meat for them at home.

(a) ate
(b) to eat
(c) eating
(d) having eaten

28. Seeing that nearly ___________ seat was taken, Jan worried that she would not get a good view of the movie.

(a) all
(b) any
(c) every
(d) many

29. Although Lloyd's grandmother passed away years ago, she ___________ one of the biggest influences on the choices he makes today.

(a) remains
(b) remained
(c) is remaining
(d) had remained

30. The drill sergeant demanded that the new recruit ___________ twenty push-ups before jogging ten miles.

(a) do
(b) does
(c) will do
(d) would do

31. The reception at the Eric Clapton concert made it clear just ___________.

(a) what he is a beloved entertainer
(b) what a beloved entertainer is he
(c) how beloved an entertainer he is
(d) how beloved is he an entertainer

32. Chris looked back on his high school years and thought about how easy life ___________.

(a) used
(b) used to
(c) used to do
(d) used to be

33. ___________ everyone that she was perfect for the job, Mona took charge of planning the company outing.

(a) Convinced
(b) To be convincing
(c) Having convinced
(d) To have convinced

34. The number of spots on the tour bus is limited, so ___________ travelers may not be able to join the tour.

(a) few
(b) any
(c) some
(d) another

35. The director considered any failure, regardless of its reason, reflective ___________ a poor work ethic.

(a) to
(b) in
(c) of
(d) by

36. Ellen was upset at her sons and worried that ___________ home long past midnight was a sign of trouble.

(a) they came to
(b) they had come
(c) their coming to
(d) their having come

37. Xerosis is a technical medical term for ___________ most people refer to as dry skin.

(a) that
(b) what
(c) which
(d) whom

38. The company will not process orders ___________ a deposit of 10% of the purchase price is received in advance.

(a) unless
(b) in case
(c) whereas
(d) as long as

39. ___________ by the need of the orphans that she volunteered to help them in any way she could.

(a) So moved was Lisa
(b) Moved so Lisa was
(c) Was Lisa so moved
(d) So Lisa was moved

40. The climbers' efforts to reach the top of the mountain were laudable, ___________.

(a) if ultimately unsuccessful
(b) ultimately unsuccessful one
(c) if ultimately unsuccessful one
(d) ultimately they were unsuccessful

GRAMMAR

Part III **Questions 41–45**

Read each sentence carefully and identify the option that contains a grammatical error.

41. (a) A: My part-time job as a receptionist is so boring. Do you know of any other jobs?

(b) B: Well, last summer I worked at a balloon art company. It was surprisingly enjoyable.

(c) A: That sounds perfect! How did you find a such unusual position?

(d) B: I found it on a website devoted to out-of-the-ordinary summer jobs for students.

42. (a) A: I can't believe we've raised enough money for this community center project.

(b) B: Yes, our fundraising goals were met much quicker than we had expected.

(c) A: People in the community have been really keen to donate money to the center.

(d) B: They know that expanding the community center is ultimate to their benefit.

43. (a) A: What do you do to stay in such good shape? I could use some advice.

(b) B: I've been doing an intensive yoga program for the past few months.

(c) A: Maybe I should try that. I wonder if there are any studios around here.

(d) B: I think there are several gyms in this area that offers similar programs.

44. (a) A: That was the best performance of *Macbeth* that I've ever seen.

(b) B: I agree. The lead actor's delivery was simply mesmerizing.

(c) A: And the actress playing Lady Macbeth has cast perfectly for the role.

(d) B: We should come to the theater more often—I really enjoyed myself.

45. (a) A: What do you think of Melanie Jackson's chances in the upcoming election?

(b) B: Her charisma has made her to be really popular, so chances are she'll win.

(c) A: But don't you think the incumbent will pose a serious challenge?

(d) B: Not at all! Most people are pretty dissatisfied with his recent service.

Part IV Questions 46—50

Read each sentence carefully and identify the option that contains a grammatical error.

46. (a) By the time Joseph Haydn died, he has become recognized as the greatest living composer. (b) His first full-time job allowed him to write music for a wealthy family's personal orchestra. (c) After that, he spent thirty years writing music for the court of Austrian Prince Paul Anton. (d) Haydn's long and prolific career helped him earn the nickname "the father of the symphony."

47. (a) The Vikings explained eclipses with a tale of two wolves pursuing the sun and moon. (b) Every so often, one of the wolves would catch its prey, and an eclipse would occur. (c) The Vikings would then attempt to scare the wolves and rescue the sun or moon. (d) They would yell at the sky, to believe that the noise would make the wolves flee.

48. (a) Historians believe that nearly 2 million sailors died of scurvy between 1500 and 1800. (b) The disease is caused by a deficiency in vitamin C, a nutrient many sailors lacked at the time. (c) However, sailors put lime into their water to cut the foul taste were healthier than others. (d) The vitamin C in limes later proved to be the reason why these sailors could stave off scurvy.

49. (a) Deciduous woodlands are among the planet's most diverse ecosystems. (b) They are peaceful when viewed from the outside, and all look similarly to untrained observers. (c) But each wooded area is actually a unique and ecologically diverse world of its own. (d) Even a single acre teems with many distinct plant and animal species.

50. (a) Unlike other mammals, whose breathing is automatic, whales actively control their respiration. (b) Because their brains must be active to regulate breathing, whales sleep a semi-conscious state. (c) That is, they sleep over short periods of time during which one side of their brain is always active. (d) Scientists believe the two sides of whales' brains take turns shutting down until both are rested.

This is the end of the Grammar section. Do NOT move on to the next section until instructed to do so. You are NOT allowed to turn to any other section of the test.

Vocabulary

Directions

This section tests your vocabulary skills. You will have 15 minutes to complete the 50 questions. Be sure to follow the directions given by the proctor.

정답 P 336

Part I Questions 1—25

Choose the option that best completes each gap.

1. A: Can I get my money back if I return this shirt?
B: We don't offer cash ___________, but you can get store credit.

(a) debts
(b) refunds
(c) receipts
(d) deposits

2. A: I wish my husband could fix things as well as yours does.
B: Yeah, it's nice to be with someone who's ___________ with tools.

(a) handy
(b) feasible
(c) portable
(d) abundant

3. A: You're a frugal shopper!
B: Well, I'm on a tight ___________ these days.

(a) purchase
(b) expense
(c) budget
(d) asset

4. A: Can I cancel this train ticket for free?
B: No, you'd have to pay a(n) ___________.

(a) excuse
(b) penalty
(c) recession
(d) extension

5. A: Are you favoring your left foot as you walk?
B: Yes, I'm ___________ because I sprained my ankle.

(a) limping
(b) yielding
(c) bending
(d) merging

6. A: Hello, Dr. Chamber's office.
B: Hi, I'd like to ___________ my appointment from 10 a.m. to 2 p.m.

(a) switch
(b) revolve
(c) suspend
(d) transform

7. A: Where does this train line ___________?
B: The last stop is Jefferson Station.

(a) navigate
(b) intersect
(c) commute
(d) terminate

8. A: Edward is never late for meetings.
B: I know. He certainly deserves his reputation for being ___________.

(a) hopeful
(b) punctual
(c) promising
(d) immediate

9. A: Did you get out of the city when you visited Dubai?
B: Yes, we went on a two-day ___________ to the desert.
(a) shift
(b) fleet
(c) excursion
(d) digression

10. A: Should I mention my hobbies at my job interview?
B: No, just discuss what's ___________ to the position.
(a) affable
(b) relevant
(c) obedient
(d) conclusive

11. A: Did you get your car to the garage after it broke down?
B: Yeah, a truck ___________ it there for me.
(a) towed
(b) hitched
(c) drained
(d) boosted

12. A: Maggie learned to use this new software really quickly.
B: Yes, she seems to have a(n) ___________ understanding of it.
(a) intuitive
(b) reluctant
(c) voluntary
(d) occasional

13. A: Rita should add some inflection to her voice when she speaks.
B: I agree. She has too ___________ a tone.
(a) hyperbolic
(b) monotonous
(c) synonymous
(d) incompatible

14. A: I heard your magazine fired a writer for her slanderous claims.
B: Yes. We were sued for ___________ because of her.
(a) adulation
(b) defamation
(c) impairment
(d) confinement

15. A: Stu owes a lot of money at the pub.
B: Yeah, he's ___________ a huge tab.
(a) run up
(b) given up
(c) stood out
(d) picked out

16. A: Ed shouldn't keep trying to convert his colleagues to his religion.
B: Right, he's too ___________ about his faith.
(a) zealous
(b) venerable
(c) pragmatic
(d) inquisitive

17. A: That dog has been barking all day.
B: I know! Its ___________ yapping is so annoying.
(a) incessant
(b) stringent
(c) retentive
(d) tentative

18. A: On TV, they showed that phone books aren't really bulletproof.

B: That's nothing new—that myth was ___________ years ago.

(a) repelled
(b) qualified
(c) debunked
(d) dissociated

19. A: How do you feel about starting college?

B: Somewhat ___________. I'm excited but also nervous.

(a) jagged
(b) negligent
(c) fortuitous
(d) ambivalent

20. A: Aren't you embarrassed to read those terrible romance novels?

B: No, I'm a(n) ___________ fan!

(a) reticent
(b) irksome
(c) profligate
(d) unabashed

21. A: Janet's team completed their project in just three days!

B: Wow! They ___________ in record time.

(a) took it in
(b) tried it on
(c) pulled it off
(d) brought it up

22. A: Did you suspect that we were trying to throw you a surprise party?

B: Not at all. I had no ___________ that you guys were planning this!

(a) caveat
(b) inkling
(c) kindling
(d) aspersion

23. A: How's your dissertation going? Finished?

B: Almost. At 600 pages, it's turned into a lengthy ___________.

(a) ploy
(b) eddy
(c) tome
(d) scribe

24. A: Jake is using Shelley's research to get himself promoted.

B: Well, there are consequences for such ___________ behavior.

(a) visceral
(b) infallible
(c) exonerated
(d) unscrupulous

25. A: Is that an Irish accent I hear in your speech?

B: Actually, my family ___________ Scotland.

(a) hails from
(b) bails out of
(c) draws from
(d) backs out of

Part II Questions 26–50

Choose the option that best completes each gap.

26. Selecting a financial adviser is an important ___________, so always pick someone with appropriate credentials.

(a) ending
(b) election
(c) decision
(d) impression

27. Although lacking definitive statistics, analysts ___________ that 10% of marriage proposals in the US occur on Valentine's Day.

(a) supply
(b) consist
(c) estimate
(d) discount

28. The company had few resources to train new recruits, so it was looking to hire someone with prior ___________.

(a) alteration
(b) experience
(c) submission
(d) dependence

29. With a minute left in the game, the score was ___________ at five to five, and neither team could get a point.

(a) fastened
(b) affixed
(c) linked
(d) tied

30. A well-known literary character from the English Restoration was the rake, ___________ for immoral and promiscuous behavior.

(a) generous
(b) infamous
(c) distracted
(d) concluded

31. Chlorinox will remove all types of stains from tile floors, leaving them absolutely ___________.

(a) obscure
(b) spotless
(c) reflexive
(d) apparent

32. The roots of the National Football League can be ___________ back to 1920, when a group of teams formed a football organization.

(a) traced
(b) conveyed
(c) persuaded
(d) subscribed

33. It had never ___________ to the professor to consider the possibility that his students were collaborating on assignments during the vacation.

(a) happened
(b) occurred
(c) recalled
(d) given

34. Gary Javadi's paintings have been ___________ by art critics and have been similarly well received by the general public.

(a) expanded
(b) conceived
(c) witnessed
(d) applauded

35. The police drove quickly to ___________ the smugglers, cutting them off just before they crossed the border.

(a) intercept
(b) intimate
(c) emulate
(d) appoint

36. Consumers should be wary of assertions about instant cures, since most of these claims are ___________ and not based on reality.

(a) rueful
(b) abrupt
(c) taciturn
(d) spurious

37. The president's reelection campaign has been ___________ by accusations of corruption.

(a) sullied
(b) evoked
(c) reputed
(d) conspired

38. Before the meeting, the director was pacing around nervously, indicating that he was extremely ___________.

(a) contested
(b) resilient
(c) agitated
(d) salient

39. In a frantic rush to leave the continent, European colonialists carved up Africa in a(n) ___________ way that disregarded tribal boundaries.

(a) arbitrary
(b) judicious
(c) indubitable
(d) circumspect

40. A recent documentary reiterated the serious threat that the planet will face if warnings about global warming continue to go ___________.

(a) unheeded
(b) unscathed
(c) articulated
(d) augmented

41. Some schools cannot provide services to special-needs children because of a ___________ in special education funding.

(a) shortfall
(b) singularity
(c) designation
(d) deformation

42. Critics who favor unadorned, straightforward prose shun the novel *Brideshead Revisited* for its ___________ style.

(a) florid
(b) leering
(c) austere
(d) tangible

43. Intelligence tests claim to ___________ people's ability to think and learn by assigning a score to their performance on various tasks.

(a) quantify
(b) multiply
(c) enumerate
(d) inaugurate

44. Avoid temptation to check on a soufflé too early, since opening the oven door ___________ may cause it to collapse.

(a) proficiently
(b) prematurely
(c) preeminently
(d) prospectively

45. Sarah has a naturally sunny personality and simply ___________ confidence and cheerfulness.

(a) casts
(b) abates
(c) exudes
(d) hampers

46. Linguists are working desperately to ___________ dying languages, in hopes of recording linguistic data that may soon be lost.

(a) document
(b) capitulate
(c) apprise
(d) situate

47. The Olympic Stadium was packed with athletes, each ___________ to win the gold medal.

(a) cloistering
(b) retaliating
(c) vetting
(d) vying

48. With the congressman already having taken an ___________ stance on the matter, there is no chance that his vote can be swayed.

(a) exorbitant
(b) ingenuous
(c) amorphous
(d) unequivocal

49. During periods of political unrest, countries often impose a ___________ on citizens to keep people off the street late at night.

(a) stigma
(b) curfew
(c) suffrage
(d) pedigree

50. Leonard's ulcer responded well to medication and he fully recovered, which ___________ the need for surgery.

(a) obviated
(b) intervened
(c) aggravated
(d) exasperated

This is the end of the Vocabulary section. Do NOT move on to the Reading Comprehension section until instructed to do so. You are NOT allowed to turn to any other section of the test.

Reading Comprehension

Directions

This section tests your ability to comprehend reading passages. You will have 45 minutes to complete the 40 questions. Be sure to follow the directions given by the proctor.

정답 P 336

Part I **Questions 1—16**

Read the passage and choose the option that best completes the passage.

1. For years, psychologists promoted the idea that strict control of one's emotions is needed for mental health. A change in experts' attitudes toward self-control, however, is slowly taking place. According to some researchers, people who practice "self-compassion," or respond to their own feelings as attentively as they would to those of their loved ones, are happier, more optimistic, and more motivated than people who strictly regulate their emotions. Psychology seems to be moving in the direction of ______________________________.

   (a) focusing on helping patients end unhealthy relationships
   (b) encouraging people to accept and embrace their emotions
   (c) basing mental health on emotional exchange in the family
   (d) helping people increase their capacity for emotional control

2. American universities have been handing out higher grades over the past fifty years but not because students are improving. Studies show that this is the result of grade inflation, a process whereby higher grades are assigned for the same quality of work. One of the motivations behind this worrying trend may be teachers' desire for recognition. Giving higher grades encourages students to give teachers more favorable reviews at the end of the semester. Thus, students' high scores may be the result of ______________________________.

   (a) teachers' use of challenging learning materials in class
   (b) a change in universities' ability to recruit top students
   (c) the desire for fairness in classroom grading procedures
   (d) a teacher review process that rewards generous grading

3. A reception is being held for painter Mark Salzburg at the Sanctuary Gallery this Saturday to highlight the artist's ________________. Salzburg, well-known for his work featuring abstract images of bleak urban landscapes, has reinvented his style. The upcoming exhibition showcases the artist's experiments with realistic images of intimate household scenes. Having received critical acclaim in London, the exhibit now comes to Sydney for the first time. The reception starts at 7 p.m. and is open to the public.

(a) continued interest in familiar household settings
(b) successful break from his previous artistic style
(c) recent works debuting on the London art scene
(d) experimental depictions of urban landscapes

4. The oil of the sandalwood tree, beloved by perfumers for centuries, has ________________. The spicy, smoky scent is used as a base in perfumes to add dimension to the other ingredients, and the oil is known for its remarkable longevity. However, the tree which produces the oil, *Santalum album*, which was plentiful for centuries, is now a protected endangered species. This means that perfumers have had to seek synthetic replacements for true sandalwood in recent years, as oil from sandalwood trees cannot be harvested.

(a) suffered a decline in quality in recent years
(b) been found to be potentially unsafe for consumers
(c) become virtually impossible for perfumers to obtain
(d) fallen out of favor as perfumers turn to modern scents

5. Many readers of the beloved Paddington Bear children's books make the mistake of assuming that the ________________. The confusion is understandable, as in the first book, Paddington Bear is found in London's Paddington rail station, from which he gets his name. When Paddington begins talking about his past, though, he says he comes from "darkest Peru," where his aunt still lives. This fact about his past is a minor detail in the book series, and since all of his adventures take place in England, the misunderstanding is common.

(a) stories were originally from Peru
(b) bear was named after a rail station
(c) books' hero is originally from Britain
(d) bear's parents come from two countries

6. The UK's Forestry Commission is battling a foreign moth species that ______________________. The oak processionary moth was accidentally introduced to Britain on a shipment of oak trees from the Netherlands in 2006 and has spread to London, Reading, and Sheffield. While the adult moth is not harmful to humans, its caterpillar form contains thousands of highly toxic hairs. When these hairs break off, they can become airborne, causing skin, eye, and throat irritation.

(a) displaces endemic species with its natural poisons
(b) poses a threat to oak trees imported from overseas
(c) endangers public health while in its caterpillar form
(d) can spread harmful toxins through the air while flying

7. When I first became a manager, I found it difficult to lead people. I wanted my staff to like me, so I offered nothing but praise. While this did make me more popular, it also led to complacency among the workforce. Productivity declined, while tardiness increased. That's when I decided to start providing firm, direct feedback on weak points. There was resistance at first, but gradually I noticed improvement. Rather than sapping their confidence, the criticism gave workers goals for which to strive. This experience taught me that ______________________.

(a) popularity cannot be gained by offering praise
(b) tactfully disguising criticism as praise works best
(c) compliments are the best way to increase productivity
(d) exclusively positive feedback can actually be detrimental

8. *The Great Gatsby* and the biblical book of Job are similar in that both focus on main characters who suffer misfortune, yet they differ in ______________________. Gatsby, who loses the girl he loves, refuses to accept his loss. He resorts to shady business deals to transform himself into a wealthy socialite, hoping to win the girl back from her husband. By contrast, Job loses everything, including all of his children, yet accepts his misfortunes and suffers in silence. In the end, Job is rewarded for his perseverance with a new family and plentiful livestock, while Gatsby's life ends with alienation and disappointment.

(a) the ways their protagonists cope with their losses
(b) how their characters attempt to justify their actions
(c) what leads their main characters to change their beliefs
(d) the means by which their protagonists eventually triumph

9.

> To Joe's Grill:
>
> I am writing to inform you of ____________________________. As you know, Grandview City restricts the number of people allowed within buildings. These limits guarantee public safety and are enforced by the police and Fire Marshal. The maximum occupancy of your premises, which was 65 people based on a previous inspection, has been reassessed at 60 people following renovations on your property. You are required to ensure that future gatherings on your property are in accordance with these updated standards.
>
> Sincerely,
> Daniel Macdonald
> Grandview Fire Department

(a) altered rules for the number of gatherings allowed
(b) modified inspection procedures for occupancy limits
(c) revisions to the regulations pertaining to renovations
(d) changes to the occupancy limit of your establishment

10. A joint white paper from the National Academy of Engineering and the National Research Council has called for American education to ____________________________. Most Americans know how to use technology—for example, cell phones and personal computers—but lack knowledge about its full range of uses. The white paper recommends that rather than limiting technological literacy instruction to computer classes, schools should integrate it into all subjects to help prepare students for the myriad ways they will engage with technology during their careers.

(a) reform students' habit of relying on technology for everything
(b) show students how to use technology for exam preparation
(c) include technological literacy across the whole curriculum
(d) focus on improving testing through the use of technology

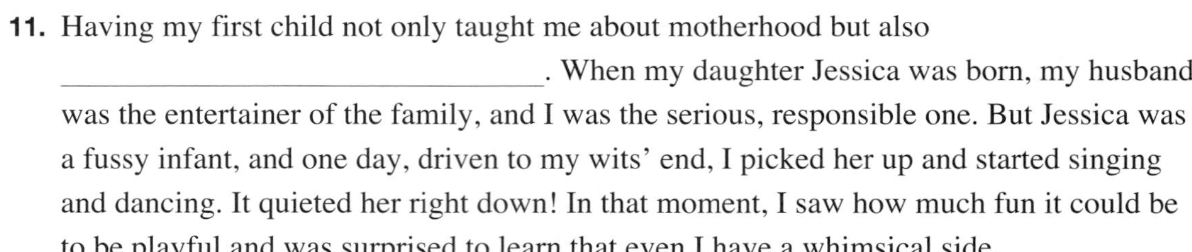

11. Having my first child not only taught me about motherhood but also ______________________. When my daughter Jessica was born, my husband was the entertainer of the family, and I was the serious, responsible one. But Jessica was a fussy infant, and one day, driven to my wits' end, I picked her up and started singing and dancing. It quieted her right down! In that moment, I saw how much fun it could be to be playful and was surprised to learn that even I have a whimsical side.

(a) helped me become a more responsible adult
(b) revealed a personality trait I never knew I had
(c) exposed the difficulty of crafting truly funny humor
(d) allowed me to become more forgiving towards others

12. In recent decades, the nation has experienced tremendous economic growth, and people of all income levels have seen their wealth grow. But social mobility has not increased with it. Those at the bottom of the income distribution have more than they used to in absolute terms, and they are unquestionably free from the shackles of poverty. But they are no more likely to reach the middle of the income distribution than they were several decades ago. Ultimately, while economic growth has brought better living conditions to many, it has ______________________.

(a) rendered traditional divisions among social classes obsolete
(b) made the structures which support society unstable
(c) not eliminated the persistence of class divides
(d) not eliminated extreme poverty from society

13. A quarterly report from fast food chain Fletcher's Restaurant released yesterday shows that its ______________________. For the past year, the company has been embroiled in a legal controversy surrounding its marketing of beef hamburgers. A lawsuit alleged that the company's new hamburgers are falsely labeled as all-beef burgers because they contain fillers. Despite successfully defending its marketing in court, however, the company's reputation has taken a beating and its latest report shows a steep drop-off in sales.

(a) strategy of reducing its burgers' beef content has paid off
(b) new lineup of healthy products has failed with the public
(c) legal triumph has not prevented its profits from slumping
(d) court battle against its main beef supplier has been a failure

14. The United Kingdom introduced a system of Anti-Social Behavior Orders in 1998 to deal with minor incidents such as loitering and vandalism. The legal orders prohibit offenders from engaging in specific actions or bar them from certain locations. But from the beginning, the effectiveness of the orders has been questioned. Reports have noted that delinquent youths regard the orders as badges of honor. Receiving restrictions on their behavior and then breaching them is a way of gaining respect from peers. In light of such reports, it appears that Britain's system of orders ________________.

(a) allows criminals to hide behind young offender legislation
(b) encourages youths to challenge their peers' criminal activities
(c) moves the site of anti-social behavior from the streets to schools
(d) promotes delinquency as a glamorous activity for defiant youths

15. William of Orange (1533-1594) was the leader of a Dutch rebellion against Spanish rule. His leadership in this rebellion resulted in the creation of the first independent Dutch state, known as the Republic of the United Provinces of the Netherlands. ________________, William is often referred to as the "Father of the Fatherland" in the Netherlands.

(a) Hence
(b) Likewise
(c) Altogether
(d) Meanwhile

16. Since 1996, computer giant IBM has been developing a sophisticated local weather forecasting system dubbed Deep Thunder. According to executives, the system is an essential tool for local governments that need short-term forecasts for highly specific locations. Despite the company's efforts to promote the system, however, potential customers are not flocking to invest in the system. ________________, there are currently only two public-sector customers who are piloting Deep Thunder systems.

(a) In fact
(b) Finally
(c) Besides
(d) Even so

Part II Questions 17—37

Read the passage, question, and options. Then, based on the given information, choose the option that best answers the question.

17. On New Year's Eve, the Riverview Club will host a private five-course dinner party for our members. Getting on the guest list is as simple as registering at the front desk or calling our reservation desk and paying a deposit one week prior to the party. Or visit our website to sign up and pay online. Space is limited, and places will fill up quickly, so register today!

Q: What is the main topic of the announcement?
(a) A year-end party for a private club's employees
(b) The grand opening of a members-only private club
(c) How to reserve a spot at a private holiday celebration
(d) How to book a restaurant to host a special private event

18. The Mortgage Lenders Association (MLA) and Federal Bureau of Investigation (FBI) have jointly produced an official Mortgage Fraud Warning Notice to be distributed to clients. As a lender, you may choose to incorporate additional elements into the warning before distribution. However, no changes may be made to the main text of the Fraud Warning Notice. This text must be displayed within a separate border, without modifications. If other elements are incorporated, they must be added separately to ensure that the warning's content remains clear.

Q: What is the main purpose of the announcement?
(a) To announce a new collaboration between the MLA and the FBI
(b) To inform lenders of rules about modifying the fraud warning notice
(c) To tell borrowers about a new security warning accompanying mortgages
(d) To publicize modifications to a previous version of the fraud warning notice

19. The third album from the Norwegian band Alternate Scenario is a blank slate in terms of music and presentation. With ellipses for a title, ten unnamed songs, and a booklet consisting of solid grey pages, it supports multiple interpretations and asks listeners to draw their own conclusions. Even the songs' lyrics, composed in a made-up language, consist of no more than random syllables. By eschewing commonly known symbols, the band encourages listeners to undertake a creative process of interpretation, allowing fans to personalize their listening experience in a groundbreaking new way.

Q: What is the writer's main point about the album?
(a) Its overly stylized symbolism muddles its meaning.
(b) Its unusual underlying concept is distinctly Norwegian.
(c) Its effort to convey a complex emotional message failed.
(d) Its design and music invite listeners' own personal analyses.

20. The Non-Profit Coordination Society cordially invites you to an upcoming event all about building positive relationships with potential donors. It will be hosted by Dr. Melinda Grady, who specializes in donor psychology and working with donors. Her presentation will give charity professionals greater insight into the assumptions, beliefs, and behaviors of those who donate to non-profit organizations. This knowledge is sure to prove helpful in meeting your fundraising goals. The talk is open to all and begins at 2 p.m. in the Dining Room of the Hamptons Hotel.

Q: What is mainly being advertised?
(a) A seminar on how to select charities to donate to
(b) A forum where non-profits can meet potential donors
(c) A speech on how to become a gift planning professional
(d) A presentation on how to best solicit charitable donations

21. Investors have a bias towards selling investments that have increased in value and holding those that have lost value. Referred to as the disposition effect, this behavior is irrational, as it shows that investors tend to focus on an investment's purchase price rather than future performance. A strictly rational investor seeking maximum profit would disregard an investment's current price relative to its purchase price and decide whether to maintain an investment based solely on its expected future performance.

Q: What is the main purpose of the passage?
(a) To explain the irrational nature of the disposition effect
(b) To provide an example of bias toward selling risky investments
(c) To caution against investing in stocks that have performed poorly
(d) To stress that a stock's price is more important than its performance

22. Researchers have investigated how illustrations in science textbooks affect high school students. The students were given chemistry lessons that were identical except for the gender of the scientists depicted in the textbooks. On a comprehension test following the lessons, students were found to have superior performance when studying from materials depicting scientists of their own gender. The study suggests that depictions of both male and female scientists are needed to ensure fairness in science education.

Q: What is the passage mainly about?
(a) Differences in the accuracy of various chemistry textbooks
(b) Disparities in the achievements of male and female chemists
(c) The influence of gendered textbook imagery on learning outcomes
(d) The most effective means of representing chemistry data in graphic form

23. The government of Fiji is taking steps to expand access to broadband Internet. Prior to the launch of a national broadband policy last year, the government opened its first three telecenters. These centers are staffed seven days a week with volunteers and can be used for free. Officials recently announced the opening of eight more centers later this year, which will also be staffed by volunteers.

Q: Which of the following is correct according to the news article?
(a) Fiji opened its first telecenter after launching its broadband policy.
(b) Volunteers are involved in the operation of Fiji's telecenters.
(c) Users are required to pay a monthly fee to use the telecenters.
(d) Fiji plans to operate eight telecenters in total by the year's end.

24. The Straton Weatherbeater tent is a two-room tent that accommodates up to ten people. Every Weatherbeater comes with a handy carrying case for storage and transport, and the tent's new flexible fiberglass poles are an improvement over earlier models' steel poles, making set-up easier than ever. The suggested retail price is $349.99, but Straton is currently offering $50 off purchases. Try Straton's Weatherbeater for your next family camping trip!

Q: Which of the following is correct about the Weatherbeater according to the advertisement?
(a) It has two rooms which can hold ten people each.
(b) Its carrying case must be purchased separately.
(c) Its poles are now being made out of flexible steel.
(d) It is being offered at a special promotional price.

25. This School Safety Guide was created by the Gwinnith County School District in 2004 and has been updated annually since 2006. It is not a comprehensive manual on health and safety laws for schools, but a guide for teachers on important safety considerations. It is based on information provided by the state's Department of Education as well as suggestions from current teachers. Any concerns regarding the guide should be addressed to the superintendent of Gwinnith County School District.

Q: Which of the following is correct according to the document?
(a) The last year in which the guide was updated was 2006.
(b) The guide contains a complete list of schools' legal duties.
(c) Practicing teachers contributed to the guide's contents.
(d) Concerns about the guide should be directed to teachers.

26. Although he is best known for his contributions to physics, Sir Isaac Newton also worked in Britain's Royal Mint during the last years of his life. Normally, the master of the Royal Mint was a ceremonial position intended to have little actual responsibility. But Newton, unlike his predecessors, took the job seriously and got personally involved in battling counterfeiting, a major problem at the time. He tackled corruption within the mint, worked to develop techniques to deter counterfeiting, and was instrumental in the criminal convictions of numerous counterfeiters.

Q: Which of the following is correct about Sir Isaac Newton according to the passage?
(a) He worked in the Royal Mint in the early years of his career.
(b) He refrained from direct involvement in tackling counterfeiting.
(c) He adopted the work ethic of former masters of the Royal Mint.
(d) He helped apprehend those who were tampering with coinage.

27. Visitors to Cambodia can obtain entry visas upon arrival. Visas are available from international airports in Phnom Penh or Siem Reap, or at authorized border crossings on roads from Thailand, Laos, or Vietnam. Applications must be accompanied by a single passport-sized photo. The costs for one-month tourist and business visas are $20 and $25 respectively. The former may be extended once for one month, while the latter can be extended indefinitely. All visas of less than six months' duration are single-entry only.

Q: Which of the following is correct according to the passage?
(a) Visa-on-arrival services are available only from airports.
(b) Tourist visas are set at higher prices than business visas.
(c) Extensions are granted for both business and tourist visas.
(d) One-month business visas grant visitors multiple entries.

28.

> To the Editor:
>
> I would like to address factual problems in your paper's article "Uranium Shipments Continue" (July 18). The US has been exporting enriched uranium to Canada for over twenty years. Your article incorrectly said that this was a recent development, beginning in the last decade. Additionally, the US government is not keeping secrets about where it stores radioactive material returned from Canada after use, despite what your article claimed. The US has clearly stated its intentions to consolidate uranium at fewer and more secure sites, and officials have made these sites publicly known.
>
> Douglas Sajewski

Q: Which of the following is correct according to the letter?
(a) The importing of US enriched uranium into Canada ceased ten years ago.
(b) The article understated how long the US has been exporting uranium.
(c) The article claimed that the location of US uranium stores was public.
(d) The US is seeking to keep its radioactive uranium at more locations.

29. Just minutes from Crawford City, the luxurious gated community of Spring Lake offers superior security and comfort. With architecture that hearkens back to the area's eighteenth-century heritage, the community's 150 townhouses are served by private guards and surveillance cameras. At the center of the community is a private park with majestic oak trees and a children's playground. Upscale shopping and entertainment are a short drive north at the recently opened Galleria Mall, and with two elementary schools and a high school nearby, Spring Lake is perfect for families.

Q: Which of the following is correct about Spring Lake according to the advertisement?
(a) It is situated in the center of the city of Crawford.
(b) The design of the buildings is old-fashioned in style.
(c) The park is available for use by the general public.
(d) Its two nearby high schools make it ideal for families.

30. Spoken by the majority of people in North India and Pakistan, Hindi and Urdu are two closely related varieties of the same language. With virtually the same grammar and colloquial forms, speakers can communicate with them nearly interchangeably in everyday usage. It is mainly in their formal or technical vocabulary and style that they diverge. The official language of Pakistan, Urdu, retains stronger Persian and Arabic influences, while the official language of India, Hindi, is more closely related to its Sanskrit roots.

Q: Which of the following is correct according to the passage?
(a) Hindi and Urdu are mutually comprehensible in everyday situations.
(b) Hindi and Urdu differ mainly in terms of common expressions.
(c) Arabic was the predominant influence on the Hindi language.
(d) The official language used by the citizens of India is Urdu.

31. Chromhidrosis is a dermatological condition in which patients perspire colored sweat. There are two types. Eccrine chromhidrosis, the rarer of the two, results in large amounts of colored sweat on the palms and feet. This is usually caused by the ingestion of food dyes. The other type, called apocrine chromhidrosis, typically involves smaller amounts of colored perspiration around the face, underarms, and chest. It results from high concentrations of lipofuscin, a byproduct of cell metabolism. Creams containing capsaicin, as well as botox treatment, can reverse the problem temporarily.

Q: Which of the following is correct about chromhidrosis according to the passage?
(a) The eccrine variety occurs in the hands and feet.
(b) The apocrine type is the less common of the two.
(c) It can result in unusually high levels of lipofuscin.
(d) It is cured permanently by applying capsaicin creams.

32. The field of hermeneutics originally referred to the explication of texts, especially those on religion, but through the work of Martin Heidegger, it came to denote the general process of interpretation. Heidegger's student Hans-Georg Gadamer later expanded the hermeneutics of his teacher and suggested that readers function within an ever-changing context of background assumptions and knowledge. Gadamer believed that the encounter between a person and a source of meaning, such as a text, involves a dialogue between different viewpoints, or "horizons," that can never be fully resolved into a definitive interpretation.

Q: Which of the following is correct about Hans-Georg Gadamer according to the passage?
(a) His work was an important precursor to that of Heidegger.
(b) He focused exclusively on the process of explicating religious texts.
(c) He posited that the assumptions people bring to interpretation are fixed.
(d) His theory suggested that the process of interpretation is open ended.

33. When rescuers discovered the site of John Mason's plane crash deep in the Rocky Mountains last week, they were hoping for survivors but were prepared for much worse. What they discovered was the pilot and his three passengers working together to build a campfire with the upholstery that they had removed from the plane. Experts say their incredible survival was possible because the pilot had managed to cushion the impact of the crash by directing the plane toward a relatively flat area covered with a thick layer of snow.

Q: What can be inferred from the passage?
(a) Mason was a novice pilot on his first flight.
(b) Mason was piloting a large commercial airliner.
(c) The rescuers located the plane weeks after the crash.
(d) The survivors escaped the crash without major injuries.

34.

> Dear Jen and Greg,
>
> We hope this note finds you well back in sunny Miami. Although our new town cannot compete with Florida in terms of weather, its beautiful scenery makes up for it. Moving to Albany has been quite a change, but we're all adjusting successfully. Richard is enjoying his busy medical practice, and I have been able to find a part-time position at the local college. Matt is into hockey and Kelly has become an avid cross-country skier. We miss you all dearly. Keep in touch.
>
> All the best,
> Karen

Q: What can be inferred about the writer from the letter?
(a) Her family used to live in Albany.
(b) She prefers Miami's weather to that of Albany.
(c) She relocated to Albany because she was offered a job.
(d) Her family plans to move back to Miami in the near future.

35. Mickey Mantle was one of baseball's greatest players. He was scouted by the New York Yankees for the 1951 season, but his rookie year fell short of recruiters' expectations, and his season was partly spent in the minor leagues. After baseball legend Joe DiMaggio retired later that year, Mantle inherited his center field position. During the following years, he helped his team win seven of their twelve World Series appearances. When Mantle retired in 1968 after 18 seasons in the big leagues, he was second only to Babe Ruth for home runs among all the Yankees players up to that point.

Q: What can be inferred about Mickey Mantle from the passage?
(a) His entry to the Yankees forced Joe DiMaggio to retire.
(b) He ultimately topped Joe DiMaggio for career home runs.
(c) He won the World Series while playing for various big-league teams.
(d) His first year in the big leagues made him a highly sought-after player.

36. Ernest Shackleton gained fame from his 1907 expedition to Antarctica, but in 2010, his name made headlines again for a completely different reason. A modern team that traveled to Shackleton's hut in Antarctica found several bottles of 103-year-old whiskey, frozen under the floorboards. Some were sent to the master blender at the Whyte and Mackay distillery, Richard Paterson, who succeeded in recreating the whiskey by chemically analyzing a small sample. The bottles have since been sent back to Antarctica according to international conservation guidelines, which restrict the removal of items from the continent.

Q: What can be inferred from the passage?
(a) Richard Paterson accompanied the expedition to recover the whiskey.
(b) Conservation guidelines only apply to plants and wildlife in Antarctica.
(c) The remaining bottles will also be sent to the Whyte and Mackay distillery.
(d) Paterson did not have access to the original recipe for Shackleton's whiskey.

37. Nigel Stevens's play *The Storm* brings more of his trademark surprises to audiences, this time a play involving two siblings. When a storm forces Bobby and Julia to spend a whole day together in an isolated cabin, the tension between them begins to intensify. At first, Bobby appears to be a selfish egotist, and by contrast, his elder sister Julia comes across as a passionate idealist. But over the course of several bitter and dramatic quarrels, Stevens executes a reversal that shows each character's true nature, forcing the audience to reevaluate their initial perceptions.

Q: What can be inferred about *The Storm* from the review?
(a) It reveals Bobby in an unexpectedly favorable light.
(b) It focuses on how Bobby is influenced by Julia's idealism.
(c) It concludes with Julia emerging as the story's moral compass.
(d) It picks up the theme of sibling rivalry from Stevens's last play.

Part III **Questions 38 – 40**

Read the passage and identify the option that does NOT belong.

38. Bighorn sheep are well known for their fierce clashes during the mating season. (a) The violent displays involve a struggle between males for the right to breed. (b) Two males charge at high speeds and crash into each other with their horns. (c) The females carry their young for six months and deliver them in the spring. (d) Those that back down from the violent collisions are excluded from mating.

39. Passengers en route to Singapore on Falcon Airlines' exclusive First Class cabin enjoy outstanding meal service. (a) We offer an international menu with carefully selected dishes from world-renowned chefs. (b) All meals are complemented with a selection of champagnes, wines, spirits, and other beverages. (c) The cuisine of Singapore results from centuries of interaction between different ethnic groups. (d) Orders can also be placed at any time on the flight for a wide variety of snacks and refreshments.

40. It is important to set the recording levels on the TSS Series professional recording decks carefully. (a) If they are too high or too low, the settings will cause distortion or unwelcome background noise. (b) As one of the more delicate recording media, vinyl records need proper handling to preserve longevity. (c) Small adjustments can be made to ensure that the recording levels match the level of the input. (d) Trial and error is a good method to use for figuring out the ideal sound levels prior to recording.

This is the end of the Reading Comprehension section. Please remain seated until the proctor has instructed otherwise. You are NOT allowed to turn to any other section of the test.

서울대 최신기출 4

Listening *Comprehension*

Grammar

Vocabulary

Reading *Comprehension*

Listening Comprehension

Directions

1. In the Listening Comprehension section, all content will be presented orally rather than in written form.
2. This section contains four parts, each with fifteen individual items. For each part, you will receive separate instructions. Listen to the instructions carefully, and choose the best answer from the options for each item.

Scripts P 301 / 정답 P 337

Part I **Questions 1–15**

You will now hear fifteen individual spoken questions or statements, each followed by four spoken responses. Choose the most appropriate response for each item.

Part II **Questions 16–30**

You will now hear fifteen short conversation fragments, followed by four spoken responses. Choose the most appropriate response to complete each conversation.

Part III **Questions 31–45**

You will now hear fifteen complete conversations. For each conversation, you will be asked to answer a question. Each conversation and its corresponding question will be read twice. Then you will hear four options which will be read only once. Based on the given information, choose the option that best answers the question.

Part IV **Questions 46–60**

You will now hear fifteen short talks. After each talk, you will be asked to answer a question. Each talk and its corresponding question will be read twice. Then you will hear four options which will be read only once. Based on the given information, choose the option that best answers the question.

TEPS

GRAMMAR

DIRECTIONS

This section tests your grammar skills. You will have 25 minutes to complete the 50 questions. Be sure to follow the directions given by the proctor.

정답 P 337

Part I Questions 1—20

Choose the option that best completes each gap.

1. A: Have you seen my phone? I can't find it.
   B: Try to remember __________ you used it last.
   (a) who
   (b) what
   (c) when
   (d) which

2. A: How's your new job?
   B: It's more involved than my previous role, but __________ enjoyable.
   (a) far
   (b) such
   (c) quite
   (d) much

3. A: Did a lot of people come to Sophie's graduation party?
   B: Yeah, we had __________ that not everyone fit inside.
   (a) a so large crowd
   (b) so large a crowd
   (c) a such large crowd
   (d) such large a crowd

4. A: Can you hear that mosquito buzzing?
   B: Yes, it's very __________! I can't concentrate.
   (a) distracted
   (b) distracting
   (c) having distracted
   (d) to have distracted

5. A: The doorbell just rang. I think the plumber's here.
   B: Oh, it __________ be him. He just called to say he's coming tomorrow.
   (a) can't
   (b) needn't
   (c) may not
   (d) might not

6. A: Am I asking too much for my car?
   B: No, $5,000 __________ reasonable.
   (a) is
   (b) are
   (c) has been
   (d) have been

7. A: Is Tom nervous now that his band got the state fair gig?
   B: No. __________ for a large audience before, he'll be fine.
   (a) Perform
   (b) To perform
   (c) Being performed
   (d) Having performed

8. A: What did your dad say about you losing his watch?
   B: Actually. I've been __________ yet.
   (a) too scared to talk to him
   (b) too scared talking to him
   (c) scared to him to talk too much
   (d) scared to him too much to talk

9. A: You should consider buying a new laptop.
B: That's ___________ luxury that I can't afford right now.
(a) few
(b) one
(c) any
(d) other

10. A: Tyson never helps out around the house.
B: I know. That's something ___________ more often.
(a) he needs to do
(b) that needs to do
(c) needs to be done
(d) that he needs doing

11. A: Have you booked our staff dinner?
B: I'm still looking for a place ___________ will accommodate us all.
(a) that
(b) where
(c) wherever
(d) whichever

12. A: Ed hasn't confirmed receipt of the shipment.
B: Then call to confirm that the merchandise ___________.
(a) will have been delivered
(b) has been delivering
(c) has been delivered
(d) delivered

13. A: Is Jim playing video games? I asked him not to.
B: He's not right now, but ___________ finally stop.
(a) only after three hours he did
(b) only after three hours did he
(c) did he only after three hours
(d) he did only after three hours

14. A: The mayor wasn't reelected.
B: Well, if he ___________ more funding, he might have won.
(a) has had
(b) had had
(c) was having
(d) has been having

15. A: What's all that construction noise next door?
B: Those rooms ___________ as executive suites.
(a) refurbish
(b) are refurbished
(c) are refurbishing
(d) are being refurbished

16. A: Why don't you support the management's new plan?
B: The changes ___________ to the staff seem unnecessary.
(a) were proposing
(b) were proposed
(c) proposing
(d) proposed

17. A: I hear a dripping sound in the bathroom.

B: The tap in there ___________ for some time now.

(a) leaks
(b) is leaking
(c) had leaked
(d) has been leaking

18. A: Do you spend much time with your roommate?

B: Not really. ___________, he's quite a private person.

(a) As much as would I like to
(b) As I would like to as much
(c) Much as I would like to
(d) Much as like I would

19. A: Why did you skip lunch?

B: I didn't have much of ___________.

(a) appetite
(b) an appetite
(c) the appetite
(d) some appetite

20. A: Jen wants to bring her boyfriend to Nick's party.

B: They don't get along. I suggest that she ___________ alone.

(a) come
(b) comes
(c) will come
(d) had come

Part II **Questions 21—40**

Choose the option that best completes each gap.

21. When Sean realized he had left his bag on the bus, he ___________ the customer center.

(a) calls
(b) called
(c) will call
(d) has called

22. The officer emphasized repeatedly that the cadets ___________ always show their superiors the utmost respect.

(a) may
(b) could
(c) might
(d) should

23. According to several sources, wages will start rising ___________ the economy begins to improve.

(a) even if
(b) as soon as
(c) as much as
(d) in order that

24. By the time Kyle is done mowing the lawn, he ___________ yard work for nearly three hours.

(a) is doing
(b) will be doing
(c) has been doing
(d) will have been doing

GRAMMAR

25. The board members were unanimous in their decision ___________ the merger's proceedings.

(a) to give the CEO control of
(b) giving to the CEO control
(c) to give to the CEO to control
(d) giving the CEO to control of

26. The dismissal bell ___________, so Ethan could not hear the teacher assigning the evening's homework.

(a) sounds
(b) is sounding
(c) has sounded
(d) was sounding

27. ___________ melons do not get sweeter after harvesting, they should not be picked until they are ripe.

(a) Since
(b) While
(c) Although
(d) Whenever

28. The gaming console that George received for Christmas was exactly what he had been hoping ___________.

(a) with
(b) for
(c) to
(d) in

29. Within the vast expanse of the universe ___________ many phenomena that physicists have yet to explain.

(a) is
(b) are
(c) was
(d) were

30. Union members debated the new contract for hours without coming any closer to ___________ a decision.

(a) reached
(b) reaching
(c) be reaching
(d) have reached

31. Jingoism, most simply ___________, is nationalism taken to an aggressively assertive level.

(a) defined
(b) defining
(c) to define
(d) was defined

32. Contaminated fish sold by a single retailer seem ___________ last week's outbreak of food poisoning.

(a) causing
(b) to cause
(c) having caused
(d) to have caused

33. Although he initially denied the principal's accusation, the student eventually confessed ___________ true.

(a) to the statement was
(b) to the statement to be
(c) that the statement was
(d) that the statement to be

34. Dylan worked late to complete his team's project even though he was not ___________.

(a) required to complete
(b) required completing
(c) required doing
(d) required to

GRAMMAR

35. Lucia was being treated at St. Vincent Hospital, which was one ___________ several large medical centers in the city.

(a) into
(b) along
(c) within
(d) among

36. Andy had difficulty adjusting to his new job because the standards of his current company were different from ___________ of his previous one.

(a) theirs
(b) those
(c) them
(d) they

37. The ambassador smiled at the nation's president, ___________ for a handshake.

(a) with hand of her outstretching
(b) with outstretching her hand
(c) her hand outstretched
(d) outstretched hand

38. Please note that anyone leaving ___________ in the park may be subject to a fine of $200.

(a) garbage
(b) garbages
(c) a garbage
(d) some garbages

39. Although Sandra disliked pumpkin pie, she ate a slice ___________ her host.

(a) so to not offend as
(b) so as not to offend
(c) to so much not offend
(d) to not offend so much

40. Martin gave ___________ notice before quitting, leaving his superiors scrambling to quickly find a replacement.

(a) no
(b) few
(c) least
(d) none of

Part III Questions 41–45

Read each sentence carefully and identify the option that contains a grammatical error.

41. (a) A: It's a shame that the school is cutting funding for the arts.
(b) B: I guess decision makers don't think those subjects are important.
(c) A: It almost seems like it won't be long before they got rid of them altogether.
(d) B: Well, there must be some way of saving them from being eliminated.

42. (a) A: I want to visit Amsterdam, but it's incredibly how expensive flights are!
(b) B: I heard rising fuel costs have driven up ticket prices recently.
(c) A: It's too much for my budget. I'm thinking about canceling my vacation.
(d) B: I'd look around a little more first. You might be able to find a deal online.

43. (a) A: So tomorrow's the big day, Steve. You're taking your driving test.
(b) B: Yes! Pretty soon I'll be able to drive myself anywhere I want.
(c) A: That's great. I know you've been practicing, but aren't you nervous?
(d) B: No. I'm certain for the driving test to be very easy for me to pass.

44. (a) A: I'd like to focus tomorrow's meeting on bettering our customer service.
(b) B: But haven't most of the staff members had training in customer service anymore?
(c) A: Yes, but it's a key element in the work our business does, so I think it bears reiterating.
(d) B: That's true. I suppose it'll help even behind-the-scenes workers understand our process better.

45. (a) A: Why was Matt up so late last night? I heard him to be working on the computer at 3 a.m.!
(b) B: I'm not sure, but I think he spent this week cramming for the bar exam.
(c) A: After years in law school, what does he think will come from one week of studying?
(d) B: He says he's just doing a final review so that everything will be fresh in his mind.

RAMMAR

Part IV **Questions 46–50**

Read each sentence carefully and identify the option that contains a grammatical error.

46. (a) Police are investigating a two-car collision that occurred on Brown Street yesterday. (b) According to eyewitnesses, both cars ran stop signs and drove right into each other. (c) Neither driver saw the stop signs, what were recently installed at the intersection. (d) With no one taking responsibility for the accident, a judge will decide who is at fault.

47. (a) When people move from one culture to another, there are often many new customs to be learned. (b) One of the first obstacles that people must overcome is eating in their new culture. (c) The food itself might not be to everyone's liking, especially when it contains new ingredients. (d) Also, many people find that the etiquette used at restaurants and family meals to be confusing.

48. (a) Writing research papers require balancing the introduction with the body of the paper. (b) Overly extensive introductions tend to set up bodies that lack in content. (c) Conversely, short introductions do not provide enough information to establish the paper's focus. (d) Ideally, the introduction should be long enough to be effective without becoming excessive.

49. (a) The Mosuo people are one of the few matrilineal ethnic groups in the world today. (b) That is, their social organization is based on women are the head of each household. (c) Mosuo families trace their heritage and lineage through their female ancestors. (d) And lineage is not bound by genetics, as adopted children are counted as part of the line.

50. (a) Previously considering a fringe treatment, acupuncture is now gaining acceptance in Western medicine. (b) Its procedures have been proven to affect the nervous system, lending credence to its advocates' claims. (c) Acupuncture stimulates the brain and nervous system to release pain-relieving chemicals called endorphins. (d) It also indirectly triggers the adrenal gland, thereby releasing hormones that help mitigate stress.

This is the end of the Grammar section. Do NOT move on to the next section until instructed to do so. You are NOT allowed to turn to any other section of the test.

VOCABULARY

DIRECTIONS

This section tests your vocabulary skills. You will have 15 minutes to complete the 50 questions. Be sure to follow the directions given by the proctor.

정답 P 337

Part I Questions 1—25

Choose the option that best completes each gap.

1. A: Why are you so worried about where Alice is?

B: She was ___________ back before 10 p.m., and it's almost 11 now.

(a) conducted
(b) admitted
(c) expected
(d) revealed

2. A: Can I borrow your laptop?

B: Yes, on the ___________ that you take good care of it.

(a) posture
(b) attitude
(c) standing
(d) condition

3. A: Do you need help picking your classes this term?

B: I'm OK. My adviser already ___________ me about what to take.

(a) counseled
(b) provoked
(c) confided
(d) audited

4. A: King Street is blocked. Do you know an alternate route to the concert hall?

B: You can ___________ down Madison Street.

(a) lag
(b) range
(c) detour
(d) branch

5. A: Is this a baroque painting?

B: I wouldn't know. I'm totally ___________ about art history.

(a) ignorant
(b) unbiased
(c) negligible
(d) indiscreet

6. A: I noticed Adam doesn't want to go to church with his family.

B: Yes. He hasn't ___________ religion like they have.

(a) embraced
(b) arranged
(c) reserved
(d) engaged

7. A: Why was Don in trouble at school?

B: He was caught ___________ during a quiz.

(a) cheating
(b) assuming
(c) degrading
(d) suspecting

8. A: Did you forget to turn off the gas again?

B: Yeah, sorry—it completely ___________.

(a) forced my hand
(b) slipped my mind
(c) stayed the course
(d) jogged my memory

9. A: This hotel isn't fancy, but it'll do.
B: Yes. It's ___________ for what we need.

(a) tactful
(b) sufficient
(c) provident
(d) competent

10. A: This copy of *Little Women* seems short. I thought the novel was over 400 pages.
B: It is. This one is shorter because it's a(n) ___________ version.

(a) collated
(b) abridged
(c) enshrined
(d) distended

11. A: Neil's done a great job, considering he has no prior experience.
B: I agree. It's hard to believe he's a ___________.

(a) zealot
(b) novice
(c) patron
(d) mentor

12. A: Do you ever imagine your dream home?
B: Sure. I ___________ a large house in the country.

(a) render
(b) position
(c) envision
(d) manifest

13. A: Would it be easier to find a job if I moved to a bigger city?
B: Yes, your employment ___________ would be better there.

(a) prospects
(b) forecasts
(c) bearings
(d) regards

14. A: My kids are always arguing.
B: Mine ___________ about small things, but they don't have major fights.

(a) testify
(b) bicker
(c) tamper
(d) collude

15. A: When will the rose bushes bloom?
B: Soon. I can already see the petals starting to ___________.

(a) unfurl
(b) exhibit
(c) discard
(d) debunk

16. A: I'm doubtful about Rick's plan to make money online.
B: I was also ___________ when he told me about it.

(a) liable
(b) lenient
(c) slender
(d) skeptical

17. A: Fiona totally resembles her mother!
B: I know. She really ___________ her.

(a) takes after
(b) looks after
(c) sees through
(d) follows through

VOCABULARY

18. A: I'm dreading tomorrow's company motivation session.

B: Me, too. I ___________ going to those meetings.

(a) refute
(b) divest
(c) loathe
(d) abdicate

19. A: I heard the Star Cinema fire burned for hours.

B: Yeah, it took firefighters until midnight to ___________.

(a) leave it out
(b) take it off
(c) turn it off
(d) put it out

20. A: Alan is too self-satisfied about his credentials.

B: He may be a bit ___________, but he did go to a top school.

(a) chic
(b) grim
(c) smug
(d) meek

21. A: Where did you go for your trip?

B: I enjoyed a week-long ___________ at the beach.

(a) niche
(b) sojourn
(c) vacancy
(d) repository

22. A: I've heard that Hector is quite a comedian.

B: He's a pretty ___________ guy, always making others laugh.

(a) garish
(b) ornery
(c) jocular
(d) meager

23. A: Is there a rule against smoking during work hours?

B: Not officially, but employees have a ___________ understanding that it should be avoided.

(a) tacit
(b) moot
(c) laden
(d) caustic

24. A: Claudia clearly wasn't happy with her meal.

B: I know. The ___________ on her face said it all.

(a) grimace
(b) snicker
(c) bluster
(d) skew

25. A: Should we drive through the city or go around it?

B: To save time, let's ___________ it instead of going through.

(a) rally
(b) skirt
(c) lapse
(d) remit

Part II **Questions 26–50**

Choose the option that best completes each gap.

26. Aesop's fables remain popular with parents because each story teaches children an important ___________ about life.

(a) chapter
(b) period
(c) lesson
(d) series

27. Friday will have a high near 15 degrees, but the temperature will ___________ dramatically to freezing at night.

(a) fall
(b) fail
(c) drip
(d) drag

28. The witness to the crime provided the key testimony that the prosecutor needed to get a ___________ during the trial.

(a) detection
(b) conviction
(c) procession
(d) succession

29. Because the music was too loud, the concert's organizers were given a $500 fine for ___________ the city's noise ordinance.

(a) violating
(b) misusing
(c) expelling
(d) obstructing

30. Not to be ___________ by the competition, Digicity Electronics broadened their advertising and matched their rivals' prices.

(a) outdone
(b) extended
(c) prevailed
(d) overruled

31. After being baked, the dessert should be ___________ in the refrigerator for about 30 minutes.

(a) chilled
(b) fetched
(c) obtained
(d) pondered

32. The skirmishes finally stopped when both nations signed a ___________ settling their border dispute.

(a) grant
(b) figure
(c) treaty
(d) league

33. Early psychologists identified a number of basic personality ___________ such as shyness, generosity, and kindness.

(a) traits
(b) stances
(c) mirages
(d) estimates

34. Investors are advised to diversify their investments to protect themselves from the ___________ of losing everything all at once.

(a) wager
(b) stake
(c) leap
(d) risk

35. Ketchup and mustard are two ___________ that typically accompany hot dogs and hamburgers.

(a) luncheons
(b) condiments
(c) appendages
(d) compositions

36. Alistair's ___________ managerial style made his employees feel like they had no power to control their own projects.

(a) diffident
(b) unwitting
(c) complaisant
(d) domineering

37. The passengers were abruptly ___________ out of their seats when the car they were in struck a large pothole.

(a) sifted
(b) jolted
(c) clipped
(d) pricked

38. Marathon runners must drink water frequently to stay ___________, since a lack of fluids can hinder performance.

(a) liquefied
(b) hydrated
(c) condensed
(d) retrenched

39. With his theory that Earth revolves around the sun, Copernicus ___________ the claim that Earth was the center of the universe.

(a) conciliated
(b) repudiated
(c) consummated
(d) emancipated

40. When visiting a friend's new home for the first time, it is always a nice ___________ to bring a housewarming gift.

(a) allure
(b) gesture
(c) gratuity
(d) intimation

41. Early humans were ___________, moving from place to place without settling in any particular area.

(a) elastic
(b) acerbic
(c) endemic
(d) nomadic

42. Those infected with tuberculosis were kept in ___________ to keep the epidemic from spreading any further.

(a) cessation
(b) desolation
(c) quarantine
(d) impediment

43. Because values are deeply ___________ in national cultures, they can be difficult to change.

(a) acclimated
(b) embedded
(c) endowed
(d) absolved

44. After the ship crashed, most of its cargo was lost at sea, but some was ___________ by passing ships.

(a) inhaled
(b) salvaged
(c) heralded
(d) launched

45. You will have no more cockroaches in your home after Pest Busters ___________ them using our guaranteed fumigation method.

(a) dodges
(b) burnishes
(c) evacuates
(d) exterminates

46. The City Council negotiations reached a stalemate, and a full two months have ___________ since any action has been taken.

(a) elapsed
(b) surpassed
(c) concurred
(d) interjected

47. The teacher ___________ her critical remarks about the student's work with some gentle words of encouragement.

(a) defrayed
(b) tempered
(c) discomfited
(d) precipitated

48. Written in the Scottish ___________, much of Robert Burns's poetry reflects the way people in his homeland really spoke.

(a) colloquy
(b) vernacular
(c) articulation
(d) enunciation

49. Upon entering the country, a duty will be ___________ at the airport for items in excess of the duty-free allowance.

(a) levied
(b) imputed
(c) accorded
(d) delegated

50. Since the party's invitation specified that it was a formal event, Simon ___________ a tuxedo he had rented.

(a) donned
(b) quaffed
(c) imparted
(d) fashioned

This is the end of the Vocabulary section. Do NOT move on to the Reading Comprehension section until instructed to do so. You are NOT allowed to turn to any other section of the test.

Reading Comprehension

Directions

This section tests your ability to comprehend reading passages. You will have 45 minutes to complete the 40 questions. Be sure to follow the directions given by the proctor.

정답 P 337

Part I **Questions 1–16**

Read the passage and choose the option that best completes the passage.

1. The Dashbury Medical Center ______________________. As you know, the staff kitchenette is stocked with coffee, cream, and sugar. Until recently, Lorna Robinson was in charge of collecting money from those staff members who drink coffee, as well as shopping for items. Since Lorna no longer works at Dashbury, we are looking for another employee to take over these duties. If you are interested, please contact Sharon Johnson.

(a) is hiring a cleaning service for the kitchenette
(b) wants staff input about their coffee preferences
(c) needs a volunteer to maintain our coffee supplies
(d) now offers free coffee in the staff kitchenette area

2. When buying "toxin-free" nail polish, consumers may not be getting what the packaging promises. In 2006, several cosmetics manufacturers announced that they would no longer use three chemical ingredients, known as the "toxic trio," in their polishes. However, recent tests showed that all three chemicals were present in products labeled "toxin-free." This misleading advertising exists because no government body regulates the cosmetics industry. So for now, what are advertised as "toxin-free" nail polishes ______________________.

(a) contain more harmful chemicals than the toxic trio
(b) still cannot compete with traditional polish formulas
(c) are the only products safe for consumers to purchase
(d) may contain the ingredients they purport to be free of

3. Having spent two years studying at an alternative high school, I believe that ______________________. Students with demanding schedules—young professionals such as gymnasts or actors—benefit from the flexibility and informality of alternative schools. But I think I actually would have benefited from the structure and discipline offered by a traditional school. In such an unstructured environment, I ended up falling woefully behind in my studies.

(a) such schools are not for everyone
(b) traditional schools are now outdated
(c) young people should have more freedom
(d) students there are under too much pressure

4. In ancient Egypt, the Nile River ______________________. Using the Nile's rich floodplain and plentiful water, ancient Egyptians harvested abundant amounts of crops such as wheat and barley, which they sold to neighboring desert territories. With these regions often stricken by famine, this agricultural affluence put Egypt in an advantageous position in diplomatic relationships in that it was able to actively dictate the terms of trade to ensure its own economic stability.

(a) forced Egyptians to diversify their crops each season
(b) led to nearly continuous conflict over water resources
(c) afforded the country economic and political advantages
(d) prompted Egyptians to devise new irrigation techniques

5. Son House was one of several blues musicians whose music ______________________. He recorded some albums in 1930, but because of the economic hardship of the Great Depression, they sold poorly and House faded into obscurity, as did his protégé, Robert Johnson. Decades later, though, America experienced a renewed interest in blues music and House, along with Johnson and several other musicians, suddenly became popular. His fame gave him the chance to perform and make new recordings.

(a) was widely accepted during the Depression
(b) was rediscovered long after its initial recording
(c) had been influenced by Robert Johnson's teachings
(d) acquired classic status immediately upon its release

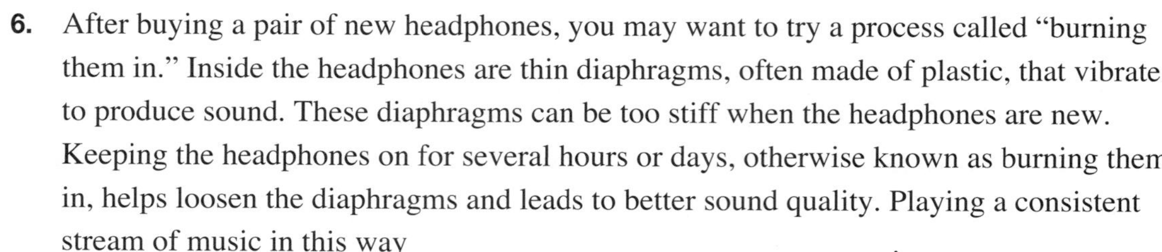

6. After buying a pair of new headphones, you may want to try a process called "burning them in." Inside the headphones are thin diaphragms, often made of plastic, that vibrate to produce sound. These diaphragms can be too stiff when the headphones are new. Keeping the headphones on for several hours or days, otherwise known as burning them in, helps loosen the diaphragms and leads to better sound quality. Playing a consistent stream of music in this way ______________________.

(a) causes the headphones to burn out unexpectedly
(b) makes the diaphragms stiffen up and vibrate faster
(c) primes the internal structures for optimum performance
(d) prolongs the condition of headphones straight from the factory

7. The Irish writer Jonathan Swift had a reputation for misanthropy largely because he disagreed with contemporary views that regarded human nature as essentially good and reasonable. However, Swift's disappointment in humanity's collective irrationality was not an expression of hatred of mankind, or a dismissal of people once and for all. Rather, Swift believed that humanity could recognize its own deficiencies in order to begin acting rationally and in its own best interests. In other words, his reputation as a misanthrope ______________________.

(a) stems from his belief that people would never act rationally
(b) overlooks the fact that he considered humanity's flaws reparable
(c) confirms that he really did espouse a despairing view of humanity
(d) explains why he gave up on the idea that people are basically good

8. Funds spent on political advertising increased dramatically in America with the emergence of so-called super political action committees, or super PACs, which are given free rein to gather and use financial resources to influence elections. Super PACs are forbidden by law from coordinating directly with candidates standing for election, but they have found a way around this restriction by hiring candidates' former staff members, who have extensive knowledge of candidates' campaign strategies. This enables super PACs to support their candidates without communicating directly with them or their current campaign staff. In this way, super PACs ______________________.

(a) spend more than the legal limit on political advertising
(b) technically obey the law without respecting its intention
(c) are allowed to coordinate openly with the candidates' staff
(d) cede control of campaign ads to current election camp aides

9. Ray Bradbury's *Fahrenheit 451*, a novel about a dystopian future in which books are banned, is often understood as an anti-censorship tome. Bradbury, however, took issue with this interpretation, declaring that the book is an exploration of the encroachment of television and mass media on reading. While most analyses of the book cast the state as the villain, Bradbury commented that people are the true culprit. In short, the book's ______________________________.

(a) unfavorable reception was a major disappointment for Bradbury
(b) critical interpretation is at odds with Bradbury's intention
(c) author's attempts to oppose censorship proved successful
(d) literary critics are divided as to its impact on society

10. Recent figures showing the number of America's per capita prisoner population ______________________________. As of 2010, there were six million people in correctional custody in the US, more than any other country in the world, and state expenditures on prisons have recently risen sharply. Analysts attribute the increase in the number of inmates partly to the fact that many prisons are run by private companies, who have lobbied for tougher sentencing laws to ensure that prison population numbers—and profits—remain high. This system of incentives has raised moral questions in the public debate.

(a) reveal that incarceration rates are tapering off
(b) have assuaged public fears over rising crime rates
(c) have created an incentive to rehabilitate more inmates
(d) are causing concern over the effects of privatizing prisons

11. Many ancient texts contain insults towards other racial or cultural groups, which has led some historians to claim that all ancient cultures, lacking modern values of tolerance and diversity, had a natural tendency to make negative generalizations about outsiders. That view is fallacious, however, because it disregards the opinions of those who were critical about stereotyping others in demeaning ways or who were more accepting of foreigners. For instance, the Greek philosopher Plato greatly admired the wisdom of the Egyptians, and Herodotus equated ethnic chauvinism with insanity. The examples of these thinkers show that ______________________________.

(a) the ancients showed no acceptance of multiculturalism
(b) there were ancients enlightened enough to dismiss racial bias
(c) their stereotypical representations were accepted by the public
(d) ethnic slurs directed toward foreigners were limited to Herodotus

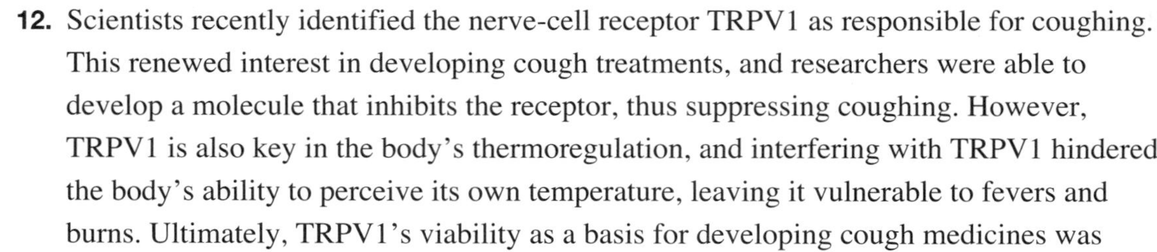

12. Scientists recently identified the nerve-cell receptor TRPV1 as responsible for coughing. This renewed interest in developing cough treatments, and researchers were able to develop a molecule that inhibits the receptor, thus suppressing coughing. However, TRPV1 is also key in the body's thermoregulation, and interfering with TRPV1 hindered the body's ability to perceive its own temperature, leaving it vulnerable to fevers and burns. Ultimately, TRPV1's viability as a basis for developing cough medicines was ____________________________.

(a) complemented by its efficacy as a cure for fevers and burns
(b) negated because of its crucial role in another bodily function
(c) confirmed upon developing several types of TRPV1 inhibitors
(d) undermined as no link was found between TRPV1 and coughing

13. In what has been one of the worst wildfire seasons to date, the governor is ____________________________. In response to extraordinarily dry conditions, bans against campfires and fireworks have been put into effect but the same cannot be done for firearms because a state law protects gun owners. Authorities are concerned because 5% of the blazes this year have been caused by sparks from guns discharged during target practice. With no means of officially restricting the use of firearms, the governor is pleading to gun owners to refrain from exercising their right to use them.

(a) issuing a strict ban on target practice shooting
(b) monitoring public lands for illegal firearm use
(c) urging citizens to voluntarily avoid using firearms
(d) restricting the use of firearms to private properties

14. Today Pythagoras is considered the first mathematician, yet many scholars hesitate to make specific claims about his contributions because ____________________________. Though he is credited with theorems essential to the understanding of modern math, there is no direct evidence that he actually created them. Compounding the confusion is the lack of first-hand, documented facts from Pythagoras's followers, who were extremely secretive about their studies and their teacher's life.

(a) the secretiveness of his work alienated his followers
(b) there is a dearth of verifiable facts about his life and work
(c) his followers took credit for some of his less famous theorems
(d) his writings were too complex to afford a unified interpretation

15. Pablo Picasso's art can be divided into five periods, the first being the Blue Period during the early part of the twentieth century. The works produced during this time all project a somber mood both through their subject matter and their largely blue or green tones. ______________________________, *The Old Guitarist*, one of Picasso's most famous paintings, uses ashen blue to depict a poverty-stricken musician.

(a) However
(b) As a result
(c) For example
(d) Nevertheless

16. Citizens are out en masse for the third week in a row to protest the Conservative-backed national pension system reforms. The new plan has been touted as more sustainable in the long term, but protesters remain convinced that the Conservative Party is being swayed by lobbyists. ______________________________, several Liberal lawmakers are putting together their own version of a plan for pension system reform, which should be unveiled in the coming weeks.

(a) Ultimately
(b) Meanwhile
(c) In other words
(d) For the most part

Part II **Questions 17—37**

Read the passage, question, and options. Then, based on the given information, choose the option that best answers the question.

17. I feel happiest when I give back to the community, so last year I went from volunteering at my local soup kitchen once a week to every weekday evening. Adjusting to less time at home has not been easy, but it is satisfying to know that I make a difference in someone's life every day. Knowing that one less person will go hungry is more worthwhile than relaxing at home.

Q: What is the passage mainly about?
(a) Why the writer first became a volunteer
(b) Why volunteering is a big time commitment
(c) The need for more volunteers in soup kitchens
(d) The writer's choice to increase his volunteer hours

18. Dan Brown's runaway bestseller *The Da Vinci Code* may never be considered great literature, but the social impact it has made cannot be dismissed. Its take on faith and the role of the Church has supplied a platform for people to discuss such issues, previously only the domain of religious scholars. The novel encouraged people everywhere to question their beliefs. In fact, *The Da Vinci Code* did more to promote a public discussion of religion in everyday life than academia has been able to.

Q: What is the writer's main point about *The Da Vinci Code*?
(a) It has incited debate over religious beliefs and institutions.
(b) It has prompted a lot of discussion over its literary merits.
(c) It has led many people to abandon their religious beliefs.
(d) It has led to divisions within various religious groups.

19. Too busy to plan and cook healthy, well-balanced meals that support your weight-loss goals? Then try the new program from DietPlus that brings fresh meals to your door! The meals help you control your appetite and boost your metabolism while providing all the essential nutrients you need. Our meals contain only organic ingredients, with no additives or preservatives. And you can customize the time and frequency of the deliveries to best fit your schedule. Give us a call to kick-start your diet today!

Q: What is the advertisement mainly about?
(a) A diet plan incorporating all-natural supplements
(b) A program that shows how to cook healthy meals
(c) A physician-approved diet and exercise regimen
(d) A healthy weight-loss meal delivery program

20. St. Stephen's Elementary School would like to inform parents of an addition to our safety policy. We are now requesting that parents send a list of caretakers who are permitted to pick students up, with an identifying photo of each caretaker. Teachers will consult the list at both end-of-day dismissal and in case of mid-day dismissal for illness. We will not allow your child to leave the premises with anyone who is not on the list, so please include names and photos of any friends or relatives who may pick your child up in the future.

Q: What is the main purpose of the announcement?
(a) To clarify the rules about mid-day dismissal for illness
(b) To inform parents of a school's new security procedures
(c) To request that students be picked up promptly upon dismissal
(d) To announce that students may not leave school unaccompanied

21.

To the Editor:

I was disappointed to see your recent editorial "No Longer Charging" applauding the end of government support for electric cars. Tax credits for purchasing electric vehicles are a much needed incentive to set the wheels in motion: they motivate people to purchase electric cars, which boosts investment in the necessary infrastructure, such as more charging stations. That, in turn, encourages more people to buy electric cars. To say tax credits were a waste, as your editorial did, lacks foresight.

Daniel Carruthers

Q: What is the writer's main point about electric cars?
(a) Revoking tax credits for them was a mistake.
(b) Using taxpayers' money to subsidize them is unfair.
(c) They have not yet proved a viable investment for companies.
(d) Investing in infrastructure is more urgent than tax credits for them.

22. Cow's milk has long been a mainstay in school cafeterias, but if the soy farmers have their way, dairy may soon be losing its corner on the market. Currently, the government reimburses schools only for cow's milk; reimbursement of dairy-free milk is limited to cases when a student cannot drink lactose. However, the soy industry is now fighting for soy milk to be given an equal status with cow's milk in schools. Dairy farmers are naturally resisting the change, claiming that soy milk is an inferior source of nutrients.

Q: What is the article mainly about?
(a) The nutritional advantages of cow's milk over soy milk
(b) A debate on whether to reimburse schools for providing soy milk
(c) The incentives for schools to offer both cow's and soy milk
(d) A push to provide lactose intolerant students with soy milk

READING COMPREHENSION

23.

> Dear Mr. Nelson,
>
> I am replying to your ad in Saturday's newspaper for a warehouse assistant job. Since graduating from high school, I have gained extensive experience working in warehouses. I worked as a part-time clerk for a small importer before working full time at a car parts company. I also worked for a cousin at his plumbing supplies business on an unofficial part-time basis. I believe my background makes me an ideal candidate.
>
> Sincerely,
> Justin Thompson

Q: Which of the following is correct about Justin Thompson according to the letter?
(a) He saw the job advertisement on an Internet bulletin board.
(b) He worked in a car-parts warehouse during high school.
(c) He has been a full-time employee in all of his positions.
(d) He was unofficially employed at his cousin's business.

24. This report by the National Survey of Family Growth shows twentieth-century trends in divorce and remarriage. In general, delayed age of marriage and a higher divorce rate led to a decrease in the amount of time people spent married in the second half of the century. The divorce rate rose from 1950 to 1970, before stabilizing at a high rate over the next twenty years. Further, remarriage generally declined from 1950 to 1990, while disruptions of second marriages increased during that time frame.

Q: Which of the following is correct according to the passage?
(a) The report examines divorce rates during the most recent decade.
(b) The divorce rate remained steady from 1970 to 1990.
(c) Remarriages generally became more common from 1950 to 1990.
(d) Disruptions of second marriages declined from 1950 to 1990.

25. Attention house hunters! We are offering an apartment for rent in the Prenzlauer Berg district of Berlin for 800 euros per month. This two-bedroom apartment is located on the ground floor of a five-story building constructed in 1918. Ideal for families with young children, the apartment is located in a very attractive green residential area with well-maintained parks nearby. Check berlinrent.com today for photos and further details—but hurry, a deal this good won't last long!

Q: Which of the following is correct about the apartment according to the advertisement?
(a) It is available for sale starting immediately.
(b) It is located on the fifth floor of its building.
(c) It is being marketed to childless young couples.
(d) It is in close proximity to public green spaces.

26. Norwegian explorer Thor Heyerdahl set out in 1947 to prove his hypothesis that Polynesian people originated in Peru. He believed they had migrated across the ocean generations before historians claimed they had seafaring technology. In order to demonstrate that the journey was possible, Heyerdahl built a raft by hand and set sail from Peru to the Pacific Islands. It took him over three months, but he successfully reached Polynesia. However, this only proved that the trip was *possible*—not that it actually happened—so Polynesians' origins remain a mystery.

Q: Which of the following is correct about Thor Heyerdahl according to the passage?
(a) His theory was that Polynesians were native to the Pacific Islands.
(b) His expedition set forth from his home country of Norway.
(c) He successfully sailed to the Pacific Islands on a handmade raft.
(d) He definitively proved that Polynesians migrated from Peru.

27. We are now recruiting players for the Brannon Club Soccer League! Previously home to only men's teams, we are now transforming into a co-ed league by adding all-women teams. Don't worry if you have no experience: in addition to our regular Thursday practices, we'll run an extra Monday night beginners' session. We welcome adults aged 18 and up, and you don't have to be a Brannon Club member to join the league—though as a player, you can get a special discount on membership!

Q: Which of the following is correct about the Brannon Club Soccer League according to the announcement?
(a) All of its teams will be co-ed from now on.
(b) It offers extra beginners' practices on Thursday.
(c) Only Brannon Club members are allowed to join.
(d) It offers a reduced rate on Brannon Club membership.

28.

Dear Madeleine Powers,

After much deliberation by the promotion board, I regretfully must inform you that we are unable to offer you the promotion to Director of Finance. Your application was quite impressive, and your performance record as Senior Financial Analyst is exemplary, but the hiring committee decided to offer the position to someone from outside of the company. Unfortunately, we have no other promotion opportunities currently available, but should another arise, we encourage you to apply.

Sincerely,
Frank Lowell
Human Resources

Q: Which of the following is correct about Madeleine Powers according to the letter?
(a) She is being rejected for the position of Senior Financial Analyst.
(b) She was denied the promotion despite excellent performance.
(c) She lost the promotion to another employee in the company.
(d) She is being directed toward another currently open position.

29. Crosstown Plaza is re-opening this April following months of renovations. The only outdoor mall in Montgomery, Crosstown offers more than just shopping. Every Saturday and Sunday we have a variety of performances in our pavilion—from live music to magic shows, there's something for the whole family. Come see a movie and stay for dinner at one of our many restaurants. We even have complimentary childcare services, so you can shop while your kids have fun!

Q: Which of the following is correct about Crosstown Plaza according to the advertisement?
(a) It will be opening to customers for the first time this April.
(b) It is one of several outdoor shopping centers in Montgomery.
(c) It features live entertainment at the pavilion every weekend.
(d) It provides shoppers with babysitting services for a small fee.

30. Polls suggest that at least 90% of Americans classify themselves as middle class, with respondents indicating that any income between $30,000 and $100,000 qualifies as such. According to the government, however, more than 12% of Americans were living below the official poverty line, suggesting that at least 2% of those who consider themselves middle class are, in actuality, lower income. To administer various social welfare programs, the government does set a standard for poverty. But it has never released an official definition of "middle class," so the confusion over the term's definition is understandable.

Q: Which of the following is correct according to the passage?
(a) Ninety percent of Americans believe that they have middle-class incomes.
(b) Respondents considered all incomes up to $100,000 to be middle class.
(c) Less than 2% of Americans have incomes under the official poverty line.
(d) The government sets an official middle class income to administer welfare.

31. After receiving a dozen complaints, Carvallo Toys is recalling several of its Bumblebee toys because the wire in the toys' antennae can scratch children. Parents with proof of purchase for the toy can bring it to the store where it was obtained for a refund; those without a receipt should contact Carvallo Toys' corporate center for a refund. This recall only applies to Bumblebee toys that are larger than eight inches, as the antennae in smaller toys do not contain a wire and are not hazardous.

Q: Which of the following is correct according to the passage?
(a) Carvallo Toys has recalled the toy after many dozens of complaints.
(b) The toy is being recalled because it poses a choking hazard to children.
(c) All consumers must apply to the corporate center for a refund.
(d) The recall does not apply to Bumblebee toys under a certain size.

32. Homeopathy is a system of alternative medicine that creates remedies by a series of dilution processes. A ground up substance is added to a liquid, either water or alcohol, and shaken. Next, a portion of the liquid is removed, diluted again, and shaken once more. After this process has been repeated numerous times, the final product is often so diluted that no trace of the original substance remains in it. Although clinical trials have not produced any scientific evidence showing that homeopathic treatments are effective, belief in their efficacy persists.

Q: Which of the following is correct about homeopathy according to the passage?
(a) It uses a mixture of water and alcohol as a basis for the dilution.
(b) Each dilution contains the same level of concentration as the original dilution.
(c) A portion of one dilution is used to produce the subsequent dilution.
(d) Scientific research supports the claim that it is an effective treatment option.

33. Many companies have adopted 360-degree feedback as a performance evaluation tool. This technique utilizes the assessments of a worker's peers as well as those of his supervisors. But research has found that when employees know each other very well, or not well enough, their feedback is often inaccurate. Studies comparing 360-degree feedback to other assessment methods show that workers who have known each other for between one to three years offer the most balanced assessments, while others with less or more familiarity often offer favorable generalizations.

Q: What can be inferred about 360-degree feedback from the passage?
(a) It produces overly negative critiques of workers' performance.
(b) It places undue emphasis on evaluations from experienced staff.
(c) It is affected by the evaluator's familiarity with his or her coworker.
(d) It is favored because it gives power over evaluation to administrators.

34. A. F. K. Organski's power transition theory, first posited in his 1958 book *World Politics*, uses the concept of hierarchy in international politics to explain how wars arise. According to the theory, when global powers are imbalanced, dominant nations use their strength to maintain the status quo, which reduces the chances of war. Armed conflicts are likely to arise when a challenger dissatisfied with the current global hierarchy gains enough strength to threaten the dominant power. When the challenger chooses to use its new strength to attain a higher status in the world's political hierarchy, war will break out.

Q: What can be inferred about power transition theory from the passage?
(a) Its main purpose is to explain domestic power struggles.
(b) It supports the use of armed forces to ensure political stability.
(c) It is based on the idea that equality in power is favorable to peace.
(d) It posits that wars are started by challengers rather than dominant powers.

35. Rhinoceros beetles have few defenses against predators since they lack the ability to bite or sting. They do have large horns, but these are used primarily in fighting other males of their species and for digging. They can fly, but their large body size and unwieldy horns limit their ability to do so efficiently. Instead, they rely primarily on their size and nocturnal habits for defense: they are too big to attract many predators, and additionally, they hide under logs or plants during the day to avoid the few that want to eat them.

Q: What can be inferred about rhinoceros beetles from the passage?
(a) They are at the base of their food chain.
(b) They spend most of the day scavenging for food.
(c) Their most effective defensive mechanism is the ability to fly.
(d) Their size is both advantageous and detrimental to their defense.

36. The protest at Weston University took another turn early yesterday when more than a dozen students staged a sit-in at the president's office. This new development is in response to the school's continued evasion of questions about why it has done nothing to improve workers' rights in factories that make clothing bearing the school name and logo. Student protesters are demanding that the school join a group that monitors these worker's rights. When questioned about the sit-in, university president Patricia Connors reiterated her previous comment that she is looking into the issue.

Q: What can be inferred from the news article?
(a) The sit-in was encouraged by President Connors.
(b) The sit-in was one in an ongoing series of protest actions.
(c) The university recently seceded from the monitoring group.
(d) The monitoring group was founded by the protesting students.

37. During the 2012 London Olympics, the British newspaper *The Guardian* gave online readers the option to hide headlines related to the Olympics, recognizing that many readers had grown tired of such stories. In effect, this so-called "reader-led curation" gives news consumers some editorial power, and thus it raises an important question: should news outlets allow readers to actively filter certain issues? The answer may be yes for something like the Olympics. But what about more important issues such as presidential elections or natural disasters? Allowing readers to willfully ignore crucial issues like that would be a mistake.

Q: Which statement would the writer most likely agree with?
(a) Headline filters should be offered for all prominent issues.
(b) *The Guardian* did not give the Olympics enough coverage.
(c) Reader-led curation is not appropriate for all news events.
(d) Readers should demand more control over online news.

Part III Questions 38–40

Read the passage and identify the option that does NOT belong.

38. SETI Live is a venture by which anyone can allow their computer to be used to help search for life in the universe. (a) Initially, the SETI institute had a problem in that they had a lot of data to analyze, but not enough computers. (b) Although the SETI uses automated algorithms, sometimes human judgment is needed to interpret the data. (c) So SETI created a freely downloadable program that harnesses the public's unused computational power. (d) While the user does other things, the program runs in the background on the user's PC and analyzes data sent to it via the Internet.

39. Recent reports show that a growing number of children are being diagnosed with asthma. (a) As recently as fifty years ago, the disease was relatively rare in children. (b) In fact, many childhood diseases, such as measles and mumps, have become rare. (c) Today, however, asthma is the most common chronic childhood disease. (d) It is estimated that nearly 10% of children have asthma, a rise that has doctors baffled.

40. Many things in American society, from pop culture to business practices, have been significantly influenced by the Japanese. (a) Merely walking down a Tokyo street shows such American influences as Starbucks coffee and McDonald's hamburgers. (b) In entertainment, the increasing relevance of Japanese manga was recently seen at the comic book festival held in California. (c) But Japanese influence has not been limited to entertainment, as the way some US companies are run now reflects Japanese principles. (d) In fact, the concept of just-in-time production, a Japanese innovation, has revolutionized manufacturing in America.

This is the end of the Reading Comprehension section. Please remain seated until the proctor has instructed otherwise. You are NOT allowed to turn to any other section of the test.

서울대 최신기출 5

Listening Comprehension

Grammar

Vocabulary

Reading Comprehension

LISTENING COMPREHENSION

DIRECTIONS

1. In the Listening Comprehension section, all content will be presented orally rather than in written form.
2. This section contains four parts, each with fifteen individual items. For each part, you will receive separate instructions. Listen to the instructions carefully, and choose the best answer from the options for each item.

Scripts P 312 / 정답 P 338

Part I **Questions 1—15**

You will now hear fifteen individual spoken questions or statements, each followed by four spoken responses. Choose the most appropriate response for each item.

Part II **Questions 16—30**

You will now hear fifteen short conversation fragments, followed by four spoken responses. Choose the most appropriate response to complete each conversation.

Part III **Questions 31–45**

You will now hear fifteen complete conversations. For each conversation, you will be asked to answer a question. Each conversation and its corresponding question will be read twice. Then you will hear four options which will be read only once. Based on the given information, choose the option that best answers the question.

Part IV **Questions 46–60**

You will now hear fifteen short talks. After each talk, you will be asked to answer a question. Each talk and its corresponding question will be read twice. Then you will hear four options which will be read only once. Based on the given information, choose the option that best answers the question.

GRAMMAR

DIRECTIONS

This section tests your grammar skills. You will have 25 minutes to complete the 50 questions. Be sure to follow the directions given by the proctor.

정답 P 338

Part I **Questions 1–20**

Choose the option that best completes each gap.

1. A: Can I help you bring your suitcases in, Tina?

B: Sure. My luggage ___________ still in the car.

(a) is
(b) are
(c) was
(d) were

2. A: Any news about our delayed flight?

B: Passengers are advised ___________ by the gate for now.

(a) to remain
(b) remaining
(c) having remained
(d) to have remained

3. A: Do I have to keep this flour in the refrigerator?

B: No. Just make sure that it is stored in ___________ area.

(a) dry
(b) a dry
(c) all dry
(d) such dry

4. A: Can I get the same discount on that TV as you did?

B: I doubt it. The offer is only available while supplies ___________.

(a) last
(b) lasted
(c) will last
(d) have lasted

5. A: How did you grade all those essays so fast?

B: The TA ___________ me grade them was really experienced.

(a) helps
(b) helped
(c) helping
(d) to have helped

6. A: It was a mistake to venture out into this rain.

B: Yeah, we ___________ have just stayed in.

(a) can
(b) will
(c) must
(d) should

7. A: Did you have lunch with all of the interviewees?

B: Most of them. One of the candidates ___________ available.

(a) wasn't
(b) weren't
(c) hasn't been
(d) haven't been

8. A: I can't decide on a wedding dress.

B: Pick ___________ you feel most comfortable in.

(a) what kind style
(b) the kind of style
(c) what kind style do
(d) the kind of style do

9. A: Does Luke ever go on business trips?
B: All the time. Meeting clients in various cities ___________ part of his job.
(a) is always being
(b) has always been
(c) are always being
(d) have always been

10. A: What did the reviewer say about the restaurant's new fusion dish?
B: She lauded it, ___________ it a great innovation.
(a) declares
(b) declared
(c) declaring
(d) to declare

11. A: Do you think Sandra could proofread my thesis tonight?
B: That ___________ on such short notice.
(a) asking her is too much
(b) asks of too much to her
(c) is too much to ask of her
(d) is asking her to too much

12. A: When can I watch TV?
B: As soon as you've finished ___________ your homework.
(a) do
(b) to do
(c) doing
(d) having done

13. A: Everybody admires our new intern's work.
B: I recommend that he ___________ permanently.
(a) is hired
(b) be hired
(c) will be hired
(d) would be hired

14. A: Why didn't you come out with us last night?
B: Because I spent all my money this month ___________ books.
(a) with
(b) on
(c) of
(d) to

15. A: This new power plant could really hurt the environment.
B: That's the part ___________.
(a) that I mostly worry
(b) I am worried the most
(c) worrying mostly to me
(d) that worries me the most

16. A: You've been meeting Sara a lot recently.
B: Well, with Sara ___________ on my film, we have to meet often.
(a) collaborates
(b) collaborated
(c) collaborating
(d) has collaborated

17. A: I want to take a taxi, but traffic is bad.

B: You might find ___________.

(a) it easier to take the subway
(b) that taking the subway easier
(c) that the subway easier to take
(d) it the subway is to be easier to take

18. A: Your sons are very different!

B: I know. Sam is studious, ___________ Pete is more of an athlete.

(a) whether
(b) whereas
(c) whenever
(d) whereupon

19. A: Does your supervisor know you have a doctor's appointment today?

B: Yeah, she gave me ___________ to leave early.

(a) permission
(b) permissions
(c) a permission
(d) her permissions

20. A: Did you tell your brother what he's doing wrong?

B: Yes, but he wouldn't listen. He's impervious ___________ criticism.

(a) to
(b) of
(c) from
(d) beyond

Part II Questions 21—40

Choose the option that best completes each gap.

21. Not until after she arrived at the office did Christine realize that she ___________ her lunch at home.

(a) has left
(b) had left
(c) was leaving
(d) would leave

22. This author's greatest strength as a novelist is that he ___________ write witty, authentic dialogue.

(a) can
(b) may
(c) must
(d) should

23. As ___________, parents often do not want them to have all the sugar and calories that it contains.

(a) kids love lemonade as much
(b) kids love as much lemonade
(c) much as kids love lemonade
(d) much lemonade as kids love

24. Many employees prefer to work at companies ___________ opportunities for personal development are provided.

(a) that
(b) who
(c) which
(d) where

25. Despite having the exams on their desks, the students were not allowed to start writing until the proctor ___________.

(a) so instructed them to do
(b) instructed them to do so
(c) had instructed so to them
(d) had them so instructed to do

26. ShinyDent claims that its products promote oral hygiene better than ___________ of its competitors.

(a) it
(b) its
(c) their
(d) those

27. When asked why she needed crutches to walk, Sheila explained that she ___________ from a recent fall.

(a) recovers
(b) recovered
(c) has recovered
(d) was recovering

28. ___________ it is approved by two-thirds of legislators, a new bill will not become a law.

(a) As if
(b) Since
(c) Unless
(d) In case

29. Knowing little about appliances, Scott ___________ to choose their new refrigerator.

(a) left to his wife it
(b) left it to his wife
(c) was leaving to his wife it
(d) was leaving to it his wife

30. Although the manager apologized about the poor service, the customers ___________ and left promptly.

(a) didn't appease
(b) hadn't appeased
(c) weren't appeased
(d) haven't been appeased

31. Though the seller set a high price, the buyer offered ___________ he thought was more appropriate in the hopes of getting a discount.

(a) that
(b) what
(c) which
(d) whom

32. ___________ in well-drained, moist soil in a sunny spot, sunflowers will grow very quickly, commonly reaching 1.5 to 3.5 meters.

(a) Planted
(b) Planting
(c) To plant
(d) Having planted

33. ___________ his naughty younger cousins' behavior was like, he would not have offered to babysit them.

(a) What had Owen known
(b) Owen had known what
(c) Had Owen known what
(d) What Owen had known

34. The guest wanted to have more dessert but wondered if it would be rude to ask for ___________ helping.

(a) other
(b) more
(c) much
(d) another

35. The latest exhibit features several famous painters, ___________ many works only the most well-known are on display.

(a) of whose
(b) of which
(c) whose
(d) which

36. The invention of the transistor ___________ the control of a large electrical signal by a much smaller signal.

(a) made it the possibility for
(b) made it possibly for
(c) made it possible
(d) made possible

37. Aden discussed the movie as though he ___________ it, when actually his experience was limited to reading the book.

(a) would see
(b) had seen
(c) has seen
(d) will see

38. Despite his grammatical errors and unclear pronunciation, Sergei can make himself ___________ in English.

(a) understand
(b) understood
(c) to understand
(d) understanding

39. Marjorie thought she had no change for the bus, so she was happy to find ___________ coins in her pocket.

(a) few
(b) little
(c) some
(d) much

40. When no one else volunteered to work the night shift, Ned graciously said that he ___________.

(a) would
(b) would be
(c) would have
(d) would have been

Part III **Questions 41–45**

Read each sentence carefully and identify the option that contains a grammatical error.

41. (a) A: Who are those people you were just speaking, dear?
(b) B: They're some tourists visiting the city for the first time.
(c) A: I saw that you talked for a good while. What did they want?
(d) B: They were asking me to recommend a good local restaurant.

42. (a) A: Erica! I haven't seen you in a long time! What brings you to New York?
(b) B: I'm living here for the past three months. What about you?
(c) A: I'm just staying here for a week with my fiancé, visiting old friends.
(d) B: How nice! You should come over for dinner before you leave.

43. (a) A: How did you touch up those old photos of your grandparents?
(b) B: I scanned them and fixed them up using some editing software.
(c) A: They look good. But that one of their first house is still a bit dark.
(d) B: I know. I tried to make as bright as possible, but it looked odd.

44. (a) A: I'm about to go out for lunch. Are you interested in joining me?
(b) B: I can't. I need to get this report done by six o'clock.
(c) A: You must really be busy if you don't even have time to take a lunch break!
(d) B: Well, if I don't work through lunch, I'll be impossible to finish the report in time.

45. (a) A: Remember when we climbed the Austrian Alps a few years back?
(b) B: Yeah. Talk about anti-climactic! With all the clouds, the visibility at the top was terrible.
(c) A: I know. It was very too cloudy to see anything, even the other members of our team.
(d) B: On our next trip, let's go when the weather is more suitable for hiking.

Read each sentence carefully and identify the option that contains a grammatical error.

46. (a) Among the dirt removed from a Phoenix construction site, workers discovered some ancient relics. (b) Although meager, the finds include pottery fragments thought to go back as far as 1,600 years. (c) To date, archeologists only uncover a few sites in the region containing such well-preserved objects. (d) The objects will be stored for preservation and research at the Pueblo Grande Museum.

47. (a) Hailstones arise when water is carried upwards and freezes in the cooler portions of clouds. (b) Subsequent cycling causes additional layers of ice to accumulate on the growing hailstones. (c) Midsummer hailstorms can be devastating particular to agriculture, shredding plants within minutes. (d) Even small pellets can cause tremendous damage to crops, ruining a full year's harvest in extreme cases.

48. (a) One great way to remember important information from a text is to highlight it. (b) Highlighting can help you review topics you need to study them for an examination. (c) The key is to highlight just enough to help you locate main points. (d) When too much is included in your highlighting, important points tend to get obscured.

49. (a) Whether viruses should consider true forms of life is a matter that is up for debate. (b) Possessing the ability to replicate and evolve, viruses do lead a dynamic existence. (c) However, they lack their own cell structure and are unable to function without a living host. (d) Also, viruses cannot react to stimuli, which further distinguishes them from true living things.

50. (a) As the hardest naturally occurring material on earth, diamonds have long been sought after and valued. (b) Diamonds are so hard because of the covalent bonds that tightly bind their carbon atoms. (c) This cubic crystal system is what makes them resistant to any shape transformations or scratches. (d) Knowledge of the structure of diamonds has enabled scientists to create substances of similarly durability in the lab.

This is the end of the Grammar section. Do NOT move on to the next section until instructed to do so. You are NOT allowed to turn to any other section of the test.

TEPS

VOCABULARY

DIRECTIONS

This section tests your vocabulary skills. You will have 15 minutes to complete the 50 questions. Be sure to follow the directions given by the proctor.

정답 P 338

Part I Questions 1–25

Choose the option that best completes each gap.

1. A: Did you remember to pick up bread at the store?
   B: No, sorry. I ___________ you'd asked me to.
   (a) lost
   (b) failed
   (c) forgot
   (d) mistook

2. A: Has the fight against poverty been a success?
   B: Yes, this report says poverty rates have been ___________.
   (a) spilled
   (b) filtered
   (c) reduced
   (d) belittled

3. A: Jessie didn't ___________ the promotion she got.
   B: I agree. She hasn't worked here long enough to earn it.
   (a) deserve
   (b) succeed
   (c) manage
   (d) provoke

4. A: My bag won't fit under the seat on the plane.
   B: It'll fit in the ___________ overhead.
   (a) parcel
   (b) cubicle
   (c) interchange
   (d) compartment

5. A: Can tomorrow's appointments be rearranged?
   B: Sure, I'll ___________ them to better suit your schedule.
   (a) whisk
   (b) flutter
   (c) justify
   (d) shuffle

6. A: Gerald always refuses to heed my advice.
   B: He's known for being ___________ like that.
   (a) barren
   (b) diligent
   (c) innocent
   (d) stubborn

7. A: Why haven't I received my magazine lately?
   B: Your subscription has ___________ and should be renewed.
   (a) disproved
   (b) discarded
   (c) expelled
   (d) expired

8. A: The sun's reflection on the water is so bright.
   B: Yes. The ___________ is so strong it's hurting my eyes.
   (a) daze
   (b) glare
   (c) ripple
   (d) streak

9. A: This car ride is making me nauseous, with all this jolting around.

B: Sorry. The road is really ___________.

(a) husky
(b) shaggy
(c) bumpy
(d) stormy

10. A: How do I sign up for swimming classes?

B: Just ___________ this registration form.

(a) get up
(b) fill out
(c) turn out
(d) make up

11. A: You need to request long vacations two weeks in advance.

B: Oh, thanks for letting me know. I was ___________ to that rule.

(a) inconsiderate
(b) preoccupied
(c) languished
(d) oblivious

12. A: Does the subway go to Lester Mall?

B: No, buses are the only available ___________ of public transit.

(a) mode
(b) post
(c) core
(d) line

13. A: The boss disliked my expensive proposal.

B: With our limited budget, she ___________ at any costly projects.

(a) balks
(b) erodes
(c) recants
(d) disavows

14. A: I hope my muffins win the baking contest.

B: They will! Everyone who has tasted them thinks they're ___________.

(a) garnished
(b) delectable
(c) flourishing
(d) demonstrable

15. A: I'm sorry your antique vase was dropped. Were you able to fix it?

B: No, it was ___________ damaged.

(a) indelibly
(b) irreparably
(c) inconsolably
(d) irreproachably

16. A: Did airport security take our sunscreen?

B: Yes. It was too big to carry on, so the guard ___________ it.

(a) revamped
(b) hampered
(c) restrained
(d) confiscated

17. A: It's amazing no one was hurt in the hurricane.

B: Luckily, everyone was able to find ___________ at shelters quickly.

(a) retort
(b) resort
(c) refuge
(d) rebuke

18. A: Sometimes I'm overwhelmed by the fear of failure.

B: Well, don't ___________ to negativity.

(a) incline
(b) conceive
(c) subsume
(d) succumb

19. A: Has anyone ever run this race so quickly?

B: No, the winner's time is totally ___________.

(a) unprecedented
(b) indisputable
(c) unassuming
(d) incisive

20. A: Is there a gift shop at this temple?

B: Not on the temple's actual ___________, but there's one outside the gate.

(a) grounds
(b) presence
(c) proximity
(d) subsistence

21. A: Paul got angry after reading the bad review of his play.

B: He always ___________ when critics pan his performances.

(a) bites the bullet
(b) runs out of steam
(c) goes out on a limb
(d) flies off the handle

22. A: Do you see James often?

B: Yes, we ___________ the same restaurant for lunch.

(a) cater
(b) occasion
(c) frequent
(d) compromise

23. A: With the way Max quit, he'll never be able to be rehired here.

B: Yeah, it's a shame he ___________ at this place.

(a) beat around the bush
(b) bent over backwards
(c) burned his bridges
(d) broke a leg

24. A: That bar was so noisy!

B: Yeah. I couldn't hear anything above all the ___________.

(a) racket
(b) earshot
(c) plunder
(d) swagger

25. A: I can't stand overly sentimental romance movies.

B: Agreed. They're way too ___________ for my taste.

(a) provident
(b) maudlin
(c) shrewd
(d) canny

VOCABULARY

Part II **Questions 26—50**

Choose the option that best completes each gap.

26. Maintaining good ____________ by sitting up straight is important for workers with desk jobs.

(a) posture
(b) spread
(c) layout
(d) lining

27. During mating season, chameleons change their skin color to ____________ a mate.

(a) detect
(b) attract
(c) extract
(d) release

28. Having won the Outstanding Teacher Award numerous times, Chris was an ____________ educator whose achievements were admired by his colleagues.

(a) attained
(b) ambivalent
(c) approximate
(d) accomplished

29. The climber's ____________ to the top of Mount Everest took many days and was exhausting.

(a) stride
(b) ascent
(c) altitude
(d) upgrade

30. Carl could not ____________ the trailer from the truck that he had used to tow it, so he left the two connected.

(a) desert
(b) detach
(c) distract
(d) disclose

31. After witnessing daily life in the developing world firsthand, many skeptics change their ____________ on the need for development aid.

(a) margins
(b) spectacles
(c) visionaries
(d) perspectives

32. After being ____________ by his doctors that his right hand was damaged from over-practicing, pianist Alexander Scriabin wrote songs for one hand.

(a) exposed
(b) informed
(c) indicated
(d) expanded

33. The movie premieres tomorrow, but select theaters are offering a(n) ____________ for fans to see it tonight.

(a) informant
(b) preview
(c) advent
(d) onset

34. Only the most reputable restoration experts are ___________ with the task of restoring priceless works of art.

(a) ministered
(b) entrusted
(c) advanced
(d) stocked

35. Melinda wasn't sure the boy in the dark theater was her nephew, since she only saw the outlines of the child's ___________.

(a) figure
(b) format
(c) quantity
(d) summary

36. Because mosquitoes can spread malaria, ___________ are often sprayed over large areas to eradicate them.

(a) insectivores
(b) pesticides
(c) torments
(d) influxes

37. Tom's loud, forceful way of speaking made others see him as a(n) ___________ person.

(a) brash
(b) naive
(c) urbane
(d) gullible

38. A construction crane in China set a world record in 2008 when it ___________ just over 20,000 metric tons into the air.

(a) rallied
(b) erected
(c) hoisted
(d) fabricated

39. With soundproof windows and walls, Wellington Apartments offers you the quiet ___________ you can't find in the bustling, noisy city outside.

(a) serenity
(b) vapidity
(c) retaliation
(d) trepidation

40. There was no time to waste preparing for the typhoon as the disaster was ___________.

(a) reticent
(b) obsolete
(c) indiscreet
(d) imminent

41. In the Middle East, several governments have experienced political ___________, leading them to be overthrown via armed revolts.

(a) layoffs
(b) lethargy
(c) upheaval
(d) pandemics

42. Differences in opinion caused a ___________ between Amy and Helen, which eventually ended their friendship.

(a) dividend
(b) dodge
(c) flaw
(d) rift

43. Leslie heard a series of noises in the hallway, so she went outside to see what was causing the ___________.

(a) composure
(b) commotion
(c) condensation
(d) condemnation

44. It was ___________ to try to convince Ann to read a book on Roman history because she found history boring.

(a) prolonged
(b) opaque
(c) futile
(d) wary

45. Libraries that once stood in Alexandria, Constantinople, and Nalanda are among the great ___________ of human knowledge now lost to us.

(a) despots
(b) tenements
(c) repositories
(d) compensations

46. The loan from Gary's parents ___________ him to open his own business.

(a) leased
(b) enabled
(c) appealed
(d) conveyed

47. Musical ___________ often display signs of their extraordinary talent from an early age.

(a) caprices
(b) tempests
(c) virtuosos
(d) syndicates

48. The president delivered a ___________ speech, rekindling national pride and inspiring hope in millions of citizens.

(a) rousing
(b) recondite
(c) quiescent
(d) bumbling

49. The spokesman's words were ___________ by reporters, who inaccurately summarized his speech.

(a) undeterred
(b) misadvised
(c) misconstrued
(d) underwhelmed

50. The peace ushered in by the Munich Agreement of 1938 proved to be ___________, as Germany invaded Poland a mere 11 months later.

(a) perennial
(b) ephemeral
(c) pugnacious
(d) emblematic

This is the end of the Vocabulary section. Do NOT move on to the Reading Comprehension section until instructed to do so. You are NOT allowed to turn to any other section of the test.

READING COMPREHENSION

DIRECTIONS

This section tests your ability to comprehend reading passages. You will have 45 minutes to complete the 40 questions. Be sure to follow the directions given by the proctor.

정답 P 338

Part I **Questions 1–16**

Read the passage and choose the option that best completes the passage.

1. Due to the early retirement of one of our marketing managers, a position on our management team is now available. The company has decided to restrict applications for this position to current employees. Interested parties are encouraged to apply no later than Friday, May 12. Interviews will commence the following week. The company's hope is that this process will allow ________________.

(a) us to bring fresh talent to the organization
(b) a suitable candidate to be recruited internally
(c) better retirement options for senior employees
(d) us to effectively outsource non-essential duties

2. Recently, several patients have gained access to restricted areas, and so we are asking all Riverside Hospital employees to ________________. The enhanced security monitoring will begin today, so please ensure that your staff badge is visible at all times. Make sure that your picture is always facing outward and not covered by clothing. Anyone without valid identification will be denied access to restricted areas, with no exceptions.

(a) observe stricter requirements for employee ID usage
(b) update their security clearance with the administration
(c) enter restricted areas by fingerprint scan rather than ID
(d) increase security measures in patients' rooms and lobbies

3. One type of worker has escaped layoffs caused by the weak economy: robots. In fact, robots may be contributing to job shortages, as they have been replacing humans in a variety of workplaces. In manufacturing, robots can do complex tasks that humans did twenty years ago; in agriculture, they are used to harvest and process food. Even in finance, artificial intelligence software sorts through documents for analysts, an onerous task that was once done by people. It would appear that machines are ________________.

(a) beginning to show their wear from overuse
(b) being reassigned away from dangerous tasks
(c) increasing their presence in various job sectors
(d) helping to create much-needed job opportunities

4. A study on patriarchy, or the system in which men occupy the dominant position in society, has ______________. The study's authors looked at the social structures of 51 countries, paying attention to the relationship between men and women. Although a definite causal relationship is difficult to establish, the researchers found a correlation between male dominance and violence: rates of violent crime were higher in countries where men were dominant. The authors noted that the correlation is strong enough to show how patriarchy is not just detrimental for women, but potentially harmful for society as a whole.

(a) posited a link between patriarchy and violence in society
(b) shown that male power deters violent and antisocial behavior
(c) revealed that gender equality in society has reached a low point
(d) suggested a new way to empower women in patriarchal societies

5. Charging your cell phone in the car is convenient, but is it good for the environment? Recent research has compared the differences between home and car charging. To produce one kilowatt-hour of electricity, a car's engine creates about 5 pounds of carbon dioxide. On the other hand, electrical power plants only produce 1.3 pounds of carbon dioxide in creating the same amount of electricity. These figures clearly show that ______________.

(a) car chargers save both time and energy
(b) wall chargers are by far the greener choice
(c) drivers should avoid using hand-held devices
(d) chargers waste energy no matter where they are

6. A recent comprehensive review of studies concerning omega-3 fatty acids and brain function concluded that ______________. Omega-3 fatty acids, found primarily in fish, have been widely promoted as beneficial in improving cognitive function and memory. But the review found that people in good health taking omega-3 fatty acids in pill form performed no better on cognitive tests than those taking a placebo. While the review does not preclude the possibility that there may be other benefits of omega-3 supplements, it seems that claims that they improve brain function may have been exaggerated.

(a) the benefits of omega-3 pills were limited to cognitive functions
(b) there is a threshold in cognitive benefits from omega-3 supplements
(c) no research exists on the effects of omega-3 pills on cognitive functions
(d) healthy people gain no cognitive benefits by taking omega-3 supplements

7. Looking back on my mid-career return to university at age forty, I see that ________________. Though I already had a well-established job in human resources, my love of mathematics and quantitative analysis called me back to university to study accountancy. In the beginning I found my classes extremely challenging and often felt like I didn't fit in with the younger students. After graduation, however, I quickly found a job I loved and haven't spent a moment regretting the path I chose.

(a) I was right to change careers from accountancy
(b) I should have studied human resources all along
(c) my love of my profession has waned in recent years
(d) my decision was a good one despite initial difficulties

8. The oral polio vaccine was administered in the US for decades, but its use was discontinued in 2000 because ________________. Since the 1960s, the oral vaccine had been favored over the injectable version because it was cheaper, easier to administer, and transmitted immunity to community members. Its drawback was that it contained live pathogens, meaning a small fraction of those taking it contracted full-blown polio, a risk not present with the injectable version, which used inactivated polio viruses. As the US got polio under control, it therefore switched to the version that presented the least risk to the public.

(a) more virulent strains of the virus were appearing
(b) it had not proved effective in halting the disease
(c) scientists developed a less expensive version
(d) a safer alternative was selected to replace it

9. When asked what makes a good leader, many people cite confidence. According to certain studies, however, the appearance of confidence actually has an inverse correlation to competence. This phenomenon, known as the Dunning-Kruger effect, refers to the tendency of incompetent people to overestimate their abilities because they do not have the knowledge to accurately evaluate themselves. Applying this idea to the selection of leaders, psychologists have suggested that people looking for leaders who appear confident are ________________.

(a) likely to underestimate their own social abilities
(b) overlooking other areas of a leader's competence
(c) accidentally selecting people who are incompetent
(d) actually lessening a leader's chances to gain support

10. After posting derogatory remarks about their school in an online forum last month, four students were temporarily suspended from Abraham Lincoln High School. The principal, who issued the punishment, called it a case of cyberbullying. But according to the students' parents, the students were simply exercising free speech, and the principal's response was too severe. After hearing the parents' appeal last night, the school board overturned the suspension, deeming that it was a(n) ______________________________.

(a) right of students to discuss their suspension online
(b) decision that would only make teachers more resentful
(c) unwarranted reaction to students expressing themselves
(d) unfortunate example of students being treated too lightly

11.

To the Editor:

The city's plan to provide free food to all kids in public schools is a brilliant initiative, yet people are complaining. Why would anyone want to block improved child nutrition? My guess is that critics simply disparage any policy put forth by our liberal mayor. On its own merits, the program is a great idea: parents will save money, taxes won't be raised, and administration will be simpler than previous need-based schemes. It seems that critics ______________________________.

Betty Fulworth

(a) are pushing instead for a plan supported by liberals
(b) are dismissing a genuinely helpful plan for political reasons
(c) have been attempting to get the program moved to another city
(d) have reason to criticize the mayor for not supporting the program

12. Filmmakers of the French New Wave of the 1950s and 1960s set out not only to use unconventional techniques, but to flaunt those techniques openly as a rejection of overblown, popular cinematic forms. Shaky, portable cameras, disjointed editing, and improvised dialogue were all used to give a documentary-type feel to New Wave films' narratives. Actors even broke cinematic conventions by addressing the camera directly. Such techniques served to ______________________________.

(a) create a style that deviated from mainstream genres
(b) preserve the time-tested conventions of early cinema
(c) impress viewers with an appearance of polished production
(d) pay tribute to the famous mass-market films that came before

13. Coccolithophores are single-celled ocean creatures ____________________________________. Their name derives from coccoliths, the tiny calcium carbonate plates they armor themselves with. Under certain conditions, coccolithophores collectively shed these shields in massive quantities, which pool together in a "coccolithophore bloom" and turn the ocean a milky white color. Much like polar ice fields, these bright coccolithophore blooms reflect sunlight, sending warming radiation back to space and cooling the earth's atmosphere slightly.

(a) whose shedding of coccoliths is limited to polar regions
(b) whose behavior has been shown to affect the climate
(c) that can speed the warming of marine ecosystems
(d) that cause ocean plants to bloom prematurely

14. In his long essay on French poet Baudelaire, Jean-Paul Sartre describes the paradoxical outcome of an intensely shy, introverted personality. He shows Baudelaire to be a man who could not hide in the anonymity of the crowd, a famous poet who sought seclusion by creating an outrageous public persona. Sartre suggests that behind the mask of a poetic madman, Baudelaire was hiding his fear of social situations and craving to be alone. Sartre's psychological portrait is of a poet who ____________________________________.

(a) was a flippant artist in pursuit of constant adoration
(b) was a deeply apprehensive person troubled by his fame
(c) assumed an introverted personality to hide his true thoughts
(d) became a victim of the public's distorted perception of his works

15. Footbag, also called Hacky Sack, is a sport in which players strive to keep a small, bead-filled bag off the ground without using their hands. Games can be played in groups, with players standing in a circle and passing the sack to and from one another. ______________________________, footbag can be played by just one person, who does a kind of performance involving freestyle tricks like kicks, spins, or ducks.

(a) Hence
(b) Overall
(c) Ultimately
(d) Alternatively

16. There is a relationship of mutual dependency between public relations and journalism. Reporters and editors use information from public relations firms to write a large part of the news. ______________________________, public relations practitioners depend upon journalists to spread their messages to the public. However, this symbiotic relationship has increasingly become controversial, as citizens demand more original content from news outlets and grow more wary of public relations firms' influence.

(a) In turn
(b) That is
(c) Otherwise
(d) Nonetheless

Part II **Questions 17—37**

Read the passage, question, and options. Then, based on the given information, choose the option that best answers the question.

17.

Dear Ms. Celia Garrison,

Thank you for your application for admission to the Veriden Conservatory. We are eager to review your application but have not yet had an opportunity to do so because we received an unexpectedly large number of applications this year. We need to extend our evaluation process by two weeks, so the original notification date of February 1 cannot be honored. We will be notifying applicants of their acceptance by February 15.

Kind regards,
William Hendricks
Admissions Director

Q: What is the main purpose of the letter?
(a) To notify Celia of the completion of her evaluation
(b) To inform Celia about a notification deadline change
(c) To advise Celia to reapply to the conservatory in 15 days
(d) To ask Celia to submit additional documents for her application

18. In 2011, the American shipping company UPS implemented an innovative change to its delivery services. The new trick? Never turn left. When delivery trucks make left turns, they have to wait for the opposing traffic to pass, and this slows down routes, wastes fuel, and increases the likelihood of accidents. By arranging its delivery routes so drivers always make right turns, the company estimates that it cut its carbon emissions by 20,000 metric tons while delivering 350,000 more packages than in the previous year.

Q: What is the report mainly about?
(a) How a company made its deliveries more efficient
(b) Drops in fuel efficiency in the shipping industry
(c) How making right turns increases driving time
(d) Drivers who changed UPS's delivery policies

19. Many fruits we eat today remain remarkably similar to the fruits eaten by our ancient ancestors. Dates, figs, grapes, plums, pears, apples, and oranges can all be found in the fossil record in forms similar to their modern appearance. Yet vegetables show a different history. Many modern vegetables have changed radically since the invention of farming. Wild carrots, for example, were inedible before humans manipulated them. Humans also took a single plant variety and turned it into cauliflower, broccoli, cabbage, and Brussels sprouts.

Q: What is the writer's main point about vegetables?
(a) They have changed more than fruits have over time.
(b) Humans' ancient ancestors ate them more than fruits.
(c) Evidence of their evolution is sparse in the fossil record.
(d) They were considered inedible before farming was invented.

20. The American flavor industry, which grew up primarily in the past half century, now generates more than a billion dollars in revenue annually. It arrived with the Second World War, when Europe's perfume industry moved to the US and brought artificial flavor manufacturing with it. In subsequent years, processed foods became prominent in the American diet, and because the methods used to preserve these products—canning, freezing, dehydrating—destroy food's natural flavors, companies that made artificial flavors found a lucrative market for their products.

Q: What is the passage mainly about?
(a) What drove the growth of America's flavor industry
(b) How artificial flavors are now closer to natural flavors
(c) How Europeans created artificial flavors before Americans
(d) Why processed foods were detrimental to the flavor industry

21. Most adults have few memories from early childhood and assume that as children, they were ignorant of their surroundings. But researchers have found that when asked specific questions, even very young children recall recent events in accurate detail. However, these early memories are quickly erased as new ones are formed because children have limited capacity to store them. As children develop and their capacity to store memories increases, they begin to store new memories at a faster rate than they lose old ones, and thus form a continuous autobiographical narrative that stretches into adulthood.

Q: What is the passage mainly about?
(a) Why children cannot remember recent events with accuracy
(b) How children develop the ability to form a memory of their lives
(c) How children can be taught to be more aware of their surroundings
(d) Why children's memories tend to record only certain types of events

22. Glass has long been mistakenly considered a liquid. This misconception originates partly from the fact that antique glass windows are thicker on the bottom; this led people to believe that the glass must be a liquid, gradually flowing downward over time. However, the glass was simply formed in this manner, since the technology of the time could not make it perfectly flat. Although glass lacks the crystalline structure of a solid, once cooled to room temperature, glass is a solid.

Q: What is the main purpose of the passage?
(a) To counter the idea that glass is a liquid
(b) To describe the properties of glass as a solid
(c) To illustrate the crystalline structure of solids
(d) To explain how glass becomes a liquid over time

23. There are cardiovascular risks involved in sleeping less than the eight hours per night that doctors recommend, and a recent study has found that these risks are even higher for women. The study compared over 4,600 people aged 35 to 55, 27% of which were women. It found that women who only slept for seven hours had higher levels of interleukin-6 compared to those who slept eight hours. Also, women who slept for five hours or less had significantly higher levels of high-sensitivity C-reactive protein. Both of these indicators are associated with higher risk of heart disease.

Q: Which of the following is correct according to the passage?
(a) Doctors recommend getting fewer than eight hours of sleep.
(b) Men are less susceptible to heart disease from lack of sleep.
(c) The study examined data collected from women only.
(d) Less sleep was associated with lower interleukin-6 levels.

24. Very little is known about playwright William Shakespeare before age 28. There is no record of his birth, but since his baptism is documented on April 26, 1564, it is generally agreed that he was born three days earlier, as the practice was to baptize infants when they were three days old. Shortly after his marriage at age 18, Shakespeare had three children, all born and christened by 1585. Following this, there are no records about his life until a critical attack on his writing in 1592, when he was presumably 28 years old.

Q: Which of the following is correct about Shakespeare according to the passage?
(a) There are no documents from his early years.
(b) People commonly agree that his birth date is April 26.
(c) He is presumed to have been baptized at age three.
(d) No record of him exists between 1586 and 1591.

25. Attention all students looking to move off-campus! Allegre Apartments, located only ten minutes from the university, is now renting two- and three-bedroom units. We are conveniently located on a bus line and offer free parking for all tenants. We have both furnished and unfurnished apartments, and residents are not responsible for any utilities except cable television. Each unit has its own washer and dryer. Contact us today to schedule a viewing!

Q: Which of the following is correct about Allegre Apartments according to the advertisement?
(a) Tenants can park on-site for a small fee.
(b) All of the apartments are fully furnished.
(c) Renters must pay to have cable television.
(d) Tenants must use shared laundry facilities.

26. Dr. William Thomas, a Harvard-educated expert on elderly care, revolutionized care of the elderly. Believing that an environment with little stimulation was detrimental to patients' health, Dr. Thomas created a care home called the Eden Alternative, which featured pets, social activities, and a garden to give senior citizens worthwhile and entertaining pursuits. The improvements in patients' outcomes were remarkable. There are now around 200 Eden Alternative nursing homes in the US and elsewhere, and the turnover rates for nurses and assistants are far lower than the US national average.

Q: Which of the following is correct about the Eden Alternative according to the passage?
(a) It was invented by a doctor who is an expert on childcare.
(b) It was based on the idea that boredom leads to poor health.
(c) It has established nursing homes exclusively in the US.
(d) It has lower staff retention rates than the national average.

27. Neoclassicism as an architectural style dates back to the mid-eighteenth century. Harking back to the classical ideas and forms of ancient Greece and Rome, it arose in reaction to the rococo style that was popular at the time. Neoclassical architecture is somewhat similar to the late baroque style, but has more of a planar quality. Architecture in the neoclassical style is abundant in both Europe and the US, and though it experienced a lull in popularity following World War II, it has had a resurgence in recent years.

Q: Which of the following is correct about neoclassical architecture according to the passage?

(a) It preceded the rococo architectural movement.
(b) It shares stylistic elements with the late baroque style.
(c) It is rare in the US but fairly common in Europe.
(d) It reached the peak of its popularity just after World War II.

28. Before he became the president of the United States, Dwight D. Eisenhower was known for his leadership in the US military during World War II. After the war, he became the president of Columbia University, which he left in order to lead the North Atlantic Treaty Organization (NATO) the year before he ran for the presidency. He went into the presidential race with no political experience, but he still won by a landslide. His military expertise proved valuable during his presidency, as he obtained a truce in Korea and worked to ease the tensions of the Cold War.

Q: Which of the following is correct about Dwight D. Eisenhower according to the passage?

(a) He commanded NATO forces before working at Columbia University.
(b) He was known as a seasoned politician before becoming president.
(c) He obtained a sweeping victory in his initial run for president.
(d) He helped forge a truce to end World War II while serving as president.

29. Residents of Clifton City are still recovering after a massive storm Monday evening left many stranded and without power. The storm far exceeded forecasters' predictions, bringing high winds and heavy rain, and rendering several bridges on the Clifton River unusable. Nearly 30,000 residents are without electricity, and power workers are hurrying to restore service as quickly as possible. However, due to a lack of manpower and the current inability to cross the river, some areas will not regain electricity until at least Thursday.

Q: Which of the following is correct according to the news report?
(a) Clifton City's electricity has been out since Monday morning.
(b) The storm was not initially predicted to be as powerful as it was.
(c) Power has already been restored for all 30,000 people who had lost it.
(d) The power company is sufficiently staffed but unable to cross the river.

30. Everton University would like to announce that all classes scheduled for MacDonald Hall will temporarily be moved to other locations. During a routine inspection by university maintenance staff, mold was found in the ventilation units, and the hall was declared a threat in accordance with city health guidelines. The ventilation system will be cleaned, which will take two weeks, and the hall will be reopened immediately thereafter. Professors teaching affected classes should plan to be back in MacDonald Hall by week three of the semester.

Q: Which of the following is correct about MacDonald Hall according to the announcement?
(a) Classes scheduled in it will be moved for the rest of the semester.
(b) Mold was discovered in it during an inspection by city officials.
(c) Its ventilation system will be cleaned to clear up a mold infestation.
(d) It will be closed to staff and students for more than three weeks.

31. Bertrand Russell, a British logician and philosopher, contributed greatly to the field of mathematics. He discovered a paradox that discredited Gottlob Frege's attempt to form a foundational theory for all math using symbolic logic. He later conceived his "theory of types," which solved this same paradox. Already a published author in the field of political philosophy, he published his first book on mathematics in 1897. This book espoused the ideas of Immanuel Kant, but Russell later dismissed Kant's theories as having no bearing on mathematics and geometry.

Q: Which of the following is correct about Bertrand Russell according to the passage?
(a) Frege's foundational theory for math was supported by his paradox.
(b) He found a solution to a paradox that he had identified himself.
(c) The first book he published was about mathematical theories.
(d) He was a lifelong defender of applying Kant's theories to math.

32. A recent survey by Marketdata Enterprises showed that the main purchaser of self-improvement books, a $9 billion-a-year industry in the United States alone, is middle-aged, financially stable women. Also, over 80% were repeat purchasers, regardless of whether they had found success with such books in the past. This is why critics characterize repeat purchasing as a type of addiction: they claim repeat purchasers mistake reading as a form of personal development in itself and avoid actually implementing the techniques that these books recommend.

Q: Which of the following is correct about self-improvement books according to the passage?
(a) They are primarily purchased by those lacking financial stability.
(b) Most Americans who purchase them stop after buying one book.
(c) Past success with them has little effect on the decision to buy again.
(d) Critics say that repeat purchasers diligently utilize their strategies.

33. Do you sometimes unconsciously turn off your alarm or sleep right through it? If so, the Shinebright Morning Call Wake-up Service is for you! For a flat fee of just $5.99 a month, get wake-up calls to any number at any time, day or night. You can arrange for recurring wake-up calls at a set time or have special one-time calls arranged whenever you need to get up extra early. Set up your Morning Call account today, and sleep more soundly tonight!

Q: What can be inferred about the wake-up call service from the advertisement?
(a) It is only available for landline telephones.
(b) It requires users to purchase a special device.
(c) It offers an unlimited number of calls per month.
(d) It is designed to be used along with an alarm clock.

34.

To Whom It May Concern:

I am writing this recommendation on behalf of Janet Pound, whom I first taught during my freshman course in English literature. I was always impressed with the hard work she did in every class, even in her senior year, when many students become distracted by the pressure to find a job. For her senior project, which I supervised, Janet read Camus's *The Stranger* in the original French and analyzed its English translations. I am privileged to know Ms. Pound, and I'm sure she will excel in whichever graduate program she chooses.

Sincerely,
Professor Miriam Roth
Johnston University

Q: What can be inferred from the letter?
(a) Professor Roth had Janet in multiple courses.
(b) Janet changed her major from English to French.
(c) Professor Roth no longer teaches English literature.
(d) Janet needs the recommendation for a job application.

35. Does your carpet look old and matted down? It doesn't need to be replaced—it needs Prime Cleaners. Our team of trained professionals can clean anything at a fraction of the price of getting new carpet. We can remove years of ground-in dirt and deep-set stains. And in public spaces that receive heavier traffic, we have a special deep cleaning service that will make your carpets look like new for your clients. We are available for late night shifts after customers and staff have gone home. Call for a quote today!

Q: What can be inferred about Prime Cleaners from the advertisement?
(a) Its services include discounted carpet replacement.
(b) It primarily targets its cleaning services at businesses.
(c) Its deep cleaning service is only available for a limited time.
(d) It is currently offering a discount on carpet cleaning services.

36. When discussing modern music, the term "mania" is used in a lighthearted way to characterize fans' devotion to performers: for instance, "Beatlemania" was well known in the 1960s. But in 1841, when pianist Franz Liszt was wowing audiences, "mania" was not used so lightly. Liszt incited great fervor, touring with his long, flowing hair, basking in adulation, and doing the unthinkable: performing without sheet music. His lovestruck female fans were said to have "Lisztomania," a specific medical condition that doctors actually feared and considered contagious—so much so that they even attempted to immunize women against it.

Q: What can be inferred from the passage?
(a) Liszt was not ashamed to receive his fans' adoration.
(b) Piano recitals were unpopular until Liszt began his career.
(c) Recitals in Liszt's time were usually performed by memory.
(d) The term "mania" lacked medical connotations during Liszt's time.

37. When a Catholic pope passes away, church leaders known as the College of Cardinals are sequestered in the Vatican while they elect the next pope. This can go on for days, as the new pope must receive a two-thirds majority vote. It is difficult to predict who will be chosen, as a candidate who starkly contrasts with his predecessor is often elected. For instance, the election of Pope John XXIII in 1958 surprised many: John himself said that he had his return train ticket in his pocket when he was chosen to assume the papacy.

Q: What can be inferred from the passage?
(a) One ballot is usually enough for the election of a new pope.
(b) Continuity in leadership is a primary concern in electing popes.
(c) Pope John XXIII had not been expecting to be elected to the papacy.
(d) The College of Cardinals solicits input from church members in elections.

Part III Questions 38 – 40

Read the passage and identify the option that does NOT belong.

38. Owning pets can be beneficial to both people's mental well-being and their physical health. (a) Owning a pet can bring a sense of nurturing and consistency to the home environment. (b) This has been shown to have physical benefits, lowering blood pressure and heart rate. (c) First-time owners are often surprised by the high cost of owning a pet. (d) Plus, having a pet that requires daily exercise also encourages the owner to exercise more.

39. The belief that the earth is flat rather than spherical can be found in many ancient cultures. (a) The ancient Norse believed that the world was completely flat and supported in the center by a pillar. (b) According to an ancient Japanese belief, the Earth's land was thought to float on the sea like a flat sheet. (c) The ancient Greeks were able to identify planets by observing how their movement was related to other stars. (d) Also, in ancient China, the standard model was of a flat Earth surrounded by a circular heaven.

40. This philosophy seminar is designed to be an engaging class discussion, which is not the same as a debate. (a) The point of a debate is to use logic and reason to convince your listener that your position is right. (b) On the other hand, in a discussion you are not necessarily trying to win anyone over to your views. (c) To effectively explore ideas and issues in the classroom, you should carefully prepare in advance. (d) Thus, the purpose of our class is to communicate ideas effectively, not to be in competition with each other.

This is the end of the Reading Comprehension section. Please remain seated until the proctor has instructed otherwise. You are NOT allowed to turn to any other section of the test.

서울대 최신기출

6

Listening *Comprehension*

Grammar

Vocabulary

Reading *Comprehension*

Listening Comprehension

Directions

1. In the Listening Comprehension section, all content will be presented orally rather than in written form.
2. This section contains four parts, each with fifteen individual items. For each part, you will receive separate instructions. Listen to the instructions carefully, and choose the best answer from the options for each item.

Scripts P 323 / 정답 P 339

Part I **Questions 1—15**

You will now hear fifteen individual spoken questions or statements, each followed by four spoken responses. Choose the most appropriate response for each item.

Part II **Questions 16—30**

You will now hear fifteen short conversation fragments, followed by four spoken responses. Choose the most appropriate response to complete each conversation.

Part III **Questions 31–45**

You will now hear fifteen complete conversations. For each conversation, you will be asked to answer a question. Each conversation and its corresponding question will be read twice. Then you will hear four options which will be read only once. Based on the given information, choose the option that best answers the question.

Part IV **Questions 46–60**

You will now hear fifteen short talks. After each talk, you will be asked to answer a question. Each talk and its corresponding question will be read twice. Then you will hear four options which will be read only once. Based on the given information, choose the option that best answers the question.

GRAMMAR

DIRECTIONS

This section tests your grammar skills. You will have 25 minutes to complete the 50 questions. Be sure to follow the directions given by the proctor.

정답 P 339

Part I Questions 1—20

Choose the option that best completes each gap.

1. A: Will you make it to Amy's party?
   B: I can't, ____________ is too bad because I really want to go.
   (a) that
   (b) what
   (c) when
   (d) which

2. A: Are there any free parking spots on your side?
   B: Nope. I'll let you know when ____________ one, though.
   (a) I see
   (b) I saw
   (c) I'll see
   (d) I'd seen

3. A: Have you started to apply for internships yet?
   B: No. I'm ____________ too busy to devote time to that.
   (a) more current
   (b) most current
   (c) currently
   (d) current

4. A: Wow, Malville's soccer team is good!
   B: Their team is OK, but not as good as ____________.
   (a) it
   (b) our
   (c) ours
   (d) other

5. A: Were you satisfied with the car rental company?
   B: No. We would ____________ to choose a different one.
   (a) advise to have been better
   (b) be better advised to have
   (c) better have to be advised
   (d) have been better advised

6. A: Max, have you chosen which kind of laptop to buy?
   B: I want to look at online reviews first. I'll decide definitively ____________ I check them.
   (a) once
   (b) since
   (c) though
   (d) because

7. A: Do you have much going on tonight?
   B: Not really. I just have ____________ housework to do.
   (a) few
   (b) little
   (c) a few
   (d) a little

8. A: My youngest son, Dylan, lies sometimes. What should I do?
   B: Well, the hardest part is getting him to admit to ____________ in the first place.
   (a) lie
   (b) lied
   (c) lying
   (d) have lied

9. A: Did Sally tell you she's moving?
B: No, ___________.

(a) it's the first hearing of it I have
(b) this is the first I've heard of it
(c) I have the first hearing of it
(d) this first of it I've heard

10. A: Ted is unsure how to move forward in his career since losing his job.
B: I sure ___________ know what to do in such circumstances, either.

(a) can't
(b) mustn't
(c) wouldn't
(d) shouldn't

11. A: How should I go about picking the planning committee members?
B: I'd simply pick those ___________ you have the most confidence.

(a) who
(b) whose
(c) in what
(d) in whom

12. A: Liz, what has ___________?
B: So far, things are great.

(a) your new job been like it
(b) it been your new job like
(c) it been like at your new job
(d) at your new job been like it

13. A: How much ice cream do we have left?
B: Two-thirds of what we bought today ___________ already gone.

(a) is
(b) are
(c) has been
(d) have been

14. A: Has the boss thought about increasing our salaries?
B: Yes, I think that matter is ___________ consideration as we speak.

(a) for
(b) into
(c) under
(d) within

15. A: How can I get reimbursed for my travel expenses?
B: Just send the accounting department receipts ___________ the date the transactions were made.

(a) show
(b) shown
(c) showing
(d) to have shown

16. A: Professor, may I sit in on your Spanish class this afternoon?
B: Sorry, but ___________ allowed to attend the class.

(a) only after registering are you
(b) only after registering you are
(c) after registering you are only
(d) after registering are you only

17. A: What did you do yesterday, Peter?
B: The weather ___________ good, I went on a hike.

(a) was
(b) being
(c) had been
(d) was being

18. A: Were you able to catch the train?
B: No. By the time I arrived at the station, it ___________.

(a) has already left
(b) had already left
(c) will have already left
(d) has already been leaving

19. A: Can you convince Macy to come skiing with us?
B: Possibly, but ___________.

(a) it is going to be so difficult doing
(b) to do so it is going to be difficult
(c) doing so is going to be difficult
(d) that is difficult to be doing so

20. A: I like the idea of going to the desert, but snakes terrify me.
B: Don't worry. Unless ___________, rattlesnakes are pretty docile.

(a) to provoke
(b) provoking
(c) provoked
(d) provoke

Part II Questions 21—40

Choose the option that best completes each gap.

21. Figure skater Monica Hewett will skip several smaller competitions ___________ her energy on the World Championship.

(a) focus
(b) focuses
(c) focused
(d) to focus

22. Even with an extension, Tim knew there was no chance he ___________ finish his project on time.

(a) can
(b) must
(c) could
(d) should

23. The snow this winter was ___________ severe that schools frequently had to close for days at a time.

(a) so
(b) far
(c) such
(d) much

24. Despite not losing a single game during the regular season, Murphy High School's football team ___________ in the district championship last week.

(a) was being defeated
(b) was defeated
(c) had defeated
(d) defeated

25. Arranging regular social gatherings outside of work hours ___________ a positive office atmosphere.

(a) cultivate
(b) cultivates
(c) is cultivated
(d) are cultivated

26. Charlie's professor recommended that he ___________ on his studies more in order to graduate with honors.

(a) concentrate
(b) concentrates
(c) will concentrate
(d) would concentrate

27. Even though the president had promised that he would improve the economy when his administration ___________, little progress has been made thus far.

(a) took over
(b) is taking over
(c) has taken over
(d) has been taking over

28. ___________ chemicals produce a colorful reaction when added to fire, but not all have this effect.

(a) Any
(b) Some
(c) Any of
(d) Some of

29. In two days' time, Jessica ___________ her project to her boss, provided she completes it by then.

(a) presented
(b) will present
(c) has presented
(d) was presenting

30. The interaction of all life forms on Earth constitutes such a delicate balance that if one element were different, ___________ could not exist.

(a) as we know life
(b) life as we know
(c) we know it as life
(d) life as we know it

31. Beth's father always encouraged her to do charity work and help others ___________ she could.

(a) unless
(b) whereas
(c) however
(d) although

32. Insulin injections are a common treatment diabetics use ___________.

(a) to keep sugar levels in check
(b) keeping in check to sugar levels
(c) for sugar levels to keep in check
(d) of keeping in check on sugar levels

33. Some feel that since men are required to serve in the military, ___________ law should be applied to women.

(a) same
(b) a same
(c) all same
(d) the same

34. Whenever budget cuts loom, state boards of education traditionally ___________ the first to suffer financially.

(a) is
(b) are
(c) was
(d) were

RAMMAR

35. ___________ about the last-minute job assignment, Erica knew she had no choice but to do it.

(a) She was as irked
(b) Irked as she was
(c) She was irked
(d) Irked was she

36. Had Sam known his weaknesses at the start, he ___________ the wrestling competition.

(a) did not enter
(b) had not entered
(c) would not enter
(d) would not have entered

37. Niihau is a privately owned island, so it is no surprise that it is ___________ the Hawaiian Islands.

(a) visited the least
(b) the least visited
(c) the least visited of
(d) of the least visited

38. So far, no other salesperson ___________ to surpass Tabitha's record of selling seven cars in one day.

(a) manages
(b) will manage
(c) has managed
(d) will have managed

39. Ford Country Club allows only club members ___________ to its three golf courses.

(a) access
(b) accesses
(c) an access
(d) the accesses

40. The hackers ___________ of maliciously infecting the company's computer network with a virus face formal charges from the police department.

(a) accused
(b) accusing
(c) had accused
(d) were accused

Part III **Questions 41–45**

Read each sentence carefully and identify the option that contains a grammatical error.

41. (a) A: Danielle, I found your bracelet at my house the other day.

(b) B: Oh, thanks! I was worried that I had lost it for good.

(c) A: It took some searching, but I finally found it under the sofa.

(d) B: I'm really grateful you kept looking at it. It's my favorite.

42. (a) A: I was sorry to hear you didn't make the baseball team this year, Marcus.

(b) B: Yeah, it was a disappointment after I spent all summer practicing so hard.

(c) A: I know, but all the guys on the team have been playing for years.

(d) B: I guess my chance of making the team was never that greatly to begin with.

43. (a) A: Excuse me, when will the bus stop at a rest station?

(b) B: In about 20 minutes, when we reach Springfield.

(c) A: Am I possible to leave my bags on the bus while we're stopped?

(d) B: You'd better take your stuff with you, since the bus won't be locked.

44. (a) A: I heard you're backing out of the annual camping trip. Why?

(b) B: I just ran into my aunt, who reminded some family obligations of me.

(c) A: But we've been planning this trip for several months now!

(d) B: Sorry, I wish things were different, but I have to put my family first.

45. (a) A: Before we end our interview, do you have any questions of your own about the job?

(b) B: Yes, actually. Could you tell me a little bit about the company's turnover rate?

(c) A: It's quite low. Almost of all our employees stay for ten years or more.

(d) B: That's good. I'm interested in really building a career at your company.

Part IV Questions 46–50

Read each sentence carefully and identify the option that contains a grammatical error.

46. (a) The nineteenth century was a time of economic and geographical growth for London. (b) This was the era in what the city became the financial and political capital of the world. (c) Migrants to London included people from Ireland and other European countries. (d) The population exploded, and new railways enabled the city to grow quickly.

47. (a) Hickory BBQ sauce had its beginning in founder Jerry Madison's small kitchen. (b) Jerry had long been known among his friends for creating delectable barbecue sauces. (c) Convincing that he had a marketable product, Jerry's friends introduced him to a distributor. (d) As word spread and demand increased, Jerry soon began selling his sauces all over the country.

48. (a) Fisherman Richard Grant is recovering after a surprise encounter with a sea lion on his boat. (b) According to onlookers, Grant was leaning over the water when the sea lion grabbed him. (c) Grant pulled ten feet under water before the sea lion let go and allowed him to surface. (d) He emerged from the incident unscathed and stated that he was more shocked than anything else.

49. (a) A recent study has looked into the cognitive benefits associated with knowing multiple languages. (b) Particularly, the study set out to explain how multilingualism offsets the effects of degenerative diseases. (c) The findings showed that these benefits extend further than researchers had originally suspected them. (d) Overall, it was found that multilingualism prevents brain atrophy, effectively keeping neurons supple and active.

50. (a) If you see someone who appears to be having a heart attack, seeking assistance is of the utmost importance. (b) Timing is key, since waiting to see if the symptoms pass is not worth the potential damage could be done to the heart. (c) Emergency personnel should be called immediately, and the sufferer should take aspirin to facilitate blood flow. (d) If an ambulance is delayed or not available, the sufferer needs to be taken to a hospital as soon as possible.

This is the end of the Grammar section. Do NOT move on to the next section until instructed to do so. You are NOT allowed to turn to any other section of the test.

VOCABULARY

DIRECTIONS

This section tests your vocabulary skills. You will have 15 minutes to complete the 50 questions. Be sure to follow the directions given by the proctor.

정답 P 339

Part I Questions 1—25

Choose the option that best completes each gap.

1. A: Why isn't our taxi driver taking Baxter Road to the airport?
   B: He said he knows a better ___________.

   (a) land
   (b) route
   (c) transfer
   (d) carriage

2. A: I don't have any ___________, but I think our neighbor broke our window.
   B: I wouldn't say anything without evidence, though.

   (a) cue
   (b) data
   (c) proof
   (d) theory

3. A: What are this airline's regulations on flying with pets?
   B: The ___________ are listed on this printout.

   (a) uses
   (b) rules
   (c) traces
   (d) effects

4. A: I'm sorry for the rude remarks I made yesterday.
   B: I can forgive your ___________ because I know you were upset.

   (a) notices
   (b) instances
   (c) amenities
   (d) comments

5. A: It's too bad Michael and Linda couldn't work out their problems.
   B: In the end, their differences were simply ___________.

   (a) incapable
   (b) undecided
   (c) unassuming
   (d) irreconcilable

6. A: Martin's not the type to brag about his accomplishments.
   B: He's always been ___________ like that.

   (a) faint
   (b) lenient
   (c) humble
   (d) perpetual

7. A: Why is the broom out here?
   B: I used it to ___________ the floor and forgot to put it back.

   (a) sweep
   (b) stroke
   (c) brush
   (d) wade

8. A: Katherine is excelling under the new administration.
   B: Oh, yes. She tends to ___________ under this type of management.

   (a) fizzle
   (b) foster
   (c) thrust
   (d) thrive

9. A: Drive carefully. It's been raining.

B: You're right. The roads will probably be ___________, so I'll go slowly.

(a) slick
(b) bland
(c) pushy
(d) clumsy

10. A: Have you found a suitable candidate for the new researcher position?

B: Not yet. I'm still ___________ through a stack of résumés trying to find someone qualified.

(a) sifting
(b) queuing
(c) vouching
(d) disclosing

11. A: Does this building have security?

B: Yes. There's a guard at the front door and one who ___________ the grounds.

(a) fastens
(b) patrols
(c) ensures
(d) upholds

12. A: Do you follow the stock market?

B: Yes, very closely. I ___________ the trends before investing.

(a) certify
(b) endorse
(c) condone
(d) scrutinize

13. A: Harry knows a lot about recent political issues.

B: Yes. He sure ___________ current events.

(a) looks up to
(b) keeps up with
(c) makes good on
(d) takes turns with

14. A: That fire drill caused a(n) __________ that could've hurt someone!

B: I know. Everyone rushed to the door in a panic.

(a) breach
(b) stopgap
(c) stampede
(d) intervention

15. A: The people from this area don't seem to have heard of Gold Beach.

B: That's because the ___________ know it as North Beach. It's just ahead of you.

(a) tenements
(b) personas
(c) premises
(d) locals

16. A: I couldn't figure out the assignment.

B: Me, neither. I was completely ___________ by it.

(a) confounded
(b) beseeched
(c) estranged
(d) ridiculed

17. A: I'd love to do something for you since you helped with my gardening.

B: Oh, there's no need to ___________!

(a) mitigate
(b) generate
(c) recuperate
(d) reciprocate

18. A: Dan isn't careful enough with his power tools.
B: Yes, I worry his ___________ could result in an injury.

(a) remission
(b) retrospect
(c) negligence
(d) temperance

19. A: What was the final outcome of the meeting?
B: The ___________ was that we need to boost sales.

(a) old flame
(b) bad apple
(c) cloud nine
(d) bottom line

20. A: Professor, a lot of chapters in this book are unrelated to my research.
B: Then just read the ones that are ___________ to your experiments.

(a) explicit
(b) pertinent
(c) equivocal
(d) schematic

21. A: The army didn't seem to have an organized plan during that battle.
B: I know. The generals weren't careful in ___________ their strategy.

(a) crossing out
(b) mapping out
(c) glossing over
(d) stowing away

22. A: I'm nervous about climbing this cliff.
B: Don't be ___________. You can do it.

(a) touted
(b) libelous
(c) sporadic
(d) intimidated

23. A: The crowd went wild when the singer appeared!
B: I know, everyone was ___________ for his attention.

(a) publicizing
(b) navigating
(c) clamoring
(d) trouncing

24. A: Harold's bankrupt? But he has a beautiful home and two cars!
B: Having the ___________ of success doesn't mean you are actually wealthy.

(a) covers
(b) truisms
(c) coatings
(d) trappings

25. A: Deanna's solution to our budget problem isn't practical.
B: I agree. We'll have to come up with a more ___________ method.

(a) feasible
(b) rampant
(c) dormant
(d) derogatory

Part II Questions 26–50

Choose the option that best completes each gap.

26. With the hottest music and movies, Networks.com has all your entertainment needs ___________.

(a) done
(b) sent
(c) lent
(d) met

27. Temporary tattoos can be ___________ with rubbing alcohol, leaving the skin without a trace of the ink.

(a) derived
(b) removed
(c) disturbed
(d) prescribed

28. The company's ___________ into Japan caused its competitor to set up a branch there as well.

(a) deduction
(b) expansion
(c) exclamation
(d) transformation

29. People often dismiss TV as a waste of time because they fail to ___________ its educational benefits.

(a) grasp
(b) submit
(c) express
(d) overlook

30. Selling ___________ music and videos constitutes copyright infringement and is punishable by law.

(a) crafty
(b) pirated
(c) debased
(d) illegible

31. In intercultural situations, choose whichever greeting most ___________ the occasion, be it a handshake, a bow, or something else.

(a) befits
(b) trusts
(c) pitches
(d) proffers

32. The comet will be ___________ to stargazers provided clouds do not block the sky.

(a) visible
(b) watchful
(c) flustered
(d) unsightly

33. Sean ___________ early on in the chess match and could not recover, ultimately losing the game.

(a) refracted
(b) dribbled
(c) faltered
(d) frisked

34. Wilson's Shop will close from January 5 to 18 to ___________ a complete renovation.

(a) undergo
(b) muster
(c) overdo
(d) sway

35. Doctors recommend wrapping injured limbs to reduce the chance of doing further ___________ to them.

(a) lag
(b) ache
(c) harm
(d) force

36. The word "Lothario," which comes from a character in a drama by Nicholas Rowe, has come to ___________ a heartless seducer.

(a) ascend
(b) denote
(c) construe
(d) elucidate

37. Abigail Adams was ___________ about women's rights at a time when it was unusual for women to speak out in such a way.

(a) oral
(b) vocal
(c) veritable
(d) impervious

38. Efficiency training was instituted in a bid to get employees to make more ___________ use of their time.

(a) inactive
(b) egregious
(c) economical
(d) clandestine

39. Jason's frequent insensitive outbursts earned him a reputation for being ___________.

(a) quaint
(b) jocular
(c) callous
(d) pristine

40. In ___________ of the Remembrance Day holiday, government offices will be closed all day tomorrow.

(a) propriety
(b) formality
(c) observance
(d) complacence

41. A good chef can ___________ a delicious meal from the most basic and commonplace ingredients.

(a) submerge
(b) saturate
(c) concoct
(d) infuse

42. A diet lacking an adequate amount of vitamins could result in a person developing nutritional ___________.

(a) pledges
(b) scruples
(c) deficiencies
(d) remittances

43. The Nereid Monument was likely ___________ in the early fourth century BC, and it remained standing until the Byzantine era.

(a) reared
(b) roused
(c) erected
(d) induced

44. After the children spent the day playing in a muddy field, they were totally ___________ and unkempt.

(a) bedraggled
(b) broached
(c) botched
(d) blurred

45. Cistercian monks live in Spartan environments, believing an ___________ lifestyle facilitates their relationship with God.

(a) obtuse
(b) ascetic
(c) urbane
(d) oblique

46. The actor's biography was bogged down with tedious details, making it rather ___________ to read.

(a) redolent
(b) stringent
(c) laborious
(d) venomous

47. Human rights are so ___________ in democratic societies that oftentimes their residents take those rights for granted.

(a) politic
(b) tentative
(c) concurrent
(d) entrenched

48. Jane hoped Reginald's poem recitation marked the end of the evening, but it was merely a(n) ___________ to the oratory that followed.

(a) influx
(b) prelude
(c) incursion
(d) premonition

49. Peterson's Chrome Cleaner will cut through the ___________ of dirt and limestone that has built up around faucets.

(a) dilution
(b) accretion
(c) simulation
(d) elaboration

50. A decade spent in news reporting had ___________ the journalist to the stress of deadlines, so they hardly fazed him anymore.

(a) vexed
(b) inured
(c) absolved
(d) conflated

This is the end of the Vocabulary section. Do NOT move on to the Reading Comprehension section until instructed to do so. You are NOT allowed to turn to any other section of the test.

READING COMPREHENSION

DIRECTIONS

This section tests your ability to comprehend reading passages. You will have 45 minutes to complete the 40 questions. Be sure to follow the directions given by the proctor.

정답 P 339

Part I Questions 1—16

Read the passage and choose the option that best completes the passage.

1. Attention, alumni! Are you looking to give back to Rodson's College, but are hesitant because you don't know exactly where your donation dollars are going? No problem. We've revamped our donation website so you can now dictate where you wish your donation to be applied. Want to aid in the construction of the new science building? Or would you rather contribute to a specific department? It's all up to you, since with our new donation system, you ______________________.

(a) receive a free gift with every donation
(b) will contribute to college policy changes
(c) are in charge of how your money is used
(d) can stay in touch with your college friends

2. The prospects of Bt corn, a kind of corn crop modified to include a gene from the pest-killing *Bacillus thuringiensis* bacteria, are looking dimmer because ______________________. Corn with the Bt gene has been remarkably popular, but scientists have long warned that over time pests would build up resistance to it. And indeed, those predictions have now come true: a new generation of worms that are resistant to the Bt gene are eating away at the Bt corn crops in Illinois and Iowa, which poses huge problems for farmers.

(a) it is causing mutations in neighboring crops
(b) the gene makes plants unsuitable for consumption
(c) genetically engineered crops will limit biodiversity
(d) some pests have adapted to its pesticidal properties

3. The colonial period in America, from the early to mid-eighteenth century, was ______________________. The primary reason for this was that settlers were largely occupied with the struggle to survive and had little time or energy to devote to the arts. The economy at the time also did not support a booming dramatic community, with theater managers being constantly on the verge of bankruptcy. Furthermore, the colonies were very religious, and denominations like the Puritans and the Quakers disapproved of acting and theater-going.

(a) the beginning of American drama as we know it today
(b) a time when theater was performed mostly in secret
(c) marked by a scarcity of theater and performing arts
(d) dominated largely by European dramatic forms

4. Starting this fall, the Marston Museum of Art ______________________. All staff will continue to receive 40% off the cost of annual membership, but now for the first time, staff members' spouses and children can also take advantage of the facilities year-round at a 20% discounted rate. Please note that members of staff's extended family are not eligible for this discount and will still be charged the normal rate.

(a) will extend discounted rates to staff's family members
(b) is implementing a staff family day to boost morale
(c) is offering an increased discount to museum staff
(d) will reduce its fees by 20% for all new members

5. Social scientists have observed that people of all ages and from all cultures tend to believe that they will ______________________. Studies on this phenomenon address both positive and negative life events. Most individuals see their chances of experiencing positive events as higher than average. They believe they will have gifted children and enjoy long life spans. As far as negative events, they believe they are less likely to get divorced or suffer debilitating diseases. This outlook is often termed the "optimism bias."

(a) avoid repeating their past mistakes
(b) have to work hard to overcome setbacks
(c) fare better in life than most other people
(d) require the help of peers to prosper in life

6. The president's new immigration act has been the subject of much criticism, but many illegal immigrants across the US consider it a landmark victory. The policy allows undocumented immigrants who entered the country as children and who meet certain criteria to work legally without risk of being forced out of the country. The act, while having no direct effect on citizenship, will benefit as many as 1.4 million immigrants who, under it, can ____________________.

(a) work without fear of being deported
(b) be granted automatic citizenship status
(c) legally bring their children into the country
(d) apply for citizenship along with their children

7. The water advisory issued last week for Riverside residents will continue while the town ____________________. The break in the town's main water pipe resulted in decreased or no water pressure for the entire area, which placed the water system at risk of bacterial contamination. Now that the break has been repaired and water pressure restored, samples have been sent to a county lab for analysis to determine whether or not such contamination occurred. As a result, the water advisory will not be lifted until the lab has officially confirmed that the water is safe to use.

(a) seeks to restore water pressure
(b) awaits water quality test results
(c) treats contaminated water sources
(d) works to repair a water main break

8.

To the Altamont Gazette:

I'm writing to request that you ____________________. I originally requested that you hold my delivery service for two weeks while I went out of town. However, my trip has been extended indefinitely, and I am no longer certain of my return date. I will contact you when I wish my newspaper delivery to be reinstated. Thank you.

Sincerely,
Janet Dobbs

(a) reinstate my newspaper delivery service
(b) credit my account for missing newspapers
(c) suspend my paper delivery until further notice
(d) forward my subscription to my temporary address

9. Desertification, a complex process in which previously productive land degrades into desert, is commonly associated with poor land management. Generally, this problem is only identified after it is already underway. At this point, however, action can be taken to stave off further desertification. Covering dunes and using straw grids, within which shrubs can be planted, for instance, will prevent sand from encroaching into land that has yet to degrade. Taking such measures ______________________.

(a) will do much to halt the process of desertification
(b) will help scientists uncover the cause of desertification
(c) can effectively prevent desertification from even beginning
(d) could actually accelerate the desertification of degraded land

10. Battlefield archaeologists analyze material remains of battles for insights into the histories of wars. This gives their analyses an advantage over those of their historian counterparts, who rely primarily on written accounts. Such written accounts are typically left by the wars' victors and for that reason are necessarily biased. Battlefields, on the other hand, provide physical evidence that is untainted by a potentially prejudiced viewpoint. This is why it can be said that battlefield archaeology ______________________.

(a) creates a more objective picture of past events
(b) fails to consider the perspective of the defeated
(c) augments the bias that typically affects historians
(d) privileges the historical interpretation of the victors

11. My decision to open my own café in an already flooded market was made with more passion than sense. By all rights, I should have gone bankrupt within the first year. But I knew the importance of getting the word out about my business, so I invested countless hours into advertising. I used social media sites, invited reviews from food critics and bloggers, and offered special discounts—and before long I had almost more business than I could handle. Ultimately, I credit all my current success to ______________________.

(a) overcoming bankruptcy in my first year
(b) attracting a small but very loyal clientele
(c) the efforts I put into promoting my business
(d) the decision to wait for a more opportune time

12. Hershel Parker, editor of the 1995 Kraken edition of Herman Melville's *Pierre*, attempted to do justice to Melville's original intentions for the novel by ______________________. Parker theorized that it was during Melville's writing of *Pierre* that negative reviews of *Moby Dick*, Melville's previous work, started surfacing; these prompted Melville to include rage-fueled diatribes against the literary establishment in *Pierre*, however gratuitous they were or however much they compromised the novel's integrity. What Parker was after in purging these passages was to recreate the novel that Melville had originally been striving to create, before the critical reception of *Moby Dick* impacted him and his writing.

(a) explicating obscure passages to make them accessible to readers
(b) taking out passages he thought detracted from the novel's coherence
(c) incorporating parts that Melville had hastily excised to please his critics
(d) placing it within the context of the literary accolades *Moby Dick* garnered

13. Brainstorming, wherein a group of people churns out suggestions, is standard practice at many organizations. Companies recognize the technique's capacity to produce a high volume of ideas in a short time. Yet research on employee productivity shows that talented and motivated employees do better work with less time wasted when they are allowed to operate independently. It seems that they excel in settings where they can avoid the pressures and distractions of being in a group. This research provides evidence that organizations can get the best work from gifted employees by ______________________.

(a) encouraging the groups that churn out the most ideas
(b) allowing talented people to collaborate with each other
(c) replacing collaboration with greater individual autonomy
(d) providing more structured guidelines for group assignments

14. Genovia has recently implemented a system designed to ______________________. The most common method of traffic control used by major metropolises suffering from severe traffic jams is imposing fees for driving during rush hour. Such measures may have some effect in mitigating the overflow of cars during rush hour, but they penalize drivers. Genovia public officials thought, why not incentivize them instead? So they have taken to rewarding drivers who alter their commutes to off-peak times by entering them into a daily lottery, in which they can win up to $50.

(a) more equitably distribute traffic around town
(b) capitalize on the severe road congestion at rush hour
(c) encourage people to stay off the road during rush hour
(d) permit only a certain number of cars on the road each day

15. Despite the rigorous laboratory testing that goes into determining the sun protection factor (SPF) level of a sunscreen, the SPF number rarely reflects a sunscreen's actual effectiveness. Several reasons account for this discrepancy. For one thing, researchers use considerably more sunscreen during testing than people use in the real world, so people generally do not get the level of protection the SPF number promises, regardless of SPF. ______________________, certain people are naturally more susceptible to sunburn, so SPF does not have the same effect on everyone.

(a) Still
(b) Also
(c) Accordingly
(d) Subsequently

16. Habitat loss is a significant factor in diminishing tiger populations. Tiger ranges have been devastated over the last 60 years, forcing tigers into small, scattered areas of remaining habitat. This has impacted the dwindling tiger population in another way: it has made tigers easy prey for poachers. ______________________, the loss of habitat has driven tigers into cramped areas where they can be easily targeted by hunters.

(a) Instead
(b) In effect
(c) Otherwise
(d) That being said

Part II **Questions 17—37**

Read the passage, question, and options. Then, based on the given information, choose the option that best answers the question.

17. Bubbly Shampoo is pulling its line of baby shampoo off the shelf after an investigation by the Campaign for Safe Cosmetics revealed that the product contains two possibly carcinogenic chemicals. One of these chemicals releases formaldehyde, which cannot only cause cancer but also irritate skin and eyes. The line is being discontinued, and consumers may return products to the manufacturer for a full refund.

Q: What is the report mainly about?
(a) A comparison of different shampoo brands
(b) How to identify dangerous chemicals in shampoo
(c) A shampoo that has been recalled for safety reasons
(d) Customer dissatisfaction with a baby shampoo brand

18.

Dear Michelle,

Congratulations on receiving your first driver's license! As a driver under the age of 18, you are limited by special restrictions governing your operation of a motor vehicle. First, nighttime driving is prohibited after 11 p.m. on weekdays and midnight on weekends. Second, you may not drive with more than one passenger in the car at a time. We at the Department of Motor Vehicles thank you for abiding by these regulations.

Sincerely,
Jesse Black
Department of Motor Vehicles

Q: What is the main purpose of the letter?
(a) To introduce a program for first-time drivers
(b) To advise the recipient of her eligibility for a license
(c) To outline the procedure for obtaining a driver's license
(d) To state restrictions that apply specifically to young drivers

19. Buddha is typically represented in different stylized poses in religious art. Buddha can be standing, or he may take one of five basic poses: ritual crouch, seated half lotus, full lotus, vigorous dance, or wheel king. Additionally, there may be any number of minor variations of these basic poses. Buddha may also be seen making different signs with his hands, called *mudra*.

Q: What is the main topic of the passage?
(a) The significance of Buddhist statues
(b) Different depictions of Buddha in art
(c) The meanings of various Buddha poses
(d) Famous Buddha statues around the world

20. Living in a city apartment often means having limited floor space and decor options. There are ways around this, however, and you do not have to sacrifice style, either. Small-space dwellers can replace bulky furniture with armless sofas and chairs to maintain an open look and use versatile furnishings that can double as storage spaces. Living areas can be kept attractive and tidy with a minimum number of statement furniture pieces that can be updated with seasonal coverings. With these tips, being short on space no longer has to mean being short on style!

Q: What is the main purpose of the passage?
(a) To offer furnishing suggestions for small spaces
(b) To describe how to fit furniture into small apartments
(c) To advise apartment-dwellers about decorating resources
(d) To state the benefits of furniture that contains storage space

21. In the tragic event of a ship going down, men typically stand back in a display of chivalry to allow women and children to board lifeboats first—at least, this is what they do according to the popular imagination. Apparently not, say two researchers out of Sweden. They did a study of 18 famous shipwrecks and found that overall a man's survival rate from a shipwreck is twice that of a woman's. So as it turns out, the idea promoted by films such as *Titanic*—that men place chivalry before their own survival during a crisis at sea—is just a myth.

Q: What is the writer's main point?
(a) Women and children should board lifeboats first in a shipwreck.
(b) Popular opinion is what spurs men to behave chivalrously in a crisis.
(c) Showing chivalry in a crisis usually ends up decreasing survival rates.
(d) The widely held belief about male chivalry during shipwrecks is a fiction.

22. According to census data, racial diversity is increasing in the predominantly Caucasian areas that make up the majority of Atlanta. This trend is not indicative of overall racial integration, though. Predominantly black neighborhoods are tending to stay predominantly black. The same goes for primarily Latino and Asian areas. So while the city is seeing an overall increase in racial diversity, this has not spread to all communities, and segregation remains the norm in many of them.

Q: What is the passage mainly about?
(a) How Atlanta is making great strides towards racial equality
(b) The negative effects of increased segregation on a community
(c) The mutually exclusive nature of racial diversity and segregation
(d) How segregation persists in Atlanta despite its rise in racial diversity

23. The Mount Pleasant Community Center will be moving locations from Grand Street to Lawn Avenue. The old center has been unable to accommodate the town's growing population, and its facilities are woefully outdated. Since no surrounding properties were available on Grand Street, the city has decided to change locations instead of expanding its current facilities. Construction is already under way for the new center, which will feature extended hours, more space, and better facilities. Until construction on the new center is finished, the old community center will remain open.

Q: Which of the following is correct about the Mount Pleasant Community Center according to the announcement?
(a) The Grand Street location is being expanded.
(b) It will cease operations during the construction.
(c) Construction has already begun on the new center.
(d) The Lawn Avenue location will have shorter hours.

24. The use of computed tomography (CT) scans in medical diagnostic imaging tripled from 1996 to 2010, while the number of magnetic resonance imaging (MRI) scans quadrupled. New research indicates that exposure to radiation given off by these scans carries a risk of cancer. In fact, a recent study that investigated the effects of CT scans found a small but significant correlation with increases in certain types of cancer. As a result, many physicians are now recommending fewer of these scans.

Q: Which of the following is correct according to the news article?
(a) CT and MRI scans quadrupled in 1996.
(b) CT and MRI scans emit radiation.
(c) Cancer risk shows no correlation with CT scans.
(d) Physicians advise making the scans more frequent.

25. In 1857, dissatisfied with existing English dictionaries, the Philological Society of London embarked on reexamining the language. Oxford University Press and James A.H. Murray were contracted to create the *New English Dictionary*. Although it was originally planned as four volumes and expected to take ten years to finish, this ended up being a modest estimate, as the first installment alone was not published until 1884. The final ten-volume set was eventually completed in 1928.

Q: Which of the following is correct about the *New English Dictionary* according to the passage?
(a) It was the first English dictionary to be published.
(b) Its first four volumes were completed by 1884.
(c) It was conceived to be a set of ten volumes.
(d) Its completion took longer than anticipated.

26. The pencil came into being in the mid-sixteenth century, when a substantial deposit of graphite was discovered in Borrowdale, England. Borrowdale's graphite was very pure and solid, and it is still the highest quality graphite ever found. Graphite was first called "black lead" because people believed it to be a darker form of lead, which explains why pencil cores are still called lead, despite never containing any actual lead. The first pencils were made by wrapping graphite in string or sheepskin; graphite only began being encased in wood later.

Q: Which of the following is correct according to the passage?
(a) Graphite deposits in Borrowdale were of low quality.
(b) The color of graphite is darker than that of lead.
(c) Graphite replaced lead as the core of pencils.
(d) Wood was the first material used to encase graphite.

27. Gossip is generally discouraged, but a recent study found that the practice of talking about and judging others who are not present is not without its benefits. Namely, gossip tends to draw attention to a person's bad behavior and warn others to protect themselves from that person. Moreover, in the study, those who engage in gossiping were also found to be prone to helping others. The act of gossiping was even found to help reduce the participants' anxiety levels.

Q: Which of the following is correct according to the study?
(a) Gossip was found to have no positive effects whatsoever.
(b) Gossip was viewed as making light of people's bad behavior.
(c) Those who gossip were seen as generally being more helpful.
(d) Those who gossip exacerbated their anxiety levels in doing so.

28. Take proper safety precautions when viewing the transit of Venus to prevent eye damage. Contrary to popular belief, sunglasses do not provide enough protection. Instead, use eclipse shades, which are similar to sunglasses but have a special filter. If using a telescope, make sure there is a solar filter on the large end. Pinhole projectors are a safe option, but they offer unmagnified views, and detailed features such as the halo around Venus will likely be indiscernible.

Q. Which of the following is correct according to the instructions?
(a) Sunglasses offer sufficient protection to view the transit of Venus.
(b) Eclipse shades provide a comparable level of protection to sunglasses.
(c) A solar filter is needed to make a telescope a safe viewing medium.
(d) Pinhole projectors offer an unparalleled view of the halo around Venus.

29.

Dear Patricia Browne,

Our records show that you have prematurely terminated your long-distance plan with SpeakUp Telecom. To win back valued customers, we are extending an exclusive offer: if you re-subscribe within the week, you'll receive a $100 credit. Also, you won't have to pay a re-registration fee. If you're not completely satisfied after taking advantage of this offer, you have up to 30 days to cancel without a fee, no questions asked. Give us another chance to serve you.

Sincerely,
Matthew Spiller
SpeakUp Telecom

Q: Which of the following is correct according to the letter?
(a) Ms. Browne allowed her long-distance plan to expire.
(b) SpeakUp Telecom is trying to entice former customers back.
(c) The $100 credit is only being offered to first-time subscribers.
(d) Backing out of the offer within 30 days incurs a small penalty.

30. *His Master's Voice*, a painting by Francis Barraud, is commonly known as the trademark image for the record company of the same name, usually abbreviated to HMV. Painted following the death of Barraud's brother, Mark, *His Master's Voice* originally depicted Mark's dog, Nipper, listening to a cylinder phonograph playing recordings of his master's voice. When the image was acquired by the Gramophone Company, later renamed His Master's Voice, the company requested that Barraud change the image to depict one of their gramophone records, which he did, and it is this image that became HMV's trademark.

Q: Which of the following is correct about the painting *His Master's Voice* according to the passage?

(a) It shares its name with a record company.
(b) It depicts Mark Barraud listening to music with his dog.
(c) It was altered to replace a gramophone with a phonograph.
(d) It took HMV's trademark image as its inspiration.

31. The Palio, a horse race held twice yearly in the Tuscan city of Siena, is a tradition dating back to medieval times. It features ten horses per race riding around a track. The horses and their jockeys represent the city's wards, but because there are only ten spots in the race and seventeen city wards, seven of the wards are excluded in any particular Palio. Those seven are automatically guaranteed a spot in the next race and the remaining three slots are filled by a draw.

Q: Which of the following is correct about the Palio according to the passage?

(a) It is a tradition that predates medieval times.
(b) Not all of the city's wards participate in each race.
(c) A city ward can go years without being included in it.
(d) All the race participants are randomly selected by a draw.

32. Sir Humphrey Gilbert was the man who founded the first English colony in North America. He was born into a wealthy family in Devonshire, England around 1539 and was educated at Eton College and the University of Oxford. After a military career, he entered parliament and later devoted himself to maritime expeditions, many of which failed. In 1583 he set sail for Newfoundland and in August of that year took possession of the harbor of St. John's. It was there that he started a colony. A month later, though, Gilbert went down with his ship near the Azores Islands.

Q: Which of the following is correct about Humphrey Gilbert according to the passage?
(a) He began his education at Eton in 1539.
(b) He left parliament for a life in the military.
(c) His sailing expeditions were all successful.
(d) His life was lost when his ship sank in 1583.

33. Stan's Fire Equipment Store is doing a safety campaign wherein we will come to your home or business to check your fire extinguishers. In compliance with government protocol, we check the extinguishers to make sure the internal pressure is at an acceptable level, that the parts are all in good working order, and that the firefighting agent—be it wet or dry chemical, or foam—is still good. An old extinguisher that has not been well maintained is a hazard and can cause injury if used, so let Stan's make sure your extinguishers are good to go!

Q: What can be inferred from the announcement?
(a) Foam is the most common firefighting agent in extinguishers.
(b) A fire extinguisher's internal pressure is irrelevant to its functioning.
(c) Firefighting agents in extinguishers lose their effectiveness over time.
(d) Maintaining fire extinguishers takes no special equipment or know-how.

34. John Keats's sonnet "On First Looking into Chapman's Homer" refers to George Chapman's translation of the Homeric epics, *The Iliad* and *The Odyssey*. This translation differed significantly from the much better-known translation by Alexander Pope. Chapman's translation, which preceded Pope's by over a century, made Keats feel liberated from the restrictions of the artificially polished poetic diction of Pope's version, and he wrote his sonnet to celebrate the epiphanic rush he felt upon first reading it. Keats's contemporary Lord Byron, who greatly admired Pope, rebuked Keats for his preference.

Q: What can be inferred about Chapman's translation of Homer from the passage?
(a) Byron was not familiar with it.
(b) It was a revision of Pope's famous translation.
(c) It was inspired by Keats's sonnet celebrating Homer.
(d) Keats had read Pope's translation of Homer before reading it.

35. Flitter Airlines has implemented a new self-boarding system in which passengers scan their own tickets and pass through turnstiles to board aircrafts. To allay employees' fears, the airline has officially stated that it does not intend to decrease the number of gate agents. The intention behind the move, the airline explains, is to free up its staff to devote more individualized attention to passengers with special needs.

Q: What can be inferred from the news article?
(a) Flitter employees need not fear being rendered redundant.
(b) The self-boarding system is intended to be completely paperless.
(c) Flitter Airlines plans to phase out the self-boarding system eventually.
(d) Automated turnstiles are exclusively for passengers with special needs.

36. As a caricature artist, I rely not only on my sight when rendering my subjects but also on my impressions of their personalities. There is comic worth in overarching an eyebrow or enlarging a nose in my drawings; it is these details that make caricatures so interesting. That is not to say that my works do not maintain a strong likeness to their subjects. However, conveying my particular take on a person inevitably entails adjustments of their physical appearance here or there. In the end, my intention for my work is for it to encompass more than a mirror reflection.

Q: What can be inferred about the writer from the passage?
(a) Mirrors form an integral part of his artistic process.
(b) He views taking artistic license as verging on arrogance.
(c) Drawing from photographs is easier for him than drawing from life.
(d) He strives to capture a subject's essence rather than a strict likeness.

37. Pedigree dogs are basically "engineered" to conform to rigid physical requirements, often to the point where meeting those requirements comes at the expense of the animal's health. For example, some dogs are bred to have flat faces, but this kind of targeted breeding can result in faces so flat that they inhibit normal breathing. An all-too-common breeding tactic—and one that is seemingly bereft of not only compassion but also common sense—used to achieve these physical characteristics is to mate dogs from restricted gene pools, thus reducing genetic diversity and increasing chances of inherited disorders.

Q: Which statement would the writer most likely agree with?
(a) Pedigree dogs are on average healthier than mixed breeds.
(b) Limiting genetic diversity is the most humane way to breed pedigree dogs.
(c) There is little use in worrying about genetic diversity among pedigree dogs.
(d) Prioritizing a pedigree dog's appearance over its health is morally questionable.

Part III **Questions 38 – 40**

Read the passage and identify the option that does NOT belong.

38. The earliest known maps were not of land but of the constellations in the night sky. (a) These maps date back to 16,500 BC and consisted of dots that corresponded with star positions painted onto cave walls. (b) The Lascaux caves, for example, house maps depicting constellations such as the Pleiades star cluster. (c) However, some archaeologists wonder if cave paintings actually served this mystical purpose or were just art for art's sake. (d) Additionally, a similar dot map, one of the Corona Borealis, has been discovered in a cave in Spain.

39. Most obese pets are not to blame for the excess weight they carry—their owners are. (a) Too many owners equate food with affection and shower their pets with treats, which leads to weight gain. (b) In fact, canine weight-loss drugs confer a feeling of satiety, preventing the dogs from overeating. (c) Another common mistake when it comes to portion control is "free choice" feeding, wherein food is available at all times for the pet. (d) This, coupled with paltry amounts of exercise, results in pets having increasing waistlines and declining health.

40. Numerous factors have caused hospitals in the United States to lose their dominance in the health care realm. (a) More medical procedures are now available on an outpatient basis, minimizing patients' hospital stays. (b) Meanwhile, after-care that used to be provided by hospitals has largely shifted to other care facilities. (c) Furthermore, as far as the number of people they employ, hospitals are the second- or third-largest industry. (d) This has allowed alternate medical care facilities to encroach on areas of health care previously dominated by hospitals.

This is the end of the Reading Comprehension section. Please remain seated until the proctor has instructed otherwise. You are NOT allowed to turn to any other section of the test.

Listening Comprehension ***Scripts***

서울대 최신기출 1

Listening Comprehension Scripts

1

M Want a hand carrying the luggage?

W ______________________

(a) I'd appreciate it.
(b) Don't mention it.
(c) Sure, I'll help out.
(d) Put it in the luggage.

2

W Has Jim found his wallet?

M ______________________

(a) It was in his wallet.
(b) Not yet, I'm afraid.
(c) He'll give it back.
(d)That was fortunate.

3

M Do you have the guidebook we bought with you?

W ______________________

(a) Actually, I forgot to bring it.
(b) Yes, the guidebook says so.
(c) No, it's a simple map.
(d) You're right, we should get one.

4

W Professor, could you reconsider my final grade?

M ______________________

(a) You are a prompt grader.
(b) No, that's against my policy.
(c) You can check online.
(d) Consider it a compliment.

5

M Let's not let these dirty dishes build up.

W ______________________

(a) I can't eat anymore.
(b) OK, I'll run the dishwasher.
(c) There aren't enough, so let's share.
(d) That's why we bought fancy dishes.

6

W Does your daughter, Jenny, know how to use chopsticks?

M ______________________

(a) Here, let me hold them.
(b) No, she's a picky eater.
(c) Use hers instead.
(d) Not really, but she tries.

7

M I'm calling to schedule a meeting with Mr. Jones tomorrow.

W ______________________

(a) No need to return my call.
(b) Sorry, he's out of the office until next week.
(c) Yes, he'll be there momentarily.
(d) It's not on his schedule.

8

W You're a journalist? How exciting!

M ______________________

(a) Maybe, but I'll never be one.
(b) I'd love to know about it.
(c) Honestly, the job is pretty routine.
(d) I'd rather publish it.

9

M Looks like I can help you move after all.

W ______________________

(a) Still, call if you need help.
(b) Too bad, but I'll manage.
(c) I'm glad to hear it.
(d) I'd love to join!

10

W I don't see how you can support company layoffs.

M ______________________________

(a) They're beneficial in the long run.
(b) No one was expecting them, though.
(c) Because I'm hesitant to lay off experienced workers.
(d) It's better than resorting to layoffs.

11

M Your flat-screen TV must've cost a fortune.

W ______________________________

(a) It was worth every penny, though.
(b) Oh, I should have bought one.
(c) No, flat-screens are very pricey.
(d) I'll budget for it beforehand.

12

W It's been a while since you saw Dan.

M ______________________________

(a) Of course! Now I remember seeing him.
(b) Too long, in fact. I should contact him.
(c) Yeah, it's unfortunate I've never met him.
(d) Right, we've been inseparable since high school.

13

M Why don't we volunteer to help clean up the oil spill?

W ______________________________

(a) I'm more than willing to.
(b) That wouldn't have prevented it.
(c) It's either that or help clean up.
(d) I'll remember to while we're doing it.

14

W With that injury, you'd better sit the rest of the game out.

M ______________________________

(a) It's fine. I'm just glad we won.
(b) With practice, we'll be ready.
(c) It's nothing I can't handle.
(d) No, my health matters more.

15

M I'm disappointed my car sold for less than its asking price.

W ______________________________

(a) You have to admit—it was in bad shape.
(b) True, you didn't bargain it down.
(c) Just splurge. Such a great car is worth it.
(d) Fixing it up might increase the price.

16

M Did you grow up in this area?

W No, in Chicago, actually.

M So when did you move here?

W ______________________________

(a) Once I get a job.
(b) My family moved often.
(c) For only a year.
(d) After graduating from university.

17

W May I help you?

M I'm looking for a video game for my son.

W Try *Speed Chase*. It's a bestseller.

M ______________________________

(a) Sounds good—I'll take it.
(b) He'll love your gift.
(c) He prefers video games.
(d) I will once it comes out.

18

M Why aren't you wearing your new sandals?

W I wasn't sure they'd match this outfit.

M Why don't you try them on and see?

W ______________________________

(a) OK, I'll do that.
(b) Yes, I'd like both.
(c) You look great, as always.
(d) Check the size first.

19

W How will we get from the hotel to the airport?

M I'm pretty sure there's a shuttle bus.

W And it stops at our hotel?

M ____________________

(a) No, it hasn't stopped yet.
(b) I think so, but I'll double-check.
(c) Any that go to the hotel.
(d) We're getting closer now.

20

M I'm having trouble sleeping.

W It's probably all the coffee you drink.

M Would three cups have that much effect?

W ____________________

(a) Sure. I'll make some coffee.
(b) I'm surprised that doesn't work.
(c) Of course. Caffeine is powerful stuff.
(d) Try sleeping a few more hours.

21

W How are you getting to work?

M By car. Why?

W Be careful—the roads are icy.

M ____________________

(a) OK, I'll leave them out of it.
(b) I noticed on my drive to work.
(c) That's why I'm taking the subway.
(d) I know. I'll go slow.

22

M You must be Ellen, the new hire.

W Yes, I am. What division do you work for?

M Corporate law. And you're in accounting, aren't you?

W ____________________

(a) No, I can't account for that.
(b) It depends on if I get hired.
(c) Yes, as a junior accountant.
(d) I haven't met them yet.

23

W Are you going to the Christmas party?

M I'd love to, but my friend's visiting so I can't.

W Why don't you both come?

M ____________________

(a) I'm excited to meet your friend.
(b) Good idea. I'll ask if she wants to go.
(c) That would mean postponing her visit.
(d) She won't mind you going.

24

M I couldn't make the mashed potatoes for the potluck dinner.

W No problem. We'll still have enough food.

M Even though we're short a dish?

W ____________________

(a) Believe me—there'll be plenty.
(b) Then bring the mashed potatoes, just in case.
(c) Better than serving too little.
(d) I didn't know you forgot them.

25

W Martin's doing well as supervisor.

M He's certainly taken to management.

W You deserve credit, too—for recognizing his potential.

M ____________________

(a) We plan to offer him the position.
(b) Still, he's better suited to management.
(c) I'm pleased to be considered for the position.
(d) He's so talented that it wasn't hard to spot.

26

M Charles said he's been depressed.

W He seemed fine to me.

M Haven't you noticed any changes in him?

W ____________________

(a) I can't say that I have.
(b) No, he definitely wasn't fine.
(c) He said he changed it, though.
(d) Yes, but he should give more notice.

27

W Do you think you got the job you interviewed for?

M I don't want to speculate.

W Don't you have a feeling about it?

M ______________________

(a) I suppose I'm cautiously optimistic.
(b) No, not even an interview.
(c) I'm just lucky I got the job.
(d) No, but thanks for saying so.

28

M Today's the wrong day for a picnic. It's overcast.

W We should've planned it for Sunday.

M But the weatherman said today would be sunny.

W ______________________

(a) Now's a better time then.
(b) It just proves how unreliable forecasts are.
(c) We should've heeded the weatherman.
(d) Good thing we rescheduled.

29

W Sorry to hear about your sister's illness.

M Thanks. It caught us all off guard.

W Oh, so she got sick suddenly?

M ______________________

(a) Oh my gosh. I had no idea.
(b) Virtually overnight. No one saw it coming.
(c) Luckily, we were able to prevent it.
(d) No one thought of asking beforehand.

30

M John wants to be a professional actor.

W If that's his dream, we shouldn't discourage him.

M But it means a life of financial struggle.

W ______________________

(a) It was too much of a struggle, so he gave up.
(b) Unlikely. Not all actors earn big salaries.
(c) I couldn't agree more. He should have a dream.
(d) Not necessarily. Besides, it's his choice to make.

31

W The living room needs an update.

M OK. What do you envision?

W Painting the walls, for one.

M Sure. What else?

W I'd also like to install a fireplace.

M That sounds like something we can do.

Q What are the man and woman mainly discussing?

(a) Turning a spare room into a living room
(b) Renovating their living room
(c) Restoring their old fireplace
(d) Rearranging their furniture

32

M Have we met before?

W You do look familiar.

M Did you go to Wilton High?

W No. Jackson Secondary School.

M Wait, now I remember! We met at Rob Hudson's party last year.

W That's it! Good memory!

Q What are the man and woman mainly doing in the conversation?

(a) Talking about their lives since high school
(b) Figuring out where they met
(c) Discussing their mutual friend Rob
(d) Reminiscing about a party they both attended

33

W Sir, the x-ray machine shows liquids in your carry-on luggage.

M It's just a bottle of sunscreen.

W It exceeds the 100 milliliter limit. It's against the policy.

M Can't you make an exception for me?

W No, you can't carry it on board.

M OK, I'll get rid of it.

Q What is mainly happening in the conversation?

(a) The woman is enforcing a policy about liquids in carry-on luggage.

(b) The man is asking if his bags need to be inspected.

(c) The woman is verifying whether an airline policy is valid.

(d) The man is determining how much sunscreen he is carrying.

34

M Are you watching that reality TV show again?

W Yes. It's how I unwind.

M But there are more stimulating shows.

W I want to relax, not think.

M You really enjoy this, though?

W We all have guilty pleasures. This one's mine.

Q What is the woman mainly doing in the conversation?

(a) Refusing to admit she watches reality TV shows

(b) Explaining why she prefers to watch a reality TV show

(c) Discussing why TV does not make her feel relaxed

(d) Admitting she watches too much TV

35

W You're really churning out a lot of writing these days.

M It's thanks to the new approach I'm using.

W What does it entail?

M Sticking to a strict writing schedule, for one.

W That's all there is to it?

M And I brainstorm ideas beforehand.

Q What is the man mainly doing in the conversation?

(a) Talking about his latest story ideas

(b) Asserting that writers should aim to produce quality work

(c) Describing how he increased his writing productivity

(d) Creating a writing schedule for the woman

36

M You should see a dentist about your toothache.

W Not after what happened last time!

M Was it that bad?

W Yes. The dentist was careless and caused me unnecessary pain.

M So now you're never going to see a dentist again?

W Truthfully, I can't bring myself to.

Q What is the conversation mainly about?

(a) Why the woman had her tooth pulled

(b) Why the woman refuses to see a dentist

(c) The woman's ability to withstand chronic tooth pain

(d) The severity of the woman's toothache

37

W This company's executives are too focused on quarterly earnings.

M You think they've become greedy?

W No, but their stressing of profits is imprudent.

M They're just trying to reach their earnings targets.

W But they shouldn't prioritize that to the exclusion of all else.

M True, other things should be considered.

Q What is the woman's main point?

(a) Company executives should account for profit shortfalls.

(b) The company's overemphasis on profits is not advisable.

(c) Making consistent profits depends on employee output.

(d) Disregarding earnings guarantees financial ruin.

38

W How'd the foreign service exam go?

M I passed, even the oral section, which I'd failed before.

W That's great! So have you been assigned to a specific post yet?

M No. I'm still waiting for my medical clearance.

W How long does that take?

M Several months, so I'll be traveling abroad in the meantime.

Q Which is correct about the man according to the conversation?

(a) He still needs to pass the exam's oral portion.

(b) He has taken the exam previously.

(c) He has been assigned to a specific post.

(d) He will not travel before receiving medical clearance.

39

M The chicken you prepared was delicious.

W Thanks. It's a recipe I created when I was a caterer.

M You were a caterer? What became of the business?

W I sold it to my sister so I could go back to advertising.

M I see. Are you happy you did?

W Extremely. Catering was just too stressful.

Q Which is correct about the woman according to the conversation?

(a) She cooked the chicken using an old family recipe.

(b) She owns a catering business with her sister.

(c) She stopped catering to pursue advertising.

(d) She regrets having given up catering.

40

M I've been homesick for weeks, and it's getting worse.

W It happens to many ESL teachers who come to Korea.

M I doubt I can make it the whole year.

W It'll pass. I struggled with it, too, my first year abroad.

M Now that you're in your third year, do you still get homesick?

W On rare occasions. It's only natural.

Q Which is correct according to the conversation?

(a) The man's homesickness is improving day by day.

(b) The man is homesick for Korea.

(c) The woman felt homesick in her first year abroad.

(d) The woman never gets homesick anymore.

41

W Hello, I'm calling from Music Magazine for an interview with Max Sayers.

M I'm his personal assistant. He's booked solid for the next month.

W I'd be willing to take whatever time I could get.

M Well, let me see. He'll be in the recording studio all day this Thursday.

W I could swing by there just to get some quotes from him.

M OK, but I can't promise more than a few minutes with him.

Q Which is correct according to the conversation?

(a) The woman is calling from Max Sayers's office.

(b) Max Sayers's schedule is open for the next month.

(c) Max Sayers cannot make it to the recording studio on Thursday.

(d) The woman is not promised much time in the studio with Max Sayers.

42

M This article says people are switching banks in record numbers.

W Five million people in five months.

M And credit unions are becoming more popular.

W Yeah, compared to banks, they have higher interest rates and lower service fees.

M Well, I'm glad my money is already in a credit union.

W I might join you. This article is making me think about what's available besides banks.

Q Which is correct according to the conversation?

(a) Five million people switched banks last month.

(b) Service fees are higher at credit unions.

(c) The man is contemplating switching to a credit union.

(d) The article has the woman considering her banking options.

43

M I'm sorry about the mistake in my fundraiser e-mail.

W It's OK. It's all cleared up now.

M I shouldn't have assumed you'd volunteer.

W It's fine. I wish I could, but I'm just too busy.

M I'll be sure to double-check with you in the future before finalizing the list.

W Thanks.

Q What can be inferred from the conversation?

(a) The man's e-mail listed the woman as a volunteer.

(b) The woman was excluded from the e-mail list by mistake.

(c) The man forgot to send an important e-mail.

(d) The woman did not receive credit for her donation to the fundraiser.

44

M Want to go to Roxy Bar tonight?

W Sure. Who else is going?

M My girlfriend, Sue. Do you think Tim would want to come?

W I'll ask him tonight.

M Actually, could you call now? I have to let Sue know who's coming.

W No problem. I'll try him at his office.

Q What can be inferred from the conversation?

(a) The woman is unfamiliar with Roxy Bar.

(b) The woman and man work with Tim.

(c) The man is anxious to finalize the plans.

(d) The man wants to set up Tim and Sue on a blind date.

45

W Did you make it to the polls to vote in the election?

M I got a flat tire on the way there and missed it.

W Well, your man won in the end.

M I know! I think he'll be good as mayor.

W As you know, I have my doubts, but I guess we'll see.

M Well, I'm pretty pleased with the outcome.

Q What can be inferred from the conversation?

(a) The woman and man supported the same candidate.

(b) The man regrets the choice he made in voting.

(c) The man had planned to meet the woman at the polls.

(d) The woman knew which candidate the man was backing.

46

I've just gotten word that Carlton PR Agency is once again the highest-earning public relations firm in Freemont, and it's all thanks to you, the employees. I could not have built this company without you. Each and every one of the employees here at Carlton PR has contributed their time and energy to making this company the best in its field. And I feel it's important that you all get the recognition you deserve. So thank you, everyone.

Q What is the speaker mainly doing?

(a) Crediting the employees for the company's success

(b) Congratulating the recipient of the employee of the month award

(c) Asking employees to put greater effort into their work

(d) Commending the staff for its positive attitude

47

John Brown was an integral part of the antislavery movement. Fervently devoted to abolition, he believed it could only be achieved through drastic action, no matter how violent. This approach, however, has made him a figure of contention. His efforts were undoubtedly effective at seizing the nation's attention, but many have questioned the extremity of his methods and his seemingly irreverent attitude towards the loss of life.

Q What is the speaker's main point about John Brown?

(a) His actions set back the antislavery movement.

(b) His tactics in the antislavery movement are seen as controversial.

(c) He escaped slavery using whatever means necessary.

(d) He was never recognized for his efforts to end slavery.

48

A new technology is helping in the fight against HIV and AIDS in Mozambique. Cell phone technology has been coupled with simple office printers to allow the immediate transmission of laboratory results to clinics in remote African villages. Before this technology was introduced, HIV test results, sent by courier, took weeks to receive. The printers, which have been successfully used in Mozambique for a year, are now being rolled out in other areas of Africa.

Q What is the report mainly about?

(a) Inefficiencies in treating AIDS patients in Mozambique

(b) The role of cell phones in educating people about HIV prevention

(c) Mozambique's pioneering of new AIDS treatments

(d) Technology that allows for the speedy transfer of HIV test results

49

Florbetaben is a drug that is being studied in connection with Alzheimer's disease. When injected, florbetaben causes amyloid plaques in the brain, which are a telltale sign of Alzheimer's, to show up brightly on brain scans. The significance of this is that doctors can detect the likelihood of Alzheimer's earlier and get patients started on treatment before the disease advances. The sooner the diagnosis, the better chance a patient has at maintaining some quality of life.

Q What is the main topic of the talk about florbetaben?
(a) Its ability to enhance the potency of Alzheimer's treatments
(b) How it breaks up amyloid plaques in the brain
(c) Its development in the brain as a precursor to Alzheimer's
(d) How it can facilitate early detection of Alzheimer's

50

Thanks for coming to the Norwood Apartments residents meeting. To start off, I'd like to stress the importance of using the security buzzer in the main lobby. Over the past month, we've had a few cases of unwanted visitors coming into the building. These have mainly been door-to-door salesmen, who are admittedly harmless but nevertheless annoying. So please, everyone, be rigorous about using the buzzer. Before you buzz someone in as a guest, make sure it is a person you know and are expecting. Thanks.

Q What is the main purpose of the announcement?
(a) To solicit suggestions to improve building safety
(b) To remind residents to use the security buzzer as directed
(c) To alert residents to a string of recent break-ins
(d) To announce the installation of a security buzzer

51

It's been a hot topic around campus, but what would it really mean to privatize Brighton University? Well, privatization would signal a profound shift in the purpose and role of the university. Brighton would go from being a publicly supported institution to an organization based on producing a product. In short, knowledge will become commodified. A deeply troubling prospect, to say the least—and one that we still have time to avert.

Q What is the speaker's main point?
(a) Privatization would radically alter Brighton University.
(b) The mingling of education and business is inevitable.
(c) Privatization would be profitable for Brighton University.
(d) Public institutions must curtail the spending of private funds.

52

Open adoptions, in which the birth parents have contact with the adoptive family, are increasingly the norm, and with good reason. Overall, these adoptions seem to be in everyone's best interests. First of all, when a birth mother is included in creating the adoption plan, she is less likely to change her mind about her decision. The adopted children often benefit as well. Having access to their birth parents can help them answer questions or alleviate concerns they might have otherwise felt about their origins.

Q What is the speaker mainly saying about open adoptions?
(a) Their increasing popularity owes to the benefits they offer.
(b) They work well for some families but not for others.
(c) The social stigma once attached to them is now abating.
(d) They pose unique challenges to the birth mother and child.

53

Got ants, mosquitoes, or other pests? No problem, with Argon brand bug sprays. Our product line is large because the variety of annoying bugs is large, too. And we're always working to come up with new products for specific problems. Our newest offering, the Argon House & Garden Ant Killer is designed to kill ants in your home and yard. As with all of our formulas, this new product is safe for use around humans and pets.

Q Which is correct about the Argon brand according to the advertisement?
(a) It has a small but powerful product line.
(b) It is continuously developing new products.
(c) Its latest product is for garden use only.
(d) Its products must not be used around pets.

54

As the very first students of the course Philosophy and Media, you can count yourselves lucky. The university has never had greater demand for a course. Over three hundred students applied for enrollment in the twenty available spaces. Since the course is new, the administration will be soliciting your evaluations at the end of the semester. The syllabus is also a work-in-progress. So if you'd like a reading to be included in the course, please speak up!

Q Which is correct according to the talk?
(a) The course was brought back this year due to popular demand.
(b) The course still has twenty available spaces for enrollment.
(c) Student evaluations will be requested at the end of each lecture.
(d) Students may suggest course materials for inclusion on the syllabus.

55

The province is attempting to help families reduce their environmental impact through a proposed amendment to the Green Homes Act. The proposed changes include offering a 25% tax credit on the cost of home renovations that include energy-efficient equipment, such as solar panels. To qualify, homeowners must schedule an energy inspection prior to the renovations and a follow-up inspection within a year. There is a $200 fee for each inspection, which is refundable only if the homeowner decides to go ahead and make the home improvements.

Q Which is correct according to the announcement?
(a) The proposal modifies the existing Green Homes Act.
(b) The proposal would provide full coverage for energy-efficient equipment.
(c) Two home inspections must be performed before renovations begin.
(d) Inspection fees will be returned if homeowners decide against renovation.

56

Coca-Cola made its debut in Atlanta, where pharmacist Dr. John Pemberton first concocted the syrup that would be mixed with carbonated water to create the popular drink. Pemberton took the syrup to Jacob's Pharmacy, where it sold for a nickel a glass. Pemberton's partner, Frank Robinson, came up with the name and originated the cursive Coca-Cola trademark, thinking the two Cs would be visually alluring. Far from an instant success, the drink made only $50 the first year, not even offsetting the $70 that it cost to produce.

Q Which is correct about Coca-Cola according to the talk?
(a) Its earliest version comprised merely carbonated water.
(b) Pemberton refused to allow Jacob's Pharmacy to sell it.
(c) Robinson created its trademark with visual appeal in mind.
(d) It made record profits in its first year on the market.

57

Mary Shelley's novel *Frankenstein* is often interpreted as a critique of nineteenth-century English imperialism and its reliance on slavery. I'd say the novel does this and more. It incorporates social criticism with philosophy, namely the master-slave dialectic espoused by Georg Hegel in his book *Phenomenology of Spirit*, which was published just over a decade before *Frankenstein*. Admittedly, no evidence exists proving that Shelley read Hegel, but she was very familiar with contemporary philosophy, especially the work of Immanuel Kant, who himself was a significant influence on Hegel.

Q Which is correct according to the talk?

(a) Critics view Shelley's *Frankenstein* as espousing English imperialism.
(b) Hegel proposed a master-slave dialectic in his work *Phenomenology of Spirit*.
(c) Shelley's *Frankenstein* predated Hegel's *Phenomenology of Spirit* by a decade.
(d) Hegel had no knowledge of Kant's philosophy.

58

Europe is facing a crisis when it comes to developing psychiatric drugs. Private pharmaceutical companies fund up to 80% of the brain research done in Europe. But more and more of these companies are withdrawing from this field of research. Drugs that treat mental illness take more time to develop, are harder to get approved, and have a high failure rate. So pharmaceutical companies are turning their attention, and their funding, to areas that offer them a better chance of recouping the funds spent on research.

Q What can be inferred from the talk?

(a) Most of the available psychiatric drugs have not been proven safe.
(b) Psychiatric drugs are proving too expensive for most consumers.
(c) A lack of financial incentives is deterring investments in psychiatric drugs.
(d) The market has become flooded with psychiatric drugs.

59

The Teach for America program has done a lot of good by having enthusiastic college graduates teach in under-performing school districts. But the program has its drawbacks as well. Putting an untested college grad in charge of a classroom creates the image that teaching is easy and that anyone with a desire to teach can do it well. The truth is, teaching takes practice. And the droves of inexperienced newcomers who volunteer for Teach for America, no matter how enthusiastic they may be, would do well to remember that.

Q Which statement about Teach for America would the speaker most likely agree with?

(a) Its main focus should be getting more volunteers into classrooms.
(b) Enthusiasm is the most important quality volunteers can bring to it.
(c) A lack of volunteers is compromising its ability to succeed.
(d) It is perpetuating an image of teaching that does not reflect reality.

60

Geologists from Russia's Chechnya region claim to have unearthed the world's largest fossilized dinosaur eggs dating back to sixty million years ago. Some are calling this discovery a little too coincidental, though, occurring as it did in the midst of the region's attempt to revamp its reputation. Paleontologists have raised questions about the discovery, stating that dinosaurs did not lay large eggs and were unlikely to roam the mountainous region. Still, that isn't stopping the Chechen government from turning the area into a tourist-friendly nature preserve.

Q What can be inferred from the talk?

(a) Several dinosaur fossils had previously been unearthed in Chechnya.
(b) The Chechen government wants to protect the dinosaur egg site from human intrusion.
(c) Paleontologists are skeptical about the authenticity of the dinosaur eggs.
(d) Chechnya never intended to publicize the dinosaur egg discovery.

서울대 최신기출 2

Listening Comprehension Scripts

1

W Who's this CD for?

M ______________________

(a) I've listened to it before.
(b) It wasn't expensive.
(c) It's a present for a friend.
(d) He's my favorite singer.

2

M Do you have any plans for spring break?

W ______________________

(a) As soon as it ends.
(b) I'd like to go camping.
(c) No, I haven't tried it before.
(d) Sure, whenever you want to.

3

W How often do you call your son in California?

M ______________________

(a) I was out when he called.
(b) Once a week, on Sundays.
(c) Only when I can't call him.
(d) He moved there two months ago.

4

M Are there overnight trains from here to London?

W ______________________

(a) No, but tickets are expensive.
(b) There's one that departs at 9 p.m.
(c) Of course you can spend the night here.
(d) It depends on where you're going.

5

W Did you set the alarm clock?

M ______________________

(a) I forgot, but I'll do it now.
(b) No, I set it an hour later.
(c) Yes, please set it for early.
(d) I don't want any more.

6

M I'll never pass this course now that I've failed the midterm.

W ______________________

(a) Ask the professor how long it takes.
(b) Maybe you can retake the course next semester.
(c) Just work hard until the midterm.
(d) You'd better prepare for the midterm, then.

7

W Isn't the man in this photo your father?

M ______________________

(a) I didn't think so, either.
(b) No, but let me try again.
(c) They look similar, but no.
(d) I don't remember whether he did.

8

M I've got to hang up. My battery's dying.

W ______________________

(a) Fine, I'll get myself another one.
(b) Try calling my office phone.
(c) That's not why I called you.
(d) OK, call me again after you charge it.

9

W Could I borrow your car?

M ______________________

(a) Let's meet there instead.
(b) As long as it's not for a long trip.
(c) Of course, I'm sorry to trouble you.
(d) OK, I promise to make it quick.

10

M I'm calling about the sales job you advertised.

W ______________________

(a) Thanks for offering me the job.
(b) Sorry, it was filled yesterday.
(c) Oh, it isn't on sale yet.
(d) You can order online.

11

W Thanks for coming to Erin's recital yesterday.

M ______________________________

(a) I hope she didn't notice my absence.
(b) She must be looking forward to it.
(c) I'm glad you liked my performance.
(d) Sure, I wouldn't have missed it.

12

M I'm wondering if I should accept this athletic scholarship offer.

W ______________________________

(a) You made the right decision.
(b) Take it. You need some solid funding.
(c) There's still a chance they might offer it.
(d) I know. I'm accepting it as well.

13

W Will it be cold this weekend?

M ______________________________

(a) Saturday works for me.
(b) It wasn't as cold as I expected.
(c) I haven't checked the forecast.
(d) I'm hoping to, so I can go skiing.

14

M You'll have to move your car—it's blocking the entrance.

W ______________________________

(a) OK, thanks for bringing it over.
(b) Oh, I didn't realize I was in the way.
(c) I'm sure that's where I left it, though.
(d) That's fine. I went around the other side.

15

W I overslept. Am I in trouble for having missed the meeting?

M ______________________________

(a) I didn't even notice you left.
(b) No, you can't make it in time.
(c) Don't worry. I covered for you.
(d) It won't happen again. I promise.

16

W Do you have any siblings?

M Yes, two brothers.

W So are you the eldest?

M ______________________________

(a) I'm the middle child.
(b) Yeah, they're older than me.
(c) No, I like the youngest one best.
(d) I don't have any of my own yet.

17

M Have you heard about Monica?

W No, why?

M She's getting promoted.

W ______________________________

(a) I'm so happy you did!
(b) I know. I wish she'd decide.
(c) Really? Good for her!
(d) Wow! That's generous of her.

18

W Hello. I'm Alexandra, your new assistant.

M Nice to meet you.

W How would you like to be addressed?

M ______________________________

(a) My secretary can help me with that.
(b) I'd prefer you do that promptly.
(c) I'll just call you Alex, then.
(d) I go by Robert around the office.

19

M That was quick. How was your run?

W A bit chilly.

M You didn't take a sweatshirt?

W ______________________________

(a) I thought you had a jacket.
(b) No, that's why I turned back early.
(c) I just wanted the exercise.
(d) Yeah, I should be back soon.

20

W Honey, I have a business trip next week.

M Really? I'll be working overtime all week.

W So how will Bobby get home from school?

M ______________________________

(a) I think he just got home now.
(b) I'll ask my mom to pick him up.
(c) His teacher told him not to be late.
(d) He's riding with a friend today.

21

M I didn't see Bill at the staff hiking trip.

W He couldn't come.

M Why not? He really wanted to.

W ______________________________

(a) He said he was swamped with work.
(b) Then you can invite him.
(c) Because attendance was required.
(d) No wonder he's enjoying it so much.

22

W Was Nicole at the concert last night?

M Yeah, and she brought her new boyfriend, too.

W What did you think of him?

M ______________________________

(a) I thought she would have brought him.
(b) Just a bit. We didn't really talk much.
(c) He seemed like a nice guy.
(d) I don't know. I didn't ask her.

23

M Hi, Cassie. How are you finding the conference?

W Pretty much as I expected it to be.

M Sounds like you've been here before.

W ______________________________

(a) No, I wasn't planning to.
(b) It'll be in Chicago this time.
(c) I think they only hold it annually.
(d) Yeah, I presented a paper here last year.

24

W We should've bought that car we test-drove last week.

M Yeah, the price was great.

W Should I call and see if it's still for sale?

M ______________________________

(a) Not before you test-drive it.
(b) Well, it's too late to take it back.
(c) No, it's probably long gone.
(d) I'd find out if it's available first.

25

M Professor, I wanted to see you about my essay.

W OK, drop by my office this afternoon.

M Great. What time would be best?

W ______________________________

(a) It should take half an hour.
(b) Any time during my office hours.
(c) I'll finish it as soon as possible.
(d) I'll see you in class at 3:00.

26

W After all that work, the experiment failed.

M We should just quit.

W Let's try again. We can make it work.

M ______________________________

(a) Well, we shouldn't give up so quickly.
(b) If you think it'll make a difference, go ahead.
(c) No, we should probably try again first.
(d) Maybe that's why it failed.

27

M Would you like these groceries delivered, ma'am?

W What time would they arrive? I might still be out.

M Probably around 1:30.

W ______________________________

(a) All right, I'll bring them at that time.
(b) I'll check if they have been delivered.
(c) Oh, I must have missed it.
(d) I'd better take them myself, then.

28

W Just one day until I leave for New Zealand!

M I'm jealous! I'm looking forward to going there again.

W You're planning a trip, too?

M ____________________

(a) It's on the agenda, but nothing definite.
(b) Last summer, and it was wonderful.
(c) It's my first time overseas.
(d) I'd love to see New Zealand for myself.

29

M Is someone coming to fix our air conditioner?

W They're coming tomorrow.

M But it's so hot! What'll we do in the meantime?

W ____________________

(a) We'll just have to make do with a fan.
(b) Let's think about it after it's repaired.
(c) Exactly. We're lucky to have a functioning air conditioner.
(d) It's fine. They don't mind waiting for a few days.

30

W You're eating potato chips? It's almost dinner time!

M But I'm really hungry.

W Isn't that going to spoil your appetite?

M ____________________

(a) I'll just have enough to tide me over.
(b) It hardly takes any time at all.
(c) Not if I eat enough at dinner.
(d) That's why I'm waiting to eat.

31

W Thanks for cleaning the office kitchen.

M You're welcome. I just tidied it up.

W Tidied it up? It looks like you scrubbed it from top to bottom!

M Well, I got tired of the mess.

W Everyone's grateful that you took the initiative.

M Thanks, I appreciate your noticing.

Q What is the woman mainly doing in the conversation?

(a) Inquiring about who cleaned the kitchen
(b) Complaining that nobody cleans the kitchen
(c) Thanking the man for helping her clean yesterday
(d) Expressing her gratitude for the man's cleaning

32

M We lucked out and lost the tournament finals.

W I think you're using that expression incorrectly.

M Lucked out? Doesn't it mean your luck ran out?

W No, it means that you got lucky.

M Are you sure? I've always said it that way.

W I'm positive.

Q What is the conversation mainly about?

(a) The correct usage of an expression
(b) Different idioms about being lucky
(c) The origin of a popular saying
(d) How the meanings of idioms change

33

W You should read *Art in Action*. It changed my life.

M Really? Sounds kind of...lightweight.

W It's not. It's about increasing your creativity.

M Isn't that a pretty trivial topic?

W Not at all! Creativity affects everything: hobbies, work, socializing...

M Seems like the kind of new age stuff I try to avoid.

Q What is the man mainly doing in the conversation?

(a) Asserting that creativity cannot be taught
(b) Dismissing the woman's book recommendation
(c) Challenging the woman's claim that creativity is trivial
(d) Suggesting the woman read less serious books

34

W This group tour of Thailand looks good.

M Hmm...I'm not sure about doing a group tour.

W But we wouldn't have to worry about planning.

M I think it'd be better to explore on our own.

W Not if it means getting lost and frustrated.

M I'd be more frustrated traveling with strangers.

Q What is the man mainly doing in the conversation?

(a) Expressing opposition to joining a group tour

(b) Complaining about a recent group tour he took

(c) Explaining why he wants to avoid Thailand

(d) Criticizing the woman's choice of travel destination

35

M Ron's looking for his cell phone. Have you seen it?

W He can't find it? Yesterday, he lost his keys!

M And before that, he couldn't find his laptop charger.

W He should be more careful.

M I know. He claims he's just forgetful.

W So am I, but I can still keep track of important things.

Q What are the man and woman mainly discussing?

(a) Ron's tendency to misplace his belongings

(b) Their search for Ron's missing cell phone

(c) Ron's disregard for other people's personal items

(d) Their annoyance with Ron's whimsical demands

36

M Did you buy a birthday gift for Jonathan?

W I'm thinking of getting him a digital camera.

M He's pretty picky about cameras. You'd better check with him first.

W But then it wouldn't be a surprise.

M Still, I wouldn't risk getting him something he doesn't like.

W I'll think about it.

Q What is the man mainly trying to do?

(a) Persuade the woman to consult Jonathan about his present

(b) Convince the woman to exchange the gift she got for Jonathan

(c) Explain why Jonathan does not like cameras

(d) Inquire about Jonathan's plans for his birthday

37

W I hate the way junk food is marketed to kids.

M What do you mean?

W You know, all the brightly colored ads and catchy jingles.

M I don't think they're aimed specifically at kids.

W Of course they are! Those are precisely the things that catch kids' attention.

M But that doesn't mean the ads aren't for adults, too.

Q What are the man and woman mainly discussing?

(a) Whether junk food ads are specifically targeted at children

(b) Why they disagree with advertising junk food

(c) What types of advertising kids pay attention to

(d) How to get their kids to stop eating junk food

38

M Did you lend Dan that money he was asking for?

W Yes, but only half the amount he wanted.

M That's smart. A thousand dollars was a lot to ask, even from family.

W I couldn't afford to lend him that much, anyhow.

M Do you think he'll pay it back soon?

W Yeah. He was pretty prompt the last time I loaned him money.

Q Which is correct about the woman according to the conversation?

(a) She gave Dan a loan for $1,000.

(b) She could not afford to give a loan to Dan.

(c) She believes that Dan will not pay her back.

(d) She had given a loan to Dan in the past.

39

W I'm considering buying a Collie.

M They're great family dogs. I had one when I was young.

W Yeah, I want one that'll be good for my kids.

M Be careful, though. My neighbor's Collie wrecked her apartment.

W I'd never keep a big dog in a small apartment like that.

M Me, neither. Your house is spacious enough, though.

Q Which is correct according to the conversation?

(a) The man has never owned a Collie.

(b) The woman wants a family-friendly pet.

(c) The woman would not mind having a big dog in a small apartment.

(d) The man thinks the woman's house is too small for a Collie.

40

W I might quit our Japanese class.

M Why? Are you dropping out of the trip to Japan this summer?

W No, I'm still going. It's just that the class isn't helpful.

M The instructor's explanations are so clear, though.

W But we never get time to practice.

M Well, some students practice after class. You should join them.

Q Which is correct according to the conversation?

(a) The woman has stopped attending Japanese class.

(b) The woman has cancelled her travel plans to Japan.

(c) The man thinks the instructor's explanations are vague.

(d) The man suggests joining a study group.

41

M Have you read Tom Bleaker's new novel?

W Not yet, but I read a good review of it.

M You're welcome to borrow my copy—I just finished reading it.

W Thanks, but I'm working through a history of Italy at the moment.

M Interesting. Maybe we can trade when you're done?

W Sure, sounds good!

Q Which is correct according to the conversation?

(a) The woman has not heard of Tom Bleaker's latest novel.

(b) The man is not done reading the new Tom Bleaker book.

(c) The woman just finished a book about Italy.

(d) The man suggests exchanging books with the woman.

42

M How'd your car get scratched?
W I scraped it trying to back into a small parking space.
M Oh no! Did you scratch another car?
W No, but I scraped the wall next to the parking space.
M Oh, so do you have to pay for the damage to the wall?
W The wall already had other scratch marks, so security said it was OK.

Q Which is correct according to the conversation?
(a) The woman scratched her car pulling out of a tight parking space.
(b) No other car was damaged when the woman scratched her car.
(c) There were no scratches on the wall prior to the incident.
(d) The woman was asked to pay for scraping the wall.

43

W Is that a new leather sofa?
M Yeah, I got it last week.
W Why? Your last one was in good shape.
M Yeah, but my allergist recommended against fabric sofas, since they trap dust.
W Oh. Well, I hope you didn't just throw away your old one.
M No, I sold it online for $300.

Q What can be inferred about the man from the conversation?
(a) His old sofa was covered in fabric.
(b) The woman did not like his previous sofa.
(c) He replaced his sofa because he disliked its color.
(d) The woman does not think his old sofa was worth selling.

44

M You should come and work at the company I'm starting up.
W Actually, I just got hired at a big corporation.
M Well, we can match your salary, plus 10%.
W That's tempting, but I've got a good, steady job now.
M What if we gave you a permanent position, rather than annual contracts?
W I don't know. Ask me again once your company is a bit more established.

Q What can be inferred about the woman from the conversation?
(a) She considers working for a start-up too risky.
(b) She prefers annual contracts to permanent ones.
(c) She got her corporate job with the help of the man.
(d) She values an immediate pay raise more than job security.

45

W Excuse me, I'm looking for Pioneer Arena.
M That closed down months ago.
W But the Tigers game is tonight. I bought tickets last week.
M Oh, they play at Warner Arena now, across town.
W So I should get back on the expressway?
M Yeah, just head east and follow the signs.

Q What can be inferred from the conversation?
(a) Pioneer Arena closed for repairs.
(b) The Tigers used to play at Pioneer Arena.
(c) The woman does not know how to access the expressway.
(d) The woman bought her tickets at Pioneer Arena.

46

Attention, folk music fans! Did you miss out on folk music legend Bobby Wilson's *Amber Harvest* tour? Well, you're in luck! Wilson has scheduled two extra shows featuring songs from his latest album: he'll be in Victoria on March 25 and Portland on April 2. Tickets for these shows go on sale starting March 11. Tickets won't last long, so call as soon as ticketing offices open!

Q What is the advertisement mainly about?
(a) How Wilson's shows have impressed concert-goers
(b) Wilson scheduling two additional shows to his tour
(c) The popularity of Wilson's most recently released album
(d) How Wilson became famous in the folk music world

47

Thank you all for coming to this teachers' meeting. The administration has noticed teachers becoming lax in their documentation of students' attendance. These records are important for when you assign students' participation scores in your classes. Also, a thorough accounting of attendance is required in order to track truancy rates, and the administration must produce a complete record for the Ministry of Education's annual audit.

Q What is the main purpose of the talk?
(a) To announce changes to recording students' attendance
(b) To address the problem of poor student attendance
(c) To emphasize the need for precise attendance records
(d) To inform teachers of yearly truancy audits

48

Fellow students, I urge you to speak up regarding the university's handling of our student activity fees. We are the ones who pay them, so why haven't we been asked for our input about their application? Activity fees are higher now than ever before. This is our money, and it should be used to our benefit in the ways that we see fit. We need to make our demands heard.

Q What is the speaker's main point?
(a) The activity fees are too high for students to afford.
(b) Students should speak out against the proposed fee hikes.
(c) Students should have a say in determining how activity fees are used.
(d) Administrators must heed opposition to fee increases.

49

Email is crucial to office communication, but messages are often crafted ineffectively. Following a few guidelines can make email communication much smoother. First, always include a clear description of the email's contents in the subject line. Second, send separate emails for separate topics to help discussions stay organized. Finally, consider whether email is the best medium for your message. Would a chat in person be quicker? These simple rules will make a big difference in your office.

Q What is the main purpose of the talk?
(a) To encourage employees to rely less on email
(b) To explain how to take effective messages for people
(c) To provide tips on improving office email communication
(d) To describe how to utilize email as an advertising tool

50

Lie detectors—or polygraphs—can show when someone is lying by measuring heart rate, sweating, and respiratory rate, all of which increase when someone is lying. But researchers at Northeastern University have found some exceptions to this. For example, when students exaggerated their grade point averages—in essence, telling lies based on their aspirations—they showed no physiological signs of anxiety. The study concluded that only guilty lies provoke anxiety reactions, and that not all lies can be detected by their physiological correlates.

Q What is the main idea of the talk?
(a) The use of polygraph tests is being questioned.
(b) Some lies cannot be detected because they do not produce physical reactions.
(c) Researchers can now detect when people are exaggerating.
(d) Lying can worsen long-term anxiety by placing stress on the body.

51

Dictionaries are useful tools for language learning. Over-reliance on these learning resources, though, can obstruct the progress toward certain learning objectives. Consulting such references every time a student encounters an unfamiliar term can hinder the development of fluency, especially in reading and speaking. Students need to be taught other strategies to compensate for their lack of vocabulary knowledge.

Q What is the speaker mainly saying about dictionaries?
(a) They are valuable for reading but not listening skills.
(b) Using them too often can impede language learning.
(c) They help students learn more than just definitions.
(d) Avoiding their use can lead to vocabulary deficiency.

52

The city of Pattersonville is facing off with its municipal police force over a $38 million lawsuit. Over 200 officers are suing for overtime pay they claim they are entitled to. The basis for the dispute is a discrepancy between state law, which requires overtime pay for any time worked over 160 hours a month, and the national Fair Labor Standards Act, which only pays overtime after 171 hours. The city claims that this act relieves them of any obligation to pay overtime during this 11-hour gap.

Q What is the news report mainly about?
(a) A discrepancy between police officers' and civil servants' pay
(b) A lawsuit filed by police officers regarding overtime payment
(c) Police officers' demands for less overtime work
(d) Police officers' complaints over an unsatisfactory pay raise

53

Welcome to today's island trek! Our tour will start here at the eastern shore, cross the island's center, and end on the western shore, where we'll be picked up and driven back. Along the way, I'll describe the island's sights and natural history. We'll stop for photographs, but please stay with the group, since you can easily become lost if you get separated. At noon, we'll stop for lunch, which will be provided for you.

Q Which is correct according to the announcement?
(a) Tour participants will hike back to the tour's point of origin.
(b) The tour guide will describe the history of the island's natural features.
(c) Hikers are urged to explore alternative trails independently.
(d) Tour participants are required to bring their own lunch.

54

If you're a serious video gamer, it's time to test your skills. Join hundreds of the best local amateur gamers at the Elite Gamers Tournament, based on the popular role-playing game *Age of Conquest*. This year's tournament will include two consecutive eight-hour sessions on the weekend of September 22 and 23. The event's top three players will earn a place in the professional Legends of Gaming Tournament this December.

Q Which is correct about the Elite Gamers Tournament according to the announcement?
(a) It does not allow amateur gamers to participate.
(b) It will be taking place on two consecutive weekends.
(c) It will test players' skills at a variety of video games.
(d) Its top three players will get a chance to compete against professionals.

55

In today's music history lecture, we're looking at Anton Dvorak's Ninth Symphony. Dvorak composed the work during a visit to America, where he drew inspiration from Native American and African American music. Music historians also see the work as highly reminiscent of the folk songs of Dvorak's native Bohemia. Its premiere in 1893 was met with thunderous applause, and it became an instant success. It is the best-known of Dvorak's works and continues to be one of the most popular pieces in the modern orchestral repertoire.

Q Which is correct about Dvorak's Ninth Symphony according to the talk?
(a) It was composed after Dvorak returned from America.
(b) It evokes the folk songs of the composer's homeland.
(c) Its premiere elicited a tepid response from the audience.
(d) Its popularity with modern orchestras has continuously waned.

56

Aristotle's *Poetics*, the earliest extant work of literary theory, comprised a detailed analysis of ancient literature. Since other literary forms, such as the novel, were not developed until much later, *Poetics* covered only poetry and drama. The work was divided into two parts, the first examining tragedy and the second comedy. However, only the first part has survived. In this, Aristotle comments on tragedy, emphasizing how it must be performed dramatically and not simply recited as poetry.

Q Which is correct about Aristotle's *Poetics* according to the lecture?
(a) It is the oldest existing treatise dealing with literary theory.
(b) It focused on ancient poetry to the exclusion of drama.
(c) It included a section on the novel that has not survived.
(d) It suggests that tragedy should be performed as poetry is.

57

I've called this meeting to explain the changes to your vacation time. As you know, personal leave was set aside for personal tasks and required a separate request form. However, from now on, personal leave will be combined into your regular vacation time and requested with the same form. As always, any vacation time left over at the end of the year will roll over. Bereavement and sick leave will still be counted separately, and the policies for requesting such time off will not change.

Q Which is correct according to the announcement?
(a) Employees' personal leave will now be counted as vacation time.
(b) Personal leave and vacation time will still have separate request forms.
(c) Vacation time has changed to carry over from year to year.
(d) Bereavement leave is now being combined with vacation time.

58

The current oil boom in Williston, North Dakota, has had a devastating effect on skilled manual labor occupations in the city. The lure of high wages in the area's petroleum industry has caused a shortage of skilled manual laborers, particularly in construction services. Paradoxically, as the oil sector booms, new residents are moving to the area, and builders, plumbers, and electricians are needed more than ever. But unless wages rise for these jobs, it's likely that labor shortages will continue in construction.

Q What can be inferred from the news report?
(a) Williston's unemployment rate has grown in recent years.
(b) Petroleum jobs are becoming harder to get.
(c) Economic prosperity has reduced the need for construction services.
(d) Jobs in the petroleum industry pay better than construction jobs.

59

It seems intuitive that people with more choices feel more autonomous and therefore experience greater satisfaction. Yet substantial research has found that as options increase, consumer satisfaction levels decrease. One of the costs of making a decision is forgoing the benefits of other options, and uncertainty about whether the selected option was the best one lowers the satisfaction gained from the chosen item. For some people, this can even cause decision paralysis: they avoid the decision-making process altogether, because the ultimate reward is not worth the frustration of choosing.

Q What can be inferred from the lecture?
(a) Decision paralysis usually leads to more satisfactory choices.
(b) People with more options are better able to choose among them.
(c) Decision paralysis occurs when there are too few attractive options.
(d) A wider range of options increases the likelihood of decision paralysis.

60

Following Emily Dickinson's death, her sister Lavinia dedicated herself to getting the poet's mostly unpublished works into print. In order to do this, she turned to her brother's wife, Susan Dickinson. But she also sought assistance from his mistress, Mabel Loomis Todd. The manuscripts of Dickinson's poetry were divided between these two women, who bitterly refused to collaborate and continuously published competing editions of Dickinson's work. This allowed Emily Dickinson's poetry to enjoy a long turn in the literary spotlight.

Q What can be inferred from the lecture?
(a) The lengthy feud turned out to be a boon for the late poet.
(b) Lavinia Dickinson wanted to honor her late sister's desire for anonymity.
(c) The initial publication of Dickinson's poems constituted her entire body of work.
(d) Lavinia Dickinson was unconvinced about the literary value of her sister's work.

서울대 최신기출 3

Listening Comprehension Scripts

1

M Sam grew up in California, didn't he?
W ____________________

(a) Only until he was eight.
(b) No, but he wants to soon.
(c) I don't think he ever would.
(d) Yes, until he moved to California.

2

W Thanks for coming! Was my house hard to find?
M ____________________

(a) This map will help you find it.
(b) Not with your directions.
(c) Just during the ride back.
(d) It's around here somewhere.

3

M This café's too noisy to study in.
W ____________________

(a) It's always quiet like this.
(b) Let's move somewhere else, then.
(c) I know! I thought it would be busier.
(d) Thanks, but I prefer the library.

4

W I didn't know you still smoked.
M ____________________

(a) Yes, I quit last year.
(b) Just every once in a while.
(c) I wouldn't mind one myself.
(d) I have no idea, either.

5

M Shouldn't the pizza we ordered be here by now?
W ____________________

(a) It only took half an hour.
(b) Let's just order in.
(c) Give it a few more minutes.
(d) We can place the order now.

6

W I didn't see you at Andrea's wedding.
M ____________________

(a) I haven't met the right person yet.
(b) Nothing will stop me from going.
(c) Unfortunately, I couldn't make it.
(d) Of course! I wouldn't have missed it.

7

M Do you recall the article Professor Nesbitt cited in her lecture?
W ____________________

(a) No, she actually conducted it herself.
(b) Not offhand. I'd have to consult my notes.
(c) Too bad she didn't mention it in the lecture.
(d) You should if you need more sources.

8

W Oh no! The car's got a flat tire!
M ____________________

(a) That's what the tread's for.
(b) That's OK—I'll put the spare on.
(c) Don't worry. I can deflate it.
(d) I knew we should have gone by car.

9

M Can I schedule a checkup for next week?
W ____________________

(a) No, you need to make an appointment.
(b) Maybe next Friday would work instead.
(c) Sure, we have an opening on Monday.
(d) Let me just cancel it for you, then.

10

W You'd love the science fiction book I just finished.
M ____________________

(a) Really? I'll lend it to you when I'm done.
(b) Any time. I can recommend other books.
(c) I bet. That's one of my favorite genres.
(d) You're welcome. I knew you'd like it.

11

M Did the home team manage to win the game?

W ______________________________

(a) I'll find out which teams are playing.
(b) Yeah, they pulled off a huge upset.
(c) Not sure. I only caught the final score.
(d) Actually, I didn't expect it, either.

12

W Did you hear a knock at the door?

M ______________________________

(a) No, I remembered my key this time.
(b) Maybe you should try again later.
(c) Not sure. Let me go and check it out.
(d) I'll call first to see if anyone's in.

13

M How much are you charging for that used guitar?

W ______________________________

(a) However long it takes to sell it.
(b) I couldn't afford it anyway.
(c) I'll consider any reasonable offer.
(d) It depends on how much you want for it.

14

W So, are you all settled into your new apartment?

M ______________________________

(a) No, it's probably about 15 years old.
(b) I sure am. No more living out of boxes for me.
(c) Of course. I can't wait to move.
(d) Mostly, I just need to find a place I like.

15

M What do you think of the business idea Nick was telling us about?

W ______________________________

(a) He couldn't convince me otherwise.
(b) It seems like a shaky proposition.
(c) I just wish he would tell us about it.
(d) You wouldn't believe him if he told you.

16

W Why do you have a Canadian passport, Pat?
M Because I'm Canadian.
W But you've lived here in America for so long.
M ______________________________

(a) No, I haven't been to Canada for years.
(b) Well, I never changed my citizenship.
(c) Still, I live here now.
(d) Yeah, but I thought you had, too.

17

M You're sure about driving in the snow?
W Yeah, the roads have been plowed.
M But it's still slippery.
W ______________________________

(a) I'll be extra careful.
(b) Don't worry. I don't intend to drive.
(c) I'll just wait until they plow, then.
(d) That's why I'm staying home.

18

W I didn't get the lead role in the musical.
M You said the audition went great.
W I know. I wonder where I went wrong.
M ______________________________

(a) It's probably a production delay.
(b) I'm sure you got the lead.
(c) I wouldn't have turned it down like that.
(d) Maybe you weren't the right fit.

19

M Hi, I'm from the real estate agency.
W Ah, yes—for the home appraisal?
M That's right. I'll be checking your property inside and out.
W ______________________________

(a) I'd start by checking with the agency.
(b) You take the outside. I'll tackle the inside.
(c) OK. I'll let you get to work right away.
(d) But I thought it needed an inspection.

20

W Any plans for spring break?

M I'm headed out of Seoul. Want to come?

W Depends on where you're going.

M ______________________________

(a) Sounds like a great idea.
(b) Some of Seoul's tourist attractions.
(c) Just to the coast to get some sun.
(d) I wouldn't mind tagging along.

21

M Welcome to EZ Car Rentals. Do you have a reservation?

W No. I'll take whatever's available.

M Would a two-door compact car be OK?

W ______________________________

(a) But I reserved something larger.
(b) No, thanks. All I need is one car.
(c) I suppose that'll have to do.
(d) Sure. It's yours all week.

22

W I'm calling to see how you're feeling.

M I'm OK. How'd you know I was sick?

W Jen told me. Can I do anything to help?

M ______________________________

(a) Yeah, we should visit her together.
(b) I'm fine, but thanks for offering.
(c) Wish her a speedy recovery for me.
(d) OK, my offer still stands.

23

M I'm thinking of seeing the latest Alan Burton movie.

W Well, I wouldn't recommend it.

M Why? I heard it was thought-provoking.

W ______________________________

(a) This one outdoes his latest one.
(b) The plot's boring, though.
(c) Maybe that's why you didn't like it.
(d) Right, you should definitely see it.

24

W Is the city library far from here?

M It takes about 15 minutes by bus.

W What about on foot?

M ______________________________

(a) I'll have to walk there then.
(b) Sorry, I've never taken the bus there.
(c) It's a long walk. I'd catch a bus.
(d) Suit yourself, but it's a nice walk.

25

M Your play's opening night was great!

W Thanks. It got good reviews, at least.

M It sounds like you weren't satisfied.

W ______________________________

(a) Yeah, but you shouldn't take offense.
(b) I'll find out at the premiere.
(c) I didn't know the critics liked it.
(d) Well, I'm my own harshest critic.

26

W Did the interviews go smoothly?

M Yeah. We've got a lot of competent candidates.

W Have you selected anyone yet?

M ______________________________

(a) No, but I doubt I'll be chosen.
(b) We've still got a few more rounds to go.
(c) We haven't even posted the job yet.
(d) Thanks, that would be really helpful.

27

M How are we getting to the ballpark tonight?

W I thought we'd take the car.

M But finding parking is so hard.

W ______________________________

(a) Not if we leave a bit early.
(b) Even so, it's better than driving.
(c) We have a good excuse.
(d) Don't worry. We'll be back soon.

28

W Do your parents live nearby?
M No, they retired to Thailand.
W Isn't it hard raising young kids with them so far away?
M ____________________

(a) Sometimes, but we manage.
(b) But we've never been there before.
(c) No, it wasn't really their choice.
(d) Sure, especially since they live so close by.

29

M Are you enrolling in Mandarin class?
W I'm considering it, but money's tight now.
M Doesn't work reimburse you for the costs?
W ____________________

(a) Only partially, so it's still expensive.
(b) No, they only pay for Mandarin classes.
(c) Some classes do, so it's manageable.
(d) Yes, they deduct it from our salary.

30

W I need to be more organized.
M I could show you some techniques I use.
W Techniques? I thought you were naturally organized.
M ____________________

(a) No, some people are just born that way.
(b) Nobody is—we all have to work at it.
(c) Yeah, but that's nothing a little effort can't fix.
(d) Right—that's why I don't use any techniques.

31

W Dan's birthday's on a Sunday this year.
M On a long weekend, right?
W Yes. Should we have a party on Sunday evening?
M Maybe Saturday would be better.
W But with the holiday on Friday, people might be away.
M Then let's just do it the following weekend.

Q What is the woman mainly doing in the conversation?
(a) Notifying the man of a party's date
(b) Determining the best day for a party
(c) Checking the man's availability for a party
(d) Considering hosting a holiday party

32

M I hate finishing a mediocre painting.
W For me, painting's about the process, not the result.
M You don't care if your work turns out badly?
W Nope, I find the act itself soothing.
M What if it's not well received?
W It doesn't matter. I just paint for my own enjoyment.

Q What is the woman mainly doing in the conversation?
(a) Stating her motivations for creating art
(b) Challenging the man on what constitutes art
(c) Disagreeing with the man's opinion of his work
(d) Explaining how to create well-received artwork

33

W Let's turn on the heat.
M It's only October, though.
W But it's chilly at night!
M Put on a sweater.
W Why, when we can run the furnace?
M Using it this soon is wasteful.

Q What is the man mainly doing in the conversation?
(a) Complaining about the room temperature
(b) Arguing that waiting to heat their home is silly
(c) Opposing the suggestion to heat the house
(d) Urging the woman to turn off the furnace

34

M I met with your friend who sells insurance.
W Did he have what you needed?
M No. He sells the same insurance that I already have.
W So you were unable to get a new plan?
M Yeah. Also, his prices were higher than my current rates.
W Sorry. I thought he could help you.

Q What are the man and woman mainly discussing?
(a) Why the woman decided to change insurance companies
(b) How the woman got the lowest rates on insurance
(c) The man's unsuccessful attempt to get a new insurance plan
(d) The man's dissatisfaction with his current insurance plan

35

W Did you decide if you're doing the optional overtime assignment?
M Not yet. I'm swamped this week.
W Well, I can't make up my mind.
M The compensation's quite generous.
W That's true. And we're already familiar with the project.
M Well, if you sign up, I will, too.

Q What are the man and woman mainly doing in the conversation?
(a) Complaining about a difficult overtime assignment
(b) Debating whether to accept additional work
(c) Rationalizing why they should decline a project
(d) Pledging to help each other with overtime work

36

W Lincoln School District outsourced its school bus service.
M That sounds short-sighted.
W Right. They might be saving now, but eventually it'll cost more.
M Exactly. Contractors' fees are bound to go up.
W Plus, the district will have less control over the service.
M I wonder who thought this was a good idea.

Q What is the main topic of the conversation?
(a) The attempt by bus companies to raise prices
(b) The downsides of outsourcing school transportation
(c) The reasons for fluctuating prices for bus services
(d) The effects of outsourcing on school bus drivers

37

M Honey, do you think I should accept that transfer to Chicago?
W Well, the cost of living there is so high.
M The company will double my salary if I take the position.
W That's encouraging. What about my job, though?
M There'll be plenty of opportunities for you there.
W Maybe, but there's still the kids' schooling to consider.

Q What is the woman mainly doing in the conversation?
(a) Raising practical concerns about relocating to Chicago
(b) Weighing the pros and cons of her new job offer
(c) Expressing regret that the man accepted a job in Chicago
(d) Encouraging the man to embrace a professional opportunity

38

W I hope this rain stops before Eric's wedding tomorrow.

M The forecast said it'll clear up in the afternoon.

W And the morning? The ceremony starts at 10 a.m.

M They're expecting light rain. The ceremony's outdoors, on the church grounds, right?

W Yeah. They'll put up a wedding tent if it rains.

M Oh, then it'll be fine.

Q Which is correct according to the conversation?

(a) Skies are expected to clear the next morning.
(b) The wedding is being held the following afternoon.
(c) The ceremony is taking place inside a church.
(d) Shelter will be provided if it rains.

39

M I applied to volunteer at the local hospital.

W I meant to, too, but I missed the deadline. Any news yet?

M I took the written test, and the results come out tomorrow.

W Wow, that's quick. Then what?

M There's a 30-hour training course for those who pass.

W I'm sure you'll make it.

Q Which is correct according to the conversation?

(a) The woman applied to volunteer at the hospital.
(b) Tomorrow is the deadline for the application.
(c) The man has already passed the written test.
(d) Selected applicants will advance to the training course.

40

M I heard you placed first in a photo contest!

W Yeah! It was my first time submitting.

M Have you ever taken any photography lessons?

W Nope, I just bought a camera and taught myself.

M Impressive! When will the photo be printed?

W In this Sunday's newspaper.

Q Which is correct about the woman according to the conversation?

(a) Her photo won second place in the competition.
(b) She had entered photo contests before.
(c) She had no formal instruction in photography.
(d) Her photo was published in last Sunday's newspaper.

41

W What do you think of these faded jeans?

M Nice! They look expensive. Did you get them online?

W No, I got some cheap off-brand jeans from the store and faded them myself.

M So they didn't have the wear-and-tear look originally?

W No. I rubbed sandpaper on the knees and hemlines.

M What a great way to mimic designer brands!

Q Which is correct about the woman according to the conversation?

(a) She purchased her jeans online.
(b) Her jeans were expensive because of their style.
(c) Her jeans were made by a designer label.
(d) She gave her jeans a worn-out look herself.

42

M I've done so much substitute teaching. I want something steadier.

W My school has a vacancy left by a retiring teacher. You should apply.

M Really? But isn't the market oversaturated with qualified applicants?

W Well, you're qualified, too!

M Thanks. Could you put in a word for me with your administration?

W Of course!

Q Which is correct according to the conversation?

(a) The man hopes to continue substitute teaching.

(b) The woman's school has found a replacement for its retiring teacher.

(c) The current job market lacks acceptable candidates.

(d) The woman agrees to recommend the man to her administrators.

43

W Oh no! I left my umbrella on the subway again.

M Didn't you just get it?

W Yeah. It's a good thing it didn't cost much.

M You must go through a lot of umbrellas.

W I constantly lose them. Don't you?

M No, I have an expensive one I've been using for years.

Q What can be inferred from the conversation?

(a) The man is careful about keeping track of his umbrella.

(b) The woman's umbrella was a gift from the man.

(c) The woman does not usually take the subway.

(d) The man prefers cheap umbrellas.

44

M I need braces. Do you know any good orthodontists?

W My family orthodontist is great.

M Where's his office located?

W In my neighborhood.

M Oh, I was hoping to find one near my house.

W Well, he's definitely worth the extra travel time.

M Don't braces involve lots of visits? I'd rather find someone closer.

Q What can be inferred about the man from the conversation?

(a) He is looking to change from his current orthodontist.

(b) He does not live in the woman's neighborhood.

(c) He is feeling reluctant about getting braces.

(d) He will visit the woman's orthodontist.

45

W The new student loan repayment scheme is brilliant.

M Agreed. Pegging repayments to income is smart.

W And payments are only required after a certain income threshold.

M I wouldn't have had to pay anything after getting my first job.

W Even the interest rate's on a sliding scale, based on graduates' income.

M Well, that's another matter. It just penalizes successful people.

Q What can be inferred from the conversation?

(a) The man objects to charging equal interest rates to all graduates.

(b) The man worked at a high-paying job right after graduation.

(c) The repayment scheme offers additional loans to graduates with low incomes.

(d) The repayment scheme assigns higher interest rates to graduates with higher incomes.

46

Are you looking for the perfect place to grow both intellectually and socially? Oslane College welcomes top students to a tight-knit community of scholars for a unique learning experience. Starting from orientation, you'll be assigned to a small group of fewer than twenty students in your major, who will be your partners in learning during your entire four years here. You'll take many classes together and develop as a group. Oslane College will create bonds that become lifelong friendships.

Q What is mainly being advertised about Oslane College?
(a) The interdisciplinary learning experiences it provides
(b) The relationships it fosters between students and instructors
(c) Its small-group-based curriculum that offers social benefits
(d) Its engaging orientation conducted in small groups

47

Athletes are often seen touching their toes or stretching their arms to warm up. But this so-called static stretching may actually increase the chances of injury. By overextending muscles and tendons, amateur athletes trick their bodies into tightening up rather than relaxing, often leading to cramps and sprains when vigorous activity begins moments later. To prevent injuries, it is best to wait until after a workout to stretch.

Q What is the main purpose of the lecture?
(a) To describe the types of injuries suffered by athletes
(b) To provide a series of exercises for safely warming up
(c) To explain why stretching before exercise can be harmful
(d) To emphasize the importance of warming up before a workout

48

Fellow students, I'd like to discuss the university's plans to demolish the Hillsborough Library. Everyone agrees that this historic building is unsuitable as a modern library. It has insufficient space for study areas and has not transitioned to the digital era smoothly. But is demolition of this campus icon really necessary? Many other universities, facing similar challenges with outdated buildings, have found new uses for them as museums or reception halls. I suggest we do likewise, to preserve one of our most treasured buildings.

Q What is the speaker's main point about the Hillsborough Library?
(a) It needs to be renovated to function as a modern library.
(b) Its demolition should be expedited to make way for a museum.
(c) Its original architecture poses a campus safety hazard.
(d) It should be re-purposed rather than torn down.

49

In-group bias, the tendency of individuals to favor those in their own group more than others, can be very destructive in a workplace. Since in-group bias often occurs when a group feels disadvantaged, managers must consider whether anyone is being treated unfairly. Is everyone being given equal opportunities? Are certain groups praised more than others? For an effective workplace, managers should monitor in-group bias to ensure that such dynamics do not develop.

Q What is the speaker's main point?
(a) In-group bias works both positively and negatively in the office.
(b) Employees should be chastised for destructive in-group behavior.
(c) Excessive scrutiny should be avoided as it can cause in-group bias.
(d) Managers should minimize in-group bias by ensuring fair treatment.

50

Protecting children from harmful advertisements requires effective legal strategies. The argument that children are a vulnerable audience will probably be ineffective in legal cases where parents have the ultimate purchasing power, since judges would likely deem parents capable of making reasonable choices. However, some products such as soda and candy are marketed directly to children as purchasers. Lawsuits focusing on curbing such advertising stand a better chance in court, and thus would be more effective for protecting children.

Q What is the speaker's main point?
(a) Advertising directed at children is detrimental to their health.
(b) Parents are ultimately responsible for making the best choices for their children.
(c) Lawsuits characterizing children as purchasers will provide better protection from ads.
(d) The legal system has failed to protect children from harmful advertising.

51

In modern art, artists may emulate famous works, but outright copying is frowned upon. However, this has not always been the case. Consider the Renaissance sculptor Pier Bonacolsi, who made high-quality replicas of classical Greek bronzes. His works were prized by the wealthy, who nicknamed him "L'Antico," meaning "the antique one." In modern times, such imitative works would be relegated to the realm of mass-market garden statuary. But clearly, a propensity for novelty has not always captivated collectors as it does today.

Q What is the main idea of the talk?
(a) Mass-market artworks should demonstrate some originality.
(b) Pier Bonacolsi's works retain their significance in modern times.
(c) The value of imitation in art has changed over time.
(d) Modern art has become too concerned with the past.

52

This week, the high-profile trial of cyber activist Marcus Valentino has run into an unexpected obstacle. After a lengthy and difficult jury selection process, the trial was set to begin on June 15. But Valentino's attorney, Lawrence Cohen, claimed that the prosecutor violated the gag order issued by the judge in an interview with local TV news reporters. The court is now delaying the start of the trial while it decides whether the prosecutor should be replaced.

Q What is mainly being reported about Marcus Valentino's trial?
(a) It is being delayed because of problems with jury selection.
(b) It has been put on hold while the prosecutor's behavior is scrutinized.
(c) The judge has issued a gag order because of its high-profile nature.
(d) The prosecutor has resigned over a conflict of interest.

53

Ladies and gentlemen, we apologize for the delay in showing the movie. There was a minor problem with the projector, which we have just resolved. To make up the lost time, we will skip the previews, but the film is going to run over by about 15 minutes. If this is an issue for anyone, you can exchange your ticket for tomorrow's screening of the movie or get a refund. Thank you for your understanding.

Q Which is correct according to the announcement?
(a) The projector is in the process of being repaired.
(b) The previews will be shown for 15 minutes.
(c) The movie will finish at its originally scheduled time.
(d) The film is being shown again the following day.

54

After monitoring online activity for the past three months, the company has learned that on average, employees spend well over 100 minutes per day on personal Internet usage. This wasted time cost us over $10,000 during this period. The employee manual clearly states that Internet usage must be job related, and though no one has been punished yet, from now on, unauthorized online activities will result in disciplinary measures.

Q Which is correct about personal Internet usage according to the announcement?
(a) Workers spend nearly 100 minutes a week on it.
(b) It costs the company $10,000 a month.
(c) The employee manual does not include a policy about it.
(d) The company has yet to take disciplinary measures because of it.

55

Over the past five years, gas prices have risen at three times the rate of household incomes, which have only increased by 15%. And lower-income families are particularly feeling the pinch. With no ability to change fixed costs like rent and utility bills, families are being forced to make cuts to areas they can control. One such area is the dining table, where fresh produce is being dropped from the menu and replaced with cheaper processed food.

Q Which is correct according to the talk?
(a) Household incomes have fallen for the last five years.
(b) Gas prices have increased by 15% in five years.
(c) Lower-income families are cutting back on food expenditures.
(d) People are replacing processed foods in their diets in a bid to save.

56

Let's look at the weekend traffic report. Road work will resume on the Lakeshore Highway this Saturday, causing two of the four eastbound lanes to be closed. The St. John Street exit will be closed, and traffic will be re-routed via the Preston Road exit. Construction is expected to be completed sometime in late September or early October. In the meantime, drivers are encouraged to plan for detours and expect delays of up to 45 minutes during peak hours.

Q Which is correct according to the news report?
(a) All eastbound lanes on the highway will be closed on Saturday.
(b) Motorists must use the St. John Street exit instead of the Preston Road exit.
(c) The exact completion date for the road work is not announced.
(d) Motorists are asked to expect 45-minute delays all day.

57

Microorganisms once thought to be unable to survive long-distance airborne journeys are turning up in the United States from as far away as Africa. The finding surprised scientists who had expected bacteria and viruses to perish from the ultraviolet radiation and harsh temperatures of the upper atmosphere. Now experts believe that these organisms are responsible for a host of ecological problems, including the destruction of coral reefs. And more organisms are expected to be carried to other places of the world as the desertification of parts of China and Africa continues.

Q Which is correct according to the talk?
(a) Microorganisms have been found to survive transoceanic journeys to America.
(b) Viruses were previously thought to be invulnerable to ultraviolet radiation.
(c) Bacteria from distant sources are now believed to facilitate coral reef growth.
(d) Desertification is expected to mitigate the long-distance transfer of bacteria.

58

Hello everyone, I need to make a brief announcement. Mrs. Pennington was scheduled to lead today's meeting in person, but pressing business matters have required her to travel to Germany. We have arranged an Internet teleconference with her while she is in Frankfurt, and because of the difference in time zones, we need to reschedule the meeting for 4 p.m. Everything else will remain unchanged, and the meeting's agenda will proceed as planned.

Q What can be inferred from the announcement?
(a) The meeting's participants are all located in different countries.
(b) Technological difficulties have delayed the meeting.
(c) Mrs. Pennington will still lead the meeting.
(d) The meeting was originally scheduled to take place in Frankfurt.

59

Last month, after a widely publicized incident of text-message bullying, the school district banned students from carrying cell phones on school property. But cell phones are simply a new medium for an age-old phenomenon, and eliminating them from schools is not going to magically eradicate bullying. Instead of banning cell phones, which do have some practical value to students, our community must take a closer look at the culture in our schools and try to encourage positive interaction among students.

Q Which statement would the speaker most likely agree with?
(a) Cell phones are not the chief cause of bullying in schools.
(b) The school district is not taking bullying seriously enough.
(c) The community should support the school district's cell phone ban.
(d) Schools have exploited cell phones' practical value.

60

Anthropologist Claude Lévi-Strauss revolutionized the concept of the primitive in his quest to reveal universal truths about mankind and civilization. Unlike his contemporaries, who believed that the "savage mind" was only concerned with the satisfaction of basic survival needs, he argued that primitive tribes possessed the capacity for logic and a thirst for knowledge. Even in the most fanciful myths of so-called primitive peoples, Lévi-Strauss found the outlines of sophisticated logic.

Q What can be inferred about Claude Lévi-Strauss from the lecture?
(a) His work corroborated the conventional wisdom about myths.
(b) He opposed depicting primitive tribes as lacking intellectual sophistication.
(c) He based his theories on unsubstantiated myths about primitive tribes.
(d) His studies portrayed primitive societies as superior to modern societies.

서울대 최신기출 4

Listening Comprehension Scripts

1

W I'm calling to speak with Ted.

M ______________________

(a) OK, I'll hold.
(b) Thanks, I appreciate the offer.
(c) Great, I'll try that.
(d) Sorry, he's on another call.

2

M Need help washing the car?

W ______________________

(a) I'd be happy to help.
(b) Sure, it looks as good as new.
(c) No, I'm just about done.
(d) Thanks for washing it.

3

W The office is so hot and stuffy.

M ______________________

(a) I know. I'm freezing.
(b) I'll open some windows.
(c) Let me put it away.
(d) Here, borrow my sweater.

4

M When will my dry cleaning be done?

W ______________________

(a) You can take it in now.
(b) This time tomorrow.
(c) About once an hour.
(d) Until I get there.

5

W Have you met your girlfriend's parents yet?

M ______________________

(a) I met her through mutual friends.
(b) I haven't introduced them yet.
(c) Yes, just after we started dating.
(d) No, they're old family friends.

6

M Is your new puppy doing well in your house?

W ______________________

(a) Great! I'm tempted to get one someday.
(b) Yeah, he's adapted quickly.
(c) Really? I didn't know you had one!
(d) Actually, the puppy belongs to me.

7

W Do my new glasses look OK on me?

M ______________________

(a) Of course. Thanks for the compliment.
(b) These? I've had them for a while.
(c) Sure. I can help you pick some out.
(d) Yeah, they really bring out your eye color.

8

M I've had trouble falling asleep lately.

W ______________________

(a) I know. I should take a rest.
(b) Maybe you should see a doctor.
(c) It's too late for that right now.
(d) Yeah, I can't stay awake, either.

9

W How thoughtless of Paul not to introduce you to his sister.

M ______________________

(a) He probably thought we were acquainted.
(b) I know. You shouldn't have ignored her like that.
(c) Yes, I appreciated his consideration.
(d) He might be too shy to introduce himself.

10

M I won't vote for any party that increases taxes.

W ______________________

(a) Well, the government has to raise money somehow.
(b) I've also been contributing more recently.
(c) Me, neither—tax policies don't affect my vote.
(d) I thought you were in favor of tax cuts, though.

11

W The books you've written are truly original.

M ______________________

(a) I prefer to read them in their original language.
(b) Wow, I'll take you up on that suggestion.
(c) Thanks. I try to avoid clichés.
(d) I'd love to find out more about them, too.

12

M Are we keeping all our knickknacks when we move?

W ______________________

(a) I hope so. That way the new place will have less junk.
(b) I'd rather not. I don't want our new place cluttered.
(c) No, we should hold onto them.
(d) Sure, I don't see why we'd move them.

13

W Can you visit Penny with me next Wednesday?

M ______________________

(a) Of course, I'll invite her.
(b) Yes, she said she would.
(c) Maybe, if I'm not scheduled to work.
(d) No, but I can visit her with you.

14

M Want to try that new Mexican restaurant tonight?

W ______________________

(a) Sure! But I don't know how to cook Mexican food.
(b) You know I can't say no to Mexican.
(c) I don't think that's on the menu.
(d) Even so, I've been wanting to try it.

15

W We're going to spend so much on this vacation.

M ______________________

(a) Next time, it can be your treat.
(b) We should've double-checked the bill before we went.
(c) The prices sure were a steal.
(d) It's OK to splurge once in a while.

16

W How long's our drive to Austin?

M About eight hours.

W I can't handle driving for that long.

M ______________________

(a) Fine, if you're sure you're up for it.
(b) Then you drive instead.
(c) OK, I'll stay in Austin.
(d) We'll take turns at the wheel.

17

M You gave an amazing performance.

W I owe it all to you.

M Me? You were the one up on stage.

W ______________________

(a) Regardless, you caught on quickly.
(b) But you helped me overcome my stage fright.
(c) That's no reason not to try.
(d) Still, it's partly my fault.

18

W Doing another crossword puzzle?
M Yep! I love them.
W Do you do one every morning?
M ______________________

(a) No, I do them on a daily basis.
(b) Of course. It's part of my routine.
(c) If you want. I still haven't solved it.
(d) Not really. I just never took to them.

19

M Hello, Starlight Planetarium.
W Hi. Do you offer group discounts?
M For groups of 15 or more. Would you like to reserve a tour now?
W ______________________

(a) Oh, that's too many. We won't all fit.
(b) I guess not, since there's more than 15 of us.
(c) I'll call back with an exact head count.
(d) We should probably reserve one instead.

20

W I need a reliable babysitter.
M Well, Julie's looking for work.
W Is she good with kids?
M ______________________

(a) Well, I wouldn't blame her.
(b) I never really tried, actually.
(c) Thanks for recommending her.
(d) You bet. She's a natural.

21

M I heard you were in an accident.
W Yeah, my car was rear-ended.
M How much will the damage cost you?
W ______________________

(a) The other party's liable, so nothing.
(b) Pretty soon, I'm sure.
(c) Not if I don't have to.
(d) I almost got into an accident.

22

W Did you get this year's student planner?
M No. Where can we get them?
W At the student center. I can get you one later.
M ______________________

(a) Right. I picked one up for each of us.
(b) Thanks. That'd save me some time.
(c) Great. That's where I got mine, too.
(d) Wow—that's practically free!

23

M Is your company still looking for a graphic designer?
W Yes, we are.
M Is previous experience required?
W ______________________

(a) Probably after a few months.
(b) That's one of the benefits we're offering.
(c) Not if you have experience.
(d) A minimum of three years.

24

W How are we faring against that newly opened salon?
M Our sales have definitely slumped.
W Any way to reverse that?
M ______________________

(a) The new salon will certainly try to.
(b) Strengthening our advertising could help.
(c) Sure, we'll want to avoid it at all costs.
(d) No need. Our sales are at their highest ever.

25

M How do you manage living by yourself?
W Just fine. It's not that hard.
M You're not lonely?
W ______________________

(a) No, I actually enjoy the company.
(b) No, that's why I prefer having roommates.
(c) Quite the opposite! I relish time alone.
(d) Once in a while, but otherwise I get lonely.

26

W An item of mine hasn't come out of the baggage carousel yet.

M Was it a suitcase?

W It was a snowboard that I checked.

M ______________________________

(a) Sorry, you can't carry that on.
(b) You can check it in at the gate.
(c) Try the over-sized baggage area.
(d) OK, just make sure it's in a case.

27

M The paper is jammed in the printer again!

W Haven't you had that printer forever?

M I've had it for a while, but it used to work fine.

W ______________________________

(a) Maybe it's time to invest in a new one.
(b) That's strange, considering it's new.
(c) No wonder it's printing so fast.
(d) It takes practice to achieve that effect.

28

W I think you rely on your brother too much.

M He does do a lot for me.

W Maybe you need to learn to do more for yourself.

M ______________________________

(a) Well, as long as it's just a one-time favor.
(b) Even so, I'd rather do things on my own.
(c) No, my goal should be more independence.
(d) Yeah, self-sufficiency is an essential skill.

29

M Why didn't you volunteer for that overtime project?

W It'd leave me no time to eat well or exercise.

M Don't you want the extra money, though?

W ______________________________

(a) Not at the expense of my health.
(b) Nonsense, I can handle the work.
(c) I know, we should've been paid by now.
(d) As long as I can earn it in overtime.

30

W We got Bob and Leslie's wedding invitation today.

M I saw that. Too bad it's being held so far away.

W So... we aren't going?

M ______________________________

(a) We'll have to try somewhere closer.
(b) We just can't spend thousands on flights to attend.
(c) I don't know. I promised them an invitation.
(d) No. Not without asking their permission first.

31

M I need to get a new passport.

W Just renew your old one by mail.

M But I lost that one, so the procedure's different.

W Did you report it missing?

M Yes. I was told I need to apply in person.

W Oh, I see.

Q What is the conversation mainly about?
(a) Reporting a missing passport
(b) Applying for a first passport
(c) Replacing a lost passport
(d) Renewing an expired passport

32

W Here's your hotel bill. Additional charges are listed at the bottom.

M Wait. I didn't order any meals.

W They were all signed to your room, though.

M But I was out all day, every day.

W Could someone you're staying with have ordered in your name?

M No, I'm here alone.

Q What is the man mainly doing in the conversation?
(a) Reporting a missing item from his room
(b) Complaining about poor room service
(c) Disputing some charges on his hotel bill
(d) Resolving a mix-up in his hotel reservation

33

M I want to get in shape, but the gym's so boring.

W You don't like using fitness machines?

M I can't stand it. It's so repetitive.

W Well, most types of exercise are pretty repetitive.

M I know. But gyms also make me feel so self-conscious.

W Yeah, it is weird to be watched by others while exercising.

Q What is the main topic of the conversation?

(a) Why the man needs to get in shape
(b) The man's plan to change to a gym he likes better
(c) Why the man dislikes working out at gyms
(d) The man's reluctance to exercise with the woman

34

M The coffee they serve here tastes really weak.

W Mine tastes fine. And I love the aroma.

M But is it worth the high prices they charge?

W Gourmet coffee is expensive everywhere.

M I guess. I just think we're overpaying for a pretentious atmosphere.

W Don't be so grumpy. I like the ambiance at this coffee shop.

Q What is the woman mainly doing in the conversation?

(a) Defending a coffee house that she enjoys
(b) Justifying her regular consumption of coffee
(c) Complaining about the price of gourmet coffee
(d) Stating her preference for another coffee house

35

W I noticed my conference expenses haven't been reimbursed.

M Sorry, the payment hasn't been sent yet.

W But I submitted the receipts three weeks ago.

M Accounting still has to authorize the transfer.

W Why the delay?

M They've been upgrading their computer systems.

Q What is the man mainly doing in the conversation?

(a) Finding out when the woman will be reimbursed
(b) Relaying confirmation of a transfer from accounting
(c) Explaining why the woman has not been reimbursed
(d) Verifying the woman's total expenses

36

M How flexible is this week's schedule?

W Why? Do you need to move something around?

M Well, I can't get this report done by Thursday.

W I thought you were given sufficient time.

M I've been staying late every night, and I still need an extra day.

W OK, I'll see if I can push the deadline back.

Q What is the man mainly doing in the conversation?

(a) Complaining about frequent changes in the schedule
(b) Requesting an extension on a project due date
(c) Confirming the final deadline for a report
(d) Asking that the report be completed by Thursday

37

M I noticed you stopped buying groceries at our local corner store.

W Yeah, I've started going to a big chain store.

M Don't you want to support local businesses, though?

W Sure. But the quality has gone downhill at that place.

M Really? I haven't noticed.

W Yeah, the produce I was getting there was terrible.

Q What is the main topic of the conversation?

(a) Why shoppers should support local corner stores

(b) Why the woman stopped patronizing a large chain store

(c) Why local businesses cannot compete with national chains

(d) Why the woman has changed where she buys groceries

38

M Are you watching the soccer match live tomorrow morning at 4?

W Yep! I've set the alarm for 3:50.

M Last time, I slept through my alarm and missed the first half.

W I can give you a wake-up call tomorrow if you want.

M Thanks, but I'll skip the live game and just watch the rebroadcast.

Q Which is correct according to the conversation?

(a) The woman set her alarm for 4 a.m.

(b) The man watched the entire previous soccer match live.

(c) The woman asks the man for a wake-up call.

(d) The man does not plan to watch the live broadcast.

39

M That hotel was so noisy! I could barely sleep.

W I know. They should've told us about the nearby construction.

M It woke me up when it started at 6 o'clock.

W Me, too. I even called the front desk and asked for a discount.

M What did they say?

W They apologized but wouldn't cut the price.

Q Which is correct according to the conversation?

(a) The man and woman were warned about the construction.

(b) The man managed to sleep through the noise.

(c) The woman complained about the noise to the hotel staff.

(d) The woman was offered a discount from the hotel.

40

W I just got back from paying my tuition at the bursar's office.

M I still need to do that.

W How are you paying?

M I tried paying online yesterday, but couldn't log into the system during peak hours.

W Yeah, I'd planned to pay by phone, but the lines were busy.

M I'll just go and pay in person, too.

Q Which is correct according to the conversation?

(a) The woman is on her way to the bursar's office.

(b) The man has yet to make his tuition payment.

(c) The woman paid her tuition over the phone.

(d) The man plans to submit his payment online.

41

M Jade Gardens opened a new restaurant downtown two months ago.
W I know. I went twice this week.
M Really? How's the atmosphere there?
W I barely noticed. I always get takeout.
M Would you recommend it?
W Sure. It's a bit pricey compared to most other Chinese places, but the food is worth it.

Q Which is correct about Jade Gardens according to the conversation?
(a) It opened its downtown location two weeks ago.
(b) The woman has not been there for two months.
(c) The woman never dines in when she goes there.
(d) It is cheaper than most other Chinese restaurants.

42

W What's the best way to drive to St. Mary's Hospital?
M Usually Lewis Street is pretty clear. When are you going?
W I have an appointment on Saturday at 9 a.m.
M Oh, Lewis Street will be closed for the farmer's market then.
W What about Waterman Street?
M Traffic's always backed up there. I'd take the subway if I were you.

Q Which is correct according to the conversation?
(a) The man usually finds Lewis Street congested.
(b) The woman's appointment is on Saturday afternoon.
(c) The farmer's market will be on Waterman Street.
(d) The man recommends the woman take public transportation.

43

W Do you think it's better to buy or lease a car?
M It depends. Each way has benefits.
W Well, I'm looking to do whatever's cheapest.
M Leasing has lower monthly payments. But buying is generally cheaper in the end.
W Would you recommend the dealership you went to?
M Definitely. They're fantastic.

Q What can be inferred from the conversation?
(a) The man prefers to lease cars.
(b) The woman is in the market for a car.
(c) The man works as a car dealer.
(d) The woman is not concerned about price.

44

W Would you like half of my sandwich?
M No, the bread contains wheat. I'm allergic.
W Oh. I didn't know that was possible.
M Yep. It's a pretty rare allergy that my father has, too.
W It must be hard to find things you can eat.
M It is. But I've always been this way, so I'm used to it.

Q What can be inferred from the conversation?
(a) The man has been avoiding wheat products since childhood.
(b) The man's mother also has the same allergy.
(c) The woman and man eat lunch together regularly.
(d) The woman knows other people with wheat allergies.

45

M Do you want to be in my movie?
W What's in it for me this time?
M Well, I've already spent my limited budget on equipment.
W So no compensation for me?
M It'd look good on your résumé.
W OK. I suppose another acting gig wouldn't hurt.

Q What can be inferred from the conversation?
(a) The man is the woman's agent.
(b) The woman will be paid for her role.
(c) The man has cast the woman in his films before.
(d) The woman wants to help direct the film rather than act.

46

The Jonestown Public Library is launching Afternoon Story Time, to be held every Saturday from 2:30 to 3:30 p.m. Storytellers will read from popular books, perform puppet shows, and do other fun reading-related activities. The event is free of charge and is a great way of getting children from the ages of 3 to 7 interested in stories and reading. We hope to see you there!

Q What is the main purpose of the announcement?
(a) To encourage parents to read to their children
(b) To invite storytellers to perform at the library
(c) To announce changes to the Story Time schedule
(d) To promote a new weekly reading event for kids

47

Multivitamins are advertised as a helpful source of necessary nutrients, but do they actually contain what they claim to? A 2011 ConsumerLab.com study examined 38 brands of multivitamins, comparing their labels to their actual chemical contents. Researchers found that 13 brands had mislabeled their products in various ways. These discrepancies mean that consumers may be missing out on vitamins and minerals they believe they're getting, or even worse, may be ingesting harmfully high levels of certain nutrients.

Q What is mainly being reported about multivitamins?
(a) They should not be relied upon as the sole source of nutrients.
(b) They should include recommended dosages on their labels.
(c) Some brands could pose health hazards because of inaccurate labels.
(d) Some brands make false claims about their shelf life.

48

Most people associate French dining with a progression of dishes—appetizer, main course, then dessert. But this style of service did not originate in France; originally, French restaurants placed dishes on the table all at once. Such presentation was impressive but inconvenient, since food sometimes went untouched or cold. In the 1880s, the French borrowed the Russian style of service in which dishes appeared following a set course order. This change produced the modern French dining experience.

Q What is the main topic of the talk?
(a) How French restaurants began serving food sequentially
(b) How chefs first popularized French cuisine
(c) The influence of French culinary customs on Russia
(d) The original style of service in Russian restaurants

49

Good morning, ladies and gentlemen. As you know, we've been in negotiations these past three months with one of our competitors in the pharmaceutical industry. Although we have done our best to acquire this company from its owners, we've been unable to arrive at terms that we think are reasonable. As a result, we've decided to abandon our efforts to take over this company and have withdrawn from negotiations with its owners.

Q What is the announcement mainly about?
(a) The halting of a bid to purchase a rival company
(b) The end of plans to open a pharmaceutical business
(c) The change in ownership of a pharmaceutical company
(d) The selling of a company's shares in its competitor

50

In light of a recent food poisoning incident, I'd like to remind cafeteria staff of the importance of preventing food-borne illness. When handling raw animal products, please be careful to avoid cross-contamination of nearby surfaces and ingredients. Handwashing and proper sanitization of utensils are essential. Also, remember that all food not served immediately must be stored at safe temperatures to prevent spoilage. Finally, always observe expiration dates strictly.

Q What is the main topic of the announcement?
(a) Procedures for safe food handling
(b) A rise in recent food-borne illnesses
(c) The cause of a particular food-poisoning incident
(d) Coping with illness from dairy and meat products

51

It has come to my attention that planning office meetings has become more challenging due to everyone's busy schedules. And having everyone take different lunch breaks doesn't help the situation. To make it easier to plan office meetings, starting next week, we'll be implementing a set lunch hour, from 12 to 1 p.m. Employees must be ready to attend meetings with a 1:15 p.m. starting time. Thanks for your cooperation.

Q What is the main topic of the announcement?
(a) Reductions to the time allotted for employee lunches
(b) Scheduling lunch breaks at a fixed time to facilitate meetings
(c) The advantages of scheduling lunch-time office meetings
(d) A plan for having employees meet for lunch

52

In this week's environmental news, the government has announced measures to reduce emissions from new power plants. While the regulations do not apply to existing plants, they essentially prevent the construction of new coal-powered plants, since these plants would not feasibly be able to comply with the new emissions standards. Natural gas facilities, however, are projected to expand as a greener alternative as they are better able to stay within the new limits.

Q What is mainly being reported?
(a) Restrictions on emissions that favor natural gas over coal-powered plants
(b) Government moves to restrict existing coal-powered plants
(c) Political maneuvers to evade issues of energy conservation
(d) The environmental effects of natural gas and coal power

53

Mel Blanc nicknamed the "man of a thousand voices," was one of the most influential voice actors in Hollywood. A shy child, Blanc was told by his teachers that he would never amount to anything. But his vocal abilities and comedic timing made him perfect for many famous cartoon roles, and he supplied the voices of Bugs Bunny, Elmer Fudd, and Barney Rubble. When he died in 1989, his voice was being heard by an estimated 20 million people every day.

Q Which is correct about Mel Blanc according to the talk?
(a) He was outspoken as a child.
(b) He succeeded despite teachers' predictions.
(c) His cartoon work involved just one famous role.
(d) His work was no longer widely broadcast by 1989.

54

In the Australian state of Victoria, koalas were nearly extinct about 100 years ago. But they've made such a strong comeback that they are now overpopulating and destroying their native eucalyptus forests. After unsuccessful attempts at relocation and surgical sterilization, scientists are turning to hormonal contraception to control koala populations. This involves giving female koalas an injection of slow-release hormones that make them infertile for approximately five years. With this, it is hoped that the population will stabilize at a sustainable level.

Q Which is correct according to the talk?
(a) Koalas overpopulated Victoria about 100 years ago.
(b) The attempt to bring koalas back to Victoria has been unsuccessful.
(c) No previous measures have been taken to control koala populations.
(d) The hormonal injection's effect lasts for about five years.

55

Many people think Cinco de Mayo is a holiday celebrating Mexico's independence from colonial rule. But the holiday actually commemorates the 1862 battle at the city of Puebla, wherein Mexican forces successfully repelled French attackers, and Mexico was a fully sovereign nation at the time. When Mexico failed to pay back loans it had borrowed from France, the French invaded Mexico in an attempt to take it over. The battle at Puebla was won by the Mexicans, but France later won the war, governing the country for three years.

Q Which is correct according to the talk?
(a) Cinco de Mayo marks the end of Mexico's colonial period.
(b) France fought Mexico to get out of paying back its loans.
(c) The battle at Puebla won the war for the Mexican forces.
(d) Mexico was ruled by the French for three years.

56

Don't miss out on Homestore's third annual Labor Day appliance sale! To celebrate the end of summer, all brands of home appliances are marked down, with savings of up to 50% on refrigerators, washers, dryers, and much more. These great deals aren't available for purchases from our online shop, so come discover the discounts waiting for you! All our Homestore locations will stay open three hours later than usual during the sale. And hurry—the sale starts Saturday and ends Monday, so these deals won't last!

Q Which is correct about Homestore according to the advertisement?
(a) This is their first ever Labor Day appliance sale.
(b) The sale applies to items purchased on their website.
(c) They will extend their opening hours during the sale.
(d) Their Labor Day sale will last for a week.

57

On June 5, 2012, Venus passed between Earth and the sun, something it only does twice every 120 years. This is known as an astronomical transit. During the Venus transit, the planet's silhouette became visible in front of the sun for seven minutes, and the sun's light dimmed slightly here on Earth. Similarly, outside our solar system, transits also occur with other stars. When light from distant stars dims for several minutes, astronomers know that a transit is likely happening. If it happens at regular intervals, this indicates the presence of an orbiting planet.

Q Which is correct about astronomical transits according to the talk?
(a) Venus completes one around Earth every 120 years.
(b) They slightly augment the sun's light.
(c) Those outside our solar system cannot be observed.
(d) They can help confirm the existence of other planets.

58

Parents in Western cultures tend to believe that sleeping in the same bed with their baby jeopardizes the baby's health. In North America particularly, public health agencies have waged intimidating ad campaigns to suggest that co-sleeping poses a suffocation risk to infants. However, when proper precautions are taken, it is not a risky practice. Such co-sleeping was widespread until the nineteenth century and is still the norm around the world. It allows for easier breast-feeding, as well as more stable sleep for both baby and parents.

Q Which statement would the speaker most likely agree with?
(a) The benefits of co-sleeping need to be verified by research.
(b) Campaigns against co-sleeping have exaggerated its risk.
(c) Co-sleeping confers greater advantages to babies than to parents.
(d) The abandonment of co-sleeping is likely to spread internationally.

59

At today's educational research conference, I want to talk about how schools overemphasize analytical skills. In many classrooms, students are rewarded for being logical and punished for daydreaming. Studies show, however, that most effective learning takes place when creative and analytical thinking are blended into a kind of creative analysis. Because students' creative faculties are not engaged in many lessons, creative analysis does not occur, leading many to lose interest.

Q Which statement would the speaker most likely agree with?
(a) Creative skills are more valuable than analytical skills.
(b) Most students unconsciously favor analytical behavior.
(c) Educators have overestimated the importance of creative analysis.
(d) Analytical skills and creativity should be balanced in classroom instruction.

60

To decrease drunk driving casualties, France has passed a law requiring all motorists to carry a breathalyzer kit in their vehicles. Drivers can test themselves to determine whether they are within the nation's alcohol limit of 50 milligrams per 100 milliliters of blood. With the exception of mopeds, all vehicles will be subject to the new law, including those arriving from other countries. Once the law goes into effect, police will conduct random checks to ensure drivers are carrying a breathalyzer.

Q What can be inferred from the report?
(a) Mopeds will be banned under the new regulations.
(b) Visitors to France will not be exempt from the new law.
(c) Most drivers in France already carry portable breathalyzer kits.
(d) France's alcohol limit is stricter than most other European nations' limits.

서울대 최신기출 5

Listening Comprehension Scripts

1

W This is Vicky calling for Alex Jones. Is he in the office?

M ______________________________

(a) I'll get back to him.
(b) OK, thanks for the reminder.
(c) He no longer works here.
(d) Sorry, Vicky's in a meeting.

2

M Excuse me, is the Steakhouse Buffet this way?

W ______________________________

(a) Sorry, I've never heard of it.
(b) I'm sure you'd be welcome.
(c) Yes, with a reservation.
(d) Only when I go there.

3

W It's freezing—are you going to wear that light jacket?

M ______________________________

(a) Just borrow mine instead.
(b) You're right. This one's too thick.
(c) The heat's bothering me, too.
(d) I'm fine. It keeps me warm enough.

4

M You're still struggling with that math problem?

W ______________________________

(a) Yeah, I don't have any left.
(b) I'm waiting for it to finish.
(c) No, I can't seem to repair it.
(d) I'm not quitting until I solve it.

5

W You're welcome to stay with me next time you're in town.

M ______________________________

(a) I'd love to, if it's no trouble.
(b) It wasn't a long visit.
(c) Of course my offer still stands.
(d) Sure, we're happy to host you.

6

M Wow! How did you get these front row seats?

W ______________________________

(a) Even waiting in line, I had no luck.
(b) Who knows? I've never sat up front.
(c) They were a gift from my company.
(d) I checked but they were sold out.

7

W Ian and I are looking for two more people for tennis. Interested?

M ______________________________

(a) I'm sure Ian's up for it.
(b) I'm in, but we'll need a fourth.
(c) Definitely. We'll only need two more then.
(d) If it's between you two, I'd ask Ian.

8

M The boss says he wants this project done within the hour.

W ______________________________

(a) Oh, I didn't know it was already done.
(b) OK, I'll start it an hour later.
(c) Seriously? It's nowhere near completed.
(d) Really? Sounds like it's overdone.

9

W Can you hand in your notice earlier when requesting leave?

M ______________________________

(a) All right, but I haven't left yet.
(b) OK, sorry I didn't request it sooner.
(c) Yep. I'll notify you when I'm back.
(d) No problem. I won't stay late tonight.

10

M Can you believe how rude that store clerk was?

W ______________________________

(a) Sure, you can count on their service.
(b) I know. I'm never setting foot in there again.
(c) Yeah. Too bad we can't shop there more often.
(d) That's not true. I was quite nice to him!

11

W This video game seems too violent for kids.

M ______________________________

(a) That's because they stopped playing.
(b) Yeah, even I find it disturbing.
(c) Even so, it has too much violence.
(d) I know. It really should be for younger audiences.

12

M Have you seen Mike anywhere?

W ______________________________

(a) I don't recognize him.
(b) I saw him leaving for lunch.
(c) I'll ask him and let you know.
(d) Oh, I suppose I could.

13

W I was too harsh with Luke, wasn't I?

M ______________________________

(a) You could've gone easier on him.
(b) Well, he didn't mean to be.
(c) Yeah, he owes you an apology.
(d) Only if he learns his lesson.

14

M Isn't it hard for you, working and being a mother?

W ______________________________

(a) Maybe once I have kids.
(b) I'll be fine after I get back to work.
(c) I've gotten better at juggling the two.
(d) It's actually easier than working.

15

W I heard Jenna just had surgery. What's her prognosis?

M ______________________________

(a) She'll save that as a last resort.
(b) She hasn't decided about it yet.
(c) She's expected to recover quickly.
(d) She won't find out until the deadline.

16

M I'll get the check.

W No, dinner's on me this time.

M I'll cover the next meal, then.

W ______________________________

(a) I've already paid for it.
(b) Sure, it's a deal.
(c) No, I'm not that hungry.
(d) I'm sorry to do that.

17

W What a surprise to see you shopping here!

M I'm just getting some Christmas presents.

W But you don't live around here.

M ______________________________

(a) Well, it's too far to drive.
(b) I happened to be in the area.
(c) I wasn't in the mood to shop.
(d) Sorry, I don't know the neighborhood.

18

M Why are you fiddling with your phone?
W The screen keeps freezing.
M Did you try turning it off and on?
W ______________________

(a) I'm waiting until the contract finishes.
(b) The battery's fully charged, though.
(c) No, even when I turn it off.
(d) Yeah, to no avail.

19

W Do you use antivirus software?
M Yes. Virus-Clean. It's free.
W Does it work well?
M ______________________

(a) I couldn't say firsthand.
(b) Not if you think it's a virus.
(c) Definitely. I recommend it.
(d) No, use a free one.

20

M How about watching a musical tonight?
W Well, I'm picky about musicals.
M I was thinking of a '50s classic'.
W ______________________

(a) Great, I love older ones.
(b) Sure. Though fifty seems a bit much.
(c) OK, but I'd rather watch a musical.
(d) Fine. I'll make it up later.

21

W What kind of car should we get?
M I really want a hybrid.
W Aren't they expensive, though?
M ______________________

(a) At first, yes. But fuel is cheaper long-term.
(b) Not if you take price into account.
(c) Well, I'd never charge that much.
(d) They were, but I got used to them.

22

M Excuse me, do I go through customs when I transfer in LA?
W Is that your point of entry to the US?
M Yes. Then I'm flying to Chicago.
W ______________________

(a) Only if there are long lines.
(b) No, you don't have to declare that.
(c) Then yes, take your bags through customs in LA.
(d) Just list your final destination as Chicago.

23

W Have you been following the show *All My Friends*?
M Not this season. I've been too busy. How's it progressing?
W Great! I was curious to know what you thought.
M ______________________

(a) I'll tell you once I catch up.
(b) I haven't missed a single episode.
(c) I think you'll like it a lot.
(d) The last season was better.

24

M What'd I miss at the meeting?
W They're scaling back all departments.
M Really? Did they say when?
W ______________________

(a) No, just some of them.
(b) Probably in order to cut costs.
(c) That hasn't been decided.
(d) Yes, right up until last week's meeting.

25

W Is it true you published a book recently?
M Yeah, sort of.
W What do you mean?
M ______________________

(a) I contributed an essay to an edited volume.
(b) I wouldn't call yourself an author just yet.
(c) It wasn't the first one I've published.
(d) I'm just reading it now, actually.

26

M Let's get a puppy.
W I'm allergic. I'd be sneezing all the time.
M Really? Have you gotten tested?
W ______________________________

(a) That doesn't mean we'll be good pet owners.
(b) It depends on what kind of pet we get.
(c) No, but it always happens when I'm around dogs.
(d) Yes, it's had all the vaccinations.

27

W How long is your business trip, again?
M I'm not sure. We're still scheduling meetings.
W Just give me an estimate.
M ______________________________

(a) The flight is 12 hours altogether.
(b) Yeah, it'll be over by then.
(c) We'll probably have two meetings a day.
(d) It should be no more than ten days.

28

M Those sneakers cost $400!
W Well, they're endorsed by a famous basketball player.
M But how can people afford them in this weak economy?
W ______________________________

(a) There's always a market for expensive items like that.
(b) I wouldn't blame that on the economy.
(c) Maybe if an athlete sponsored them.
(d) That's why they are affordable.

29

W Do you practice your music in this small apartment?
M Yeah. My piano's not really portable.
W Don't the neighbors complain?
M ______________________________

(a) Actually, they've complimented my playing.
(b) No, I don't bother them with complaints.
(c) Oh, they're not that loud usually.
(d) Yeah, that's why I only practice here.

30

M I'm applying for a GoldExpress card.
W Don't. You have enough credit cards already.
M But it offers rewards for every dollar spent.
W ______________________________

(a) Then it's twice as expensive.
(b) You know I don't need those.
(c) The benefits you'll get are negligible.
(d) It's not worth it to turn down a line of credit.

31

W Hello, Gabriel's Plumbing?
M Yes, how may I help you?
W This is Susan Kendrick. I've been waiting for your plumber for an hour.
M I'm sorry. He must be caught in traffic.
W Well, I can't wait much longer.
M My apologies. He should be arriving shortly.

Q What is the woman mainly complaining about?
(a) A plumbing job that took a long time
(b) A plumber not showing up on time
(c) A repair job that was unsatisfactory
(d) A phone line that was busy for too long

32

M Would your company sponsor our softball team?
W We'd consider it. What benefits are there?
M Brand exposure. And you're supporting the community.
W How much would it cost?
M We have two sponsorship packages: basic and premium.
W Then we might consider the basic one.

Q What is the man mainly doing in the conversation?
(a) Describing various donation packages
(b) Convincing the woman to become a softball coach
(c) Persuading the woman to join his softball team
(d) Seeking financial support for his sports team

33

W That movie wasn't what I was expecting.

M Yeah, from the poster, it looked like an action movie.

W I know! The trailer was full of action scenes, too.

M Who would've guessed it was actually a romance?

W A slow-moving one at that. No suspense at all.

M Right. I hate being deceived like that.

Q What is the conversation mainly about?

(a) The lack of romance in a movie
(b) Why a movie's ending was unexpected
(c) A discrepancy between movie reviews
(d) How a movie's advertising was misleading

34

M Where are you getting the textbook for our physics class?

W The campus bookstore probably. Why?

M Just wondering. I'm trying to get it at a discount.

W The bookstore has a 10% sale going on.

M Only 10%? Do you think it'd be cheaper online?

W I'm not sure. It'd be easy to find out, though.

Q What are the man and woman mainly discussing?

(a) Which book to buy for their physics course
(b) Where to get the best price for a textbook
(c) Whether or not to purchase a physics course text
(d) How to get a good resale price for their textbooks

35

W Can I ask a favor while I'm away on vacation?

M Sure. Need me to swing by and check up on your apartment?

W Actually, I was wondering if you could just stay there.

M For the whole three weeks?

W Yeah, I'd feel better knowing someone's there.

M OK—I'm sure my roommates won't miss me too much.

Q What is the woman mainly asking the man to do?

(a) Move in and become her roommate
(b) Accompany her on her vacation
(c) Take care of her home by occupying it while she is away
(d) Check up on her place occasionally while she is on vacation

36

M We need to start organizing our meetings better.

W How about summarizing the main points at intervals?

M OK. How would that work?

W Someone could announce a summary every 20 minutes or so.

M That's good. It would keep the discussion on track.

W Exactly. And everyone can follow along.

Q What is the woman mainly doing in the conversation?

(a) Helping the man with the meeting's agenda
(b) Suggesting an organizational strategy for meetings
(c) Questioning the man's rules for business meetings
(d) Volunteering to summarize meeting agendas

37

M This report says 40% of food in the US is wasted.
W Really? Wow, that's a lot.
M Well, I think retailers are mostly at fault.
W True. Supermarkets do overstock fresh produce.
M And so much of it spoils before it's sold.
W Not to mention all of the ready-to-eat food they can't sell.

Q What are the man and woman mainly discussing?
(a) Why large portions should be blamed for food waste
(b) How retailers contribute to food waste
(c) Reasons why only 40% of food is consumed
(d) Increases in US food consumption

38

W Check out the designer purse I got today.
M Looks nice. Was it expensive?
W It's from this season's collection, and I got it for only $150.
M That's its retail price?
W No, the manager took $50 off because of a small flaw.
M Well, that's still too much for a purse.

Q Which is correct about the purse according to the conversation?
(a) The woman bought it yesterday.
(b) The woman only paid $50 for it.
(c) It is from last season's collection.
(d) It was discounted because of a defect.

39

W Want to taste this chocolate? It has half the fat of normal chocolate.
M Sounds weird. Is the fat replaced with an artificial substitute?
W Pure fruit juice, actually.
M Does it taste the same as normal chocolate?
W It has a fruity taste, but the texture is the same. And it even costs less.
M OK, I guess I'll try it.

Q Which is correct about the chocolate according to the conversation?
(a) It does not contain any fat.
(b) It uses artificial substitutes to replace fruit juice.
(c) Its texture is identical to that of regular chocolate.
(d) It is more expensive than normal chocolate.

40

W Did you close the car windows after we got home tonight?
M Yes, was I not supposed to?
W Remember? Mike spilled water on the backseat.
M I forgot! And we were going to air it out.
W I'll go out and roll them down.
M Better not—there's rain in the forecast tonight.

Q Which is correct according to the conversation?
(a) The man forgot to leave the car windows open.
(b) The woman accidentally spilled water on the backseat.
(c) The man asks the woman to go out to open the car windows.
(d) The weather is predicted to be dry during the night.

41

M Hey Becca! This is the first time I've seen you this semester.
W Yeah, I've been really busy with my internship.
M Really? I'm starting my internship next semester.
W Well, good luck. I can't wait for mine to be over.
M Why? Aren't you getting an income for your work?
W I am, but I'd still rather just be doing coursework.

Q Which is correct according to the conversation?
(a) The man and woman encountered each other frequently this semester.
(b) The man will begin his internship later this semester.
(c) The woman's internship is unpaid.
(d) The woman prefers studying to doing an internship.

42

W Hi, I ordered a sweater online, but this shirt was delivered, so I'd like a refund.
M Did you contact our online store for our return policy?
W No, I wanted to get the refund in person.
M Well, we don't offer refunds here in the store, only exchanges.
W Really? So I have to ship it back to get a refund?
M Yes. But they'll give you one, no questions asked.

Q Which is correct according to the conversation?
(a) The woman ordered the wrong item from the online store.
(b) The woman has already contacted the online store for a refund.
(c) The man cannot give the woman a direct refund.
(d) The online store does not offer refunds for returned goods.

43

M Do hotels around here offer free shuttles from the airport?
W Most do. Where are you staying, sir?
M I'll be at the Marion Hotel.
W They have a shuttle—it leaves from the main arrivals area.
M OK. And the ride isn't too long?
W Check with the driver—I think it's about 5 minutes.

Q What can be inferred from the conversation?
(a) The woman works as a shuttle driver.
(b) The man's hotel is not far from the airport.
(c) The woman and man are traveling together.
(d) The man usually stays at the Marion Hotel.

44

W Where are you thinking of going for our vacation?
M I don't know, maybe somewhere around here.
W You don't want to go back to Mexico?
M Not after what happened there last summer.
W But we'll stay at a fancy resort this time. The food will be much safer.
M Maybe, but I'm not interested in being hospitalized again.

Q What can be inferred from the conversation?
(a) The woman has never been to Mexico.
(b) The man thinks traveling domestically is boring.
(c) The man had a foodborne illness while in Mexico.
(d) The woman is not interested in trying food in Mexico.

45

M These job applications I'm reviewing are atrocious.
W Why's that?
M They're plagued with poor grammar.
W Small errors don't matter, though.
M In this job they do. We can't have editors who let mistakes slide.
W True. Still, you're really narrowing the candidate pool.

Q What can be inferred from the conversation?
(a) The man is ruling out applicants based on grammar.
(b) The woman is hoping to be hired as an editor.
(c) The job in question requires applicants to teach writing.
(d) The man is interviewing the woman for a job.

46

The City Parks and Recreation Commission has a vision to create a new park in the Jackson Heights neighborhood. To this end, the commission is hosting a competition for a design that will take into consideration the area's history as well as the park's functionality. The winning design will be chosen by the commission on August 1, so submissions must be received by July 1. For further information, please visit our website.

Q What is the main purpose of the announcement?
(a) To invite applications for a job maintaining parks
(b) To announce the winner of a design competition
(c) To seek public support for a newly opened park
(d) To invite design submissions for a new park

47

In discussions of the environment, the effects of carbon emissions on the atmosphere receive a great deal of attention. However, nitrogen also has a profound environmental impact, and the public should become more aware of this. Factory nitrogen emissions cause acid rain, and runoff of nitrogen fertilizer used in agriculture pollutes waterways, endangering many aquatic species. Nitrogen pollutants have already exceeded safe levels, and fragile ecosystems are being irreversibly affected.

Q What is the talk mainly about?
(a) The role agriculture plays in nitrogen pollution
(b) The threat nitrogen poses to the environment
(c) The damage nitrogen is doing to agriculture
(d) The ways nitrogen and carbon interact to pollute the atmosphere

48

As a society, we need to revamp the way kids are taught. Accustomed to having continuous access to information via the Internet, our youth have cognitive capabilities that are different from previous generations. For instance, kids today are often accused of having short attention spans. While that might be true, they also demonstrate a remarkable ability to multitask, and they understand how to use the wisdom of the crowd to approach problem-solving. Teachers should recognize these abilities and integrate them into their pedagogical strategies.

Q What is the speaker's main point?
(a) Schools should teach children how to think without relying on the Internet.
(b) The Internet has harmed children by shortening their attention spans.
(c) The Internet should be harnessed as a tool for training teachers.
(d) Education should adapt to the cognitive abilities of Internet-savvy kids.

49

Author Brent Jacobson's latest novel *The Thrillseeker* is a disappointing example of what happens when successful genre writers don't stick to what they're good at. Venturing into the science fiction genre for the first time, Jacobson loses the touch that made his historical novels so wonderful. His attempt at sci-fi is marred by a clear lack of technical knowledge and an inability to create believable futuristic scenarios. Let's hope Jacobson goes back to writing historical fiction, a genre where his knowledge of the past serves him well.

Q What is the speaker's main point about *The Thrillseeker*?
(a) It would have been better without so much historical detail.
(b) It is spoiled by writing that is overly colloquial.
(c) Its author failed in his attempt to master a new genre.
(d) Its plot was based too much on a futuristic premise.

50

Today, I'd like to talk about drug research carried out by pharmaceutical companies. Many doctors have become wary of these companies' influence and are unfairly skeptical, even dismissive, of the research they sponsor. Admittedly, there have been occasional ethical and scientific lapses in such studies. But drug companies have conducted a huge number of clinical trials, and the vast majority are legitimate. As medical professionals, we need to set our prejudices aside and evaluate published research on its own merits.

Q What is the speaker's main point?
(a) Pharmaceutical companies have been unfairly dismissive of doctors' criticisms.
(b) Excessive skepticism about drug companies' studies is unwarranted.
(c) Drug companies have used their research budgets to wield undue influence.
(d) Doctors should not endorse drugs without researching them extensively.

51

When interviewing job candidates, do you ask a lot of rapid-fire questions? If so, you may be making a mistake. Try following American journalist Jim Lehrer's advice. When interviewing public figures, Lehrer says he always waits for five seconds after a reply before asking his next question, because it allows interviewees to go into more depth. If you try this in your next interview, you'll find that candidates usually expand on their answers in a way that yields valuable information—and helps make your decision easier.

Q What is the talk mainly about?
(a) A strategy for making interview questions more relevant
(b) A technique for eliciting more detailed responses from job interviewees
(c) How interviewees make the mistake of asking too many questions
(d) How a journalist's advice can help job candidates in interviews

52

Despite ample photographic documentation of the moon landing in 1969, some people still question whether it really occurred. Skeptics suggest that the photos are fake, questioning the lack of stars in the sky and saying that the flag the astronauts put up should not have been waving, since there is no wind on the moon. But such conspiracy theories are misguided. Stars were not visible because the bright sunlight on the moon's surface obscured them, and the flag was moving because of the motion caused by astronauts placing it in the soil.

Q What is the main purpose of the talk?
(a) To explain why some people think the moon landing was faked
(b) To refute the claims of those who deny the moon landing
(c) To show how hoax theories spread quickly among skeptics
(d) To argue that conspiracy theories should be taken seriously

53

Attention employees: I'd like to remind you that the inside of our office is a completely smoke-free environment. Smoking is permitted only on our company's outdoor premises, provided that it is not within thirty yards of the building. Anyone found violating this rule will be fined $20 for the first offense and $50 for each subsequent violation. After a third violation, employees' personnel records will reflect their offenses. Thank you for your cooperation.

Q Which is correct according to the announcement?
(a) Smoking is allowed on some parts of the company's property.
(b) Employees can smoke anywhere outside the building.
(c) Initial noncompliance with the rule will cost $50.
(d) Punishment for smoking is limited to monetary fines.

54

The distinction between clinical depression and a bout of the "blues" can be blurry, sometimes even for medical professionals. However, official medical guidelines have a firm definition for depression. They classify clinical depression as a genuine physical illness that alters brain chemistry, and list depression's physiological symptoms, such as significant weight loss or gain, insomnia, and excessive sleeping. In order to be diagnosed with clinical depression, the guidelines state that at least five of the nine symptoms must present themselves within two weeks of each other.

Q Which is correct according to the lecture?
(a) Clinical depression does not manifest itself physically.
(b) Both upward and downward changes in weight can indicate depression.
(c) Depression guidelines do not take sleep patterns into consideration.
(d) All symptoms must be present simultaneously for a depression diagnosis.

55

Tired of TV news? Then the G1000 satellite radio is for you! Tune in to one of over a thousand channels from around the world. With 200 channels exclusively dedicated to news, the G1000 gives you up-to-the-minute reports. Program up to 20 preset stations and listen to them with the push of a button. And since it only requires four AA batteries, you're free from needing a wall outlet, so you can take your G1000 with you anywhere!

Q Which is correct about the G1000 radio according to the advertisement?
(a) It accesses channels from various countries.
(b) It offers 1,000 channels dedicated to news.
(c) It can have 200 stations preset on it.
(d) It must be plugged into a power outlet to work.

56

In the early days of Manhattan's expansion, city commissioners set about organizing its streets. In 1811, they proposed a plan involving a grid design originally conceived by the New York State Legislature, and the plan was implemented later that year. This was Manhattan's first successful design proposal, as earlier designs that were proposed were rejected by the city council. Of course, the regular, rigid street patterns of the grid did earn it considerable criticism, but not enough to stop its implementation.

Q Which is correct about Manhattan's Commissioners' Plan of 1811 according to the talk?
(a) It was implemented a year after it was proposed.
(b) It was originally conceived by the legislature of New York State.
(c) It was the first design to be proposed to the city council.
(d) It was praised for its rigid, regular street patterns.

57

Torrential rains stranded hikers for hours on a back-country trail in Sunrise National Park yesterday, leading Governor Patrick Smith to question the park's lack of a weather warning system. The hikers left for their 12-hour trek accompanied by a guide, unaware of the severe thunderstorm warning that had already been announced by the national weather service. Fortunately, none of the twenty hikers suffered any injuries. In light of the incident, Governor Smith is demanding that a park-wide alert system be set up immediately.

Q Which is correct according to the news report?
(a) The park did not have a weather warning system.
(b) No guide was available to go with the group of hikers.
(c) The storm warning was announced after the hikers set out.
(d) Twenty of the hikers suffered injuries while stranded.

58

Earlier today, the prestigious Blackstone College announced that it will be making its gym facilities available to the Adamsville community. This marks one of several initiatives by the college to become more integrated into the community, a change from its longstanding exclusivity. Also, Adamsville residents will be able to enjoy select free exercise classes offered by the sports center. College president Simon Heath has hinted that residents may find him stretching alongside them in next month's yoga course.

Q What can be inferred about Blackstone College from the news report?
(a) Its facilities used to be closed to community residents not affiliated with it.
(b) It will not allow staff to participate in community exercise classes.
(c) It has recently moved into the Adamsville area.
(d) Its programs are funded by the community.

59

Attention all globetrotters! This month at Fantastic Travel our special location is Paris. We're offering incredible discounts on plane tickets, hotels, and everything you need to enjoy Paris. We have a ten-day vacation already set up, so just let us know your travel dates! Or stop in and plan your own Paris trip while still taking advantage of our fantastic deals. Not interested in Paris? Check with us next month for an entirely new set of deals somewhere on the globe.

Q What can be inferred from the advertisement?
(a) Fantastic Travel has the same set of discounts every month.
(b) The travel package does not include tours in Paris.
(c) Travelers do not have to stick to the prearranged itinerary.
(d) Fantastic Travel specializes in travel to France.

60

I am alarmed by the recent proposals to substantially increase taxes on middle- and lower-income workers. Advocates of these proposals claim they are an unfortunate necessity in the face of our nation's flagging economy. However, the government needs to take more from those who have more, not from those who are in need, especially in a financial crisis. The nation's highest earners have been paying absurdly low taxes, and it's time they contributed their long-due share.

Q Which statement would the speaker most likely agree with?
(a) All income brackets will be impacted equally by the proposed tax hike.
(b) A flagging economy calls for higher taxes on lower-income workers.
(c) Those above a certain income bracket should pay higher taxes.
(d) Current tax rates are fair and should remain unchanged.

서울대 최신기출 6

Listening Comprehension Scripts

1

M Have you read the poem I wrote?
W ______________________

(a) Sorry, not yet.
(b) Keep reading it.
(c) I'll write one.
(d) He's my favorite poet.

2

W Do you warm up before exercising?
M ______________________

(a) Yes, use mine.
(b) No, but check first.
(c) Definitely. It's essential!
(d) Only before I warm up.

3

M What do you usually have for breakfast?
W ______________________

(a) Anytime you're free.
(b) Thanks, but I ordered already.
(c) It's not that unusual.
(d) Nothing. I skip it.

4

W Hello, I'm calling to speak with Dave.
M ______________________

(a) Oops, I dialed incorrectly.
(b) Not at the moment.
(c) He just stepped out.
(d) Tell him to hold.

5

M May I check an extra bag on the flight?
W ______________________

(a) Try the baggage carousel.
(b) No, it isn't required.
(c) Yes, for a fee.
(d) I should've booked in advance.

6

W Is the storm expected to hit tonight?
M ______________________

(a) It was smaller than we expected.
(b) According to the forecast, it is.
(c) No wonder you're soaked!
(d) I know better than to do that.

7

M Would I be able to catch an airport taxi to my hotel?
W ______________________

(a) Sure. There are plenty lined up outside the terminal.
(b) Yes, wherever there's a room available.
(c) No, there's only one way to the airport.
(d) Well, you can take the shuttle from your hotel.

8

W I don't use my gym membership enough.
M ______________________

(a) True, you hardly ever go.
(b) Fine, if you don't mind paying extra.
(c) Perhaps you should join.
(d) Sorry, I need to cancel my membership.

9

M Are there any playgrounds in your neighborhood?
W ______________________

(a) No, the children are on the playground.
(b) Unfortunately, none that I can spare.
(c) Yes, two within walking distance.
(d) Sure, I'm new to the neighborhood.

10

W Excuse me. Has the number 3 bus come recently?

M ________________________

(a) As often as you wish.
(b) It's more recent than that.
(c) I've taken it many times.
(d) Not in the last 15 minutes.

11

M How can the administration justify these tuition hikes?

W ________________________

(a) Agreed. These rates can't get any better.
(b) It's the administration that's increasing them, actually.
(c) True, but it means cutbacks in tuition.
(d) I know. There's no excuse for raising fees.

12

W Could you help me set up this ladder?

M ________________________

(a) I'll give you a hand in just a minute.
(b) Yes, you've got my permission.
(c) Sure. I really appreciate the hand.
(d) Only if you're done using it.

13

M We shouldn't have had second helpings. I'm stuffed!

W ________________________

(a) But we don't have space for more.
(b) Order another serving for yourself, then.
(c) No kidding. We definitely overdid it.
(d) I wish they'd gotten the order right.

14

W I'm stumped on this last calculus problem. Any ideas?

M ________________________

(a) I'm just as lost as you are.
(b) That sounds correct, but test it out first.
(c) Yes, thanks for your help.
(d) If you don't mind showing me how to.

15

M Have I got what it takes to start my own business?

W ________________________

(a) With your determination, of course.
(b) You can take as many as you like.
(c) I'd keep it off your résumé for now.
(d) Granted, you'd run your own business, in that case.

16

W Is this the Jameson Building?
M It's the Royal Bank Building.
W Isn't this 243 Elm Street?
M ________________________

(a) Thanks for the information.
(b) Royal Bank is a block away.
(c) No, it's 243 Oak Street.
(d) Yes, it's a nice building.

17

M Any plans for the summer?
W I'm going to France for a friend's wedding.
M Have you been there before?
W ________________________

(a) It'll be my first time.
(b) I can't believe you're getting married.
(c) I wish I were going.
(d) The wedding was wonderful.

18

W That movie was great!
M I thought the dialogue was terrible.
W Really? I didn't think it was all that bad.
M ________________________

(a) That makes two of us.
(b) You shouldn't be so negative.
(c) I did. It was totally unrealistic.
(d) Then maybe I will see it.

19

M Welcome to the party, Kim.
W Thanks. Glad to be here.
M Was it easy to find the place?
W ______________________________

(a) I found it rather pleasing.
(b) No. It wasn't there, actually.
(c) Yeah, I had good directions.
(d) It was OK for a party.

20

W Was your school reunion fun?
M Yes, but also strange. We've all changed so much.
W In what way?
M ______________________________

(a) I wish I could've made it.
(b) Everyone looks so different.
(c) The nostalgia kept us going for hours.
(d) We instantly connected.

21

M How was your doctor's appointment?
W He told me my blood pressure's too high.
M Do you know what's to blame for it?
W ______________________________

(a) Keep exercising it.
(b) No, I don't blame the doctor.
(c) Stress is my best guess.
(d) Medicine might help.

22

W The realtor has more homes for us to look at.
M But my schedule's packed this week.
W We might miss out if we wait, though.
M ______________________________

(a) You're right. We can wait a bit longer.
(b) OK, I'll make time for it, then.
(c) Just tell the realtor they're not for sale.
(d) Still, this week is better for me.

23

M Are you going to continue watching TV?
W No, nothing good's on.
M Can I turn it off, then?
W ______________________________

(a) Please, go right ahead.
(b) I haven't seen that episode.
(c) Yes, there must be something on TV.
(d) I prefer watching it by myself.

24

W I haven't heard from Uncle Ralph recently.
M Me, neither. It's been about a month.
W I wonder what's up with him.
M ______________________________

(a) You're wrong. He hasn't been in touch.
(b) We ought to call him and find out.
(c) I know. I wish he'd stop calling so often.
(d) That's why I've been hearing him out.

25

M Could you help me with this month's rent?
W I wish I were able to, but I can't.
M Just this one time?
W ______________________________

(a) Don't worry, I'll return it soon.
(b) No, but there are places for rent.
(c) All right, I'll let you pay just this once.
(d) Sorry, money is tight for me, too.

26

W The weekend went by so quickly.
M Yes, all I did was relax at home.
W Didn't you feel like going out?
M ______________________________

(a) Well, I reserve that for weekends.
(b) Yes, but I needed to spend time at work.
(c) No, staying in was just what I needed.
(d) A little. I would've loved to relax.

27

M I heard you ran into a bear while hiking!

W Yes, but thankfully it was at a distance.

M How did it react to the encounter?

W ______________________________

(a) Close enough to see its face.
(b) It was a noteworthy experience nonetheless.
(c) Mostly it ignored me and kept on its way.
(d) It was the best way to handle it.

28

W I have to go to the immigration office to renew my visa tomorrow.

M Prepare yourself. The lines there are brutal.

W Do you think I'll be able to get out by 10 a.m.?

M ______________________________

(a) You really should wait your turn.
(b) No, it's best to process your visa quickly.
(c) If you get there early, perhaps.
(d) It's outrageous that they made you late.

29

M I hate it when people leave their dogs in the car.

W On hot summer days, it seems pretty heartless.

M There must be a law against it, right?

W ______________________________

(a) Truly, I'd rather it were legalized.
(b) In that case, there's no way to obey it.
(c) It's easiest for dog-owners.
(d) If there isn't, there really should be.

30

W Did you buy the concert tickets?

M Yes, they were $60 apiece. Pay me back whenever.

W Sure, but didn't we decide on getting the $90 seats?

M ______________________________

(a) Those were sold out, so I had to get cheaper ones.
(b) No, that's OK. Another $30 is affordable.
(c) Right, together they were $120.
(d) Splitting the cost evenly will solve that.

31

W Do you have lunch plans?

M I brought a sandwich I made.

W Do you always do that?

M On most days.

W Great idea. I should do that, too.

M It saves money, and it's healthier.

Q What are the man and woman mainly discussing?

(a) When to eat lunch
(b) Where to go for lunch
(c) Sharing their lunch with each other
(d) Bringing lunch from home

32

M Welcome to our office! You must be Laurie.

W Yes, that's right. I'm the new accountant.

M I'm Simon. I work in your department.

W Oh, nice to meet you.

M The pleasure's mine. Shall I show you around?

W Yes, please.

Q What is the man mainly doing in the conversation?

(a) Greeting a new colleague
(b) Asking about his new job
(c) Agreeing to hire the woman
(d) Explaining the accountant position

33

W Mr. Brown, would it be OK if I left work now?

M Is there a problem?

W My daughter's daycare just called and said she has a fever.

M Oh. You'd better go pick her up, then.

W Thanks for understanding.

M No problem. You're only leaving an hour early, anyway.

Q What is the woman mainly trying to do?

(a) Get permission to leave work early
(b) Apologize for being late
(c) Determine what is wrong with her daughter
(d) Arrange a ride for her daughter to get to daycare

34

M Thank you for doing such a great job on the website!
W No problem at all.
M I know you put in a lot of overtime.
W There were some minor problems to be fixed.
M Well, your effort is appreciated.
W Thanks. It's nice to get the recognition.

Q What is the man mainly doing in the conversation?
(a) Accepting the woman's praise
(b) Evaluating feedback from a website
(c) Offering the woman overtime pay
(d) Expressing gratitude for the woman's work

35

W My savings are disappearing fast.
M I thought you were following a budget.
W I was, but I keep having to pay for unexpected things.
M Like what?
W Last week's trip to the emergency room, for one.
M I see. You certainly couldn't have planned for that.

Q What is the main topic of the conversation?
(a) How the woman can reduce her monthly expenses
(b) How unforeseen expenses are depleting the woman's savings
(c) How the woman is budgeting to increase her savings
(d) How an emergency room trip cost more than the woman expected

36

M Where should we take your aunt during her stay?
W I was thinking she'd enjoy the shopping district.
M Is she a big shopper?
W Yes. Also, there are lots of tourist attractions there.
M True. There's the museum, cathedral, and park.
W Plus, we can have dinner at the rooftop restaurant.

Q What are the man and woman mainly discussing?
(a) Where the woman's aunt is staying during her visit
(b) Plans to visit the woman's aunt
(c) Places the woman's aunt has already seen
(d) What to do with the woman's aunt during her visit

37

W All Charlie does in his free time is read comic books.
M At least he's reading something.
W But he doesn't learn anything. And they're filled with violence.
M Even if they're not educational, I don't see any reason for alarm.
W I do. It's a shame he wastes so much time on them.
M If I were you, I'd just let Charlie enjoy them.

Q What is the woman mainly doing in the conversation?
(a) Blaming comic books for Charlie's bad behavior
(b) Arguing that comic books are legitimate reading material
(c) Extolling the educational value of comic books
(d) Lamenting Charlie's predilection for comic books

38

M The sculpture in your dining room is beautiful!
W Thanks. It was made by a Brazilian artist.
M You have many things from Brazil.
W Well, I lived there for ten years before moving to Korea.
M And when did you move to Korea?
W A year ago, just after my son was born.

Q Which is correct about the woman according to the conversation?
(a) She made the sculpture in her dining room.
(b) Her only souvenir from Brazil is the sculpture.
(c) Her son was born about a year ago.
(d) She relocated to Korea ten years ago.

39

W Are there any vending machines in this building?
M There are two in the basement.
W Thanks. I'm looking for a cold drink.
M Oh, I think one sells snacks and the other only hot coffee.
W Is there a convenience store in this building, then?
M No, but there's one across the street.

Q Which is correct according to the conversation?
(a) The basement has three vending machines.
(b) The woman is looking for a hot coffee.
(c) The vending machines do not sell beverages.
(d) The building does not have a convenience store.

40

M Did you see last night's *Idol Quest*?
W Of course. I love singing competition shows like that.
M I was surprised to see Jeremy let go.
W It was heartbreaking. I was rooting for him to win!
M Really? I thought he was pretty good, but not enough to win.
W Come on, he's miles better than the three remaining contestants.

Q Which is correct according to the conversation?
(a) The woman missed last night's *Idol Quest*.
(b) Jeremy was eliminated as a contestant on *Idol Quest*.
(c) Both the man and woman expected Jeremy to win *Idol Quest*.
(d) Four contestants are left in the *Idol Quest* competition.

41

W This sweater is just my style. I have to have it.
M You'd better be sure. Since it's on clearance, it can't be exchanged.
W I am sure. I just don't have enough cash for it.
M How much do you need?
W I have a twenty, so I need another ten, since it's $30, right?
M The tag says $20 right here. See?
W Oh, then I do have enough. Perfect!

Q Which is correct according to the conversation?
(a) The woman is not sure if she likes the sweater.
(b) The sweater is on sale for $30.
(c) The sweater is less expensive than the woman expected.
(d) The woman needs to borrow $10 to buy the sweater.

42

M Your son, Eli, has been struggling in class.

W Is it his grades? He does his homework every night.

M Academically, he's excelling. It's his socializing I'm worried about.

W Oh. Is he being boisterous?

M Just the opposite. He's shy and withdrawn.

W That's definitely unlike him. I'll talk to him.

Q Which is correct about Eli according to the conversation?

(a) He is struggling because he is neglecting his homework.

(b) His social interactions are the cause of the man's concern.

(c) His raucous classroom behavior is proving disruptive.

(d) He is typically shy and withdrawn at home.

43

M Thanks for calling Gary's Roofing. How may I help you?

W Yes, how much does roof repair work cost?

M I'd have to inspect the damage to quote you a price.

W When can you come?

M Not until Friday. We're extra busy because of yesterday's storm.

W No problem, it can wait until then.

Q What can be inferred from the conversation?

(a) The woman has hired Gary's Roofing to repair her roof before.

(b) Gary's Roofing charges a flat rate for all repairs.

(c) Yesterday's storm damaged several roofs in the area.

(d) The woman is preparing her roof for an impending storm.

44

M Are you enjoying the digital camera you got for your birthday?

W Yeah! I'm having so much fun with it.

M Taking lots of pictures?

W Tons. I never knew taking photos was so fun.

M Sounds like you've got a new hobby.

W I certainly do!

Q What can be inferred about the woman from the conversation?

(a) She is looking to buy a new digital camera.

(b) Her hobbies do not leave much time for her to pursue photography.

(c) She works as a professional photographer.

(d) Her new camera has ignited her interest in photography.

45

W Unpaid internships are ruining the workforce.

M You used to be all for them.

W That was before hearing the talk Sue Layton gave at the university.

M She must've made a convincing argument.

W She did. Why don't you see if her talk has been posted on the Internet?

M Maybe I will. It sounds interesting.

Q What can be inferred from the conversation?

(a) The woman is alarmed over dwindling internship opportunities.

(b) The woman heard Sue Layton's talk over the Internet.

(c) Sue Layton offers unpaid internships for university students.

(d) Sue Layton's talk changed the woman's opinion of unpaid internships.

46

Welcome to Johnson Elementary School's Annual Science Fair. You may notice the exhibits share a common overarching theme. The students worked hard to put together exhibits that explore the scientific explanation for phenomena we encounter every day. For instance, you can visit the soap bubble booth to learn about surface tension or the music booth to learn about the physics of sound. We hope you enjoy the fair!

Q What is the main purpose of the announcement?
(a) To invite audience questions
(b) To state the topics students may choose to work on
(c) To name the most popular exhibit
(d) To describe the fair's theme of the science behind daily life

47

Until recently, Nelson Mandela had difficulty entering the United States. This goes back to his involvement with the African National Congress, also known as the ANC, which South Africa's old apartheid regime had designated a terrorist organization. The US followed suit and restricted ANC members from entering the US without a waiver, which was a policy that remained in place even decades after the group became South Africa's leading political party. It took the actions of former US Secretary of State Condoleezza Rice to lift these restrictions.

Q What is mainly being reported about Nelson Mandela?
(a) His efforts to win US support for the ANC
(b) How his travels to the US created controversy in South Africa
(c) His opposition to the ANC's terrorist activities
(d) Why his access to the US was restricted for many years

48

North Americans are indebted to railroads for the establishment of standardized time zones. Before railroads, most towns used their own local solar time based on when the sun peaked in the sky. The speed of train travel, though, meant that moving between towns became much quicker, and having to grapple with local times that differed for each town made scheduling extremely difficult. So in 1883, railroad companies delineated time zones, similar to those used today.

Q What is the main topic of the lecture?
(a) Why trains used to have trouble arriving on time
(b) How standardized time zones were instituted in North America
(c) Why railroad companies insisted on schedules using solar time
(d) How train travel changed people's perception of time

49

Former Representative Mary Stockholm wants her seat in Congress back. Last night she took on current Congressman Daniel Potter in a live debate and wowed everyone. Going on the offensive early, Potter repeatedly criticized Stockholm's stances on economic policy, health care, and employment, but Stockholm was armed and ready with her responses. Indeed, Stockholm deflected Potter's attacks at every turn and repeatedly had him on the defensive, producing a strong showing for herself.

Q What is the news report mainly about?
(a) Stockholm's refusal to clarify her stance on key issues
(b) The issues that have voters split between Potter and Stockholm
(c) Stockholm's deft handling of her debate opponent's attacks
(d) A campaign aimed at smearing Stockholm's image

50

Supporters of compulsory religious education in public schools contend that exposure to a variety of belief systems cultivates tolerance. This is a powerful argument, but one that needs to be qualified. Learning about other religions does not necessarily make students more open-minded. Negative or biased education may actually promote the opposite qualities. Those looking to promote a tolerant society need to realize that it can only happen if religious education is done right.

Q What is the speaker's main point about compulsory religious education?
(a) It must afford students the freedom to worship openly.
(b) It assists students in forming strong belief systems.
(c) It has not resulted in a consensus on religious issues.
(d) It does not necessarily promote religious tolerance.

51

Traditionally, E. coli infections have not been treated with antibiotics because doing so heightens patients' risk of developing hemolytic uremic syndrome, which can be life-threatening. But now a study out of Germany may change that. In the study, E. coli patients treated with the antibiotic azithromycin were able to rid their bodies of the bacteria more quickly than those who did not receive antibiotics. Moreover, none of the patients developed hemolytic uremic syndrome—another point in azithromycin's favor.

Q What is the main topic of the news report?
(a) The reasons antibiotics can worsen infections
(b) How E. coli has become resistant to antibiotics
(c) A study that suggests azithromycin can safely treat E. coli
(d) Azithromycin's questionable efficacy in preventing infections

52

Ocean iron fertilization has been proposed as a way to counter global warming, but it has secondary impacts that deserve more attention than they have thus far received. Ocean iron fertilization works by producing phytoplankton blooms, which suck global-warming-causing carbon dioxide from the atmosphere. However, ocean iron fertilization might also produce toxic tides of algae and cause disruptions to marine ecosystems. Such unintended consequences have not been fully investigated and could prove hazardous.

Q What is the speaker's main point about ocean iron fertilization?
(a) It comes with side effects that are potentially dangerous.
(b) It is only effective on a large scale.
(c) It is based on discredited theories about climate.
(d) It has resulted in ecological catastrophes.

53

This Saturday and Sunday only, come to Sharps Furniture Warehouse and take advantage of our spring sale. Save 50% on all four-piece bedroom sets and 30% on all kitchen and dining furniture. And it gets even better: we're offering free delivery on all furniture purchased this weekend. To give you more time to shop, we're extending our hours until 8 p.m. on both days. See you at Sharps this weekend!

Q Which is correct according to the advertisement?
(a) Sharps is having a week-long sale.
(b) All kitchen and dining sets will be 50% off.
(c) The sale offer does not include delivery.
(d) Sharps will be open until 8 p.m. this weekend.

54

When purchasing ink sticks for calligraphy, consider three things. First, check that the ink stick has a dense and uniform structure, a sign that it has been well kneaded. Next, make sure the stick's surface is free of cracks or irregularities. Finally, quality ink sticks should be air-dried. To check if an ink stick has been sufficiently dried, tap it with a fingernail. A metallic sound indicates that the stick is good.

Q Which is correct about calligraphy ink sticks according to the instructions?
(a) Their makeup should be light rather than dense.
(b) Their surface ought to have no cracks.
(c) They should not be exposed to air while drying.
(d) They should make no noise when tapped.

55

This is a reminder to Summerville residents to adhere to recycling procedures. Only items placed in the standard 32-gallon recycling cans provided to each resident by the township will be accepted by waste management personnel. The receptacles should be placed by the curb on Wednesday evenings for pick-up the following morning. As a reminder, large or heavy items should be brought to the Summerville Drop-off Center.

Q Which is correct according to the announcement?
(a) Residents share a communal 32-gallon recycling can.
(b) Recycling should not be left by the curb.
(c) Recycling is picked up every Wednesday evening.
(d) Residents should bring large items to the drop-off center.

56

I know many of you are disappointed by Mayor Smithson's decision to scrap Freemont City's plan for a light-rail system. To be sure, the plan was ideal for a mid-sized city like Freemont. While funding was a factor in the mayor's decision, it wasn't the decisive one. The overwhelming response from citizens in public opinion polls was that taxpayer dollars should go towards building upon our existing subway system, and the mayor has agreed to do so.

Q Which is correct about the plan for a light-rail system according to the announcement?
(a) It was deemed impractical for a city of Freemont's size.
(b) Insufficient funding was the deciding factor in its rejection.
(c) Public opinion had no bearing on the mayor's decision against it.
(d) It was dismissed in favor of expanding the subway system.

57

Since the launch of the Hubble Space Telescope into space in 1990, there have been five servicing missions to replace various instruments. The most important of these missions was the first one, in 1993. The purpose of this mission was to replace a defective mirror that was distorting all of the images taken by the Hubble's camera. This mission was declared a success after a new mirror was installed.

Q Which is correct about the Hubble Space Telescope according to the talk?
(a) It was launched into outer space in 1993.
(b) It is serviced five times a year on average.
(c) The first images it sent back were distorted by a faulty part.
(d) The first mission to service it failed to replace the defective mirror.

58

Many believe they can rely on their memory when a particularly good idea hits them, but the human mind has too many ideas in a day to retain all of them. Therefore, the most important tip for writers is to jot everything down. Granted, the majority of these ideas will never develop into a fully-formed story. But every once in a while, an idea that did not seem particularly gripping at the time could develop into something worthwhile once you actually set pen to paper and begin writing about it.

Q Which statement would the speaker most likely agree with?

(a) An idea's potential is not always immediately apparent.

(b) It is rare for writers to get story ideas out of the blue.

(c) Collecting too many ideas can overwhelm novice writers.

(d) Writers should have a fully-formed idea before starting to write.

59

US history shows that military recruitment efforts work best when tailored to the circumstances of the time. During World Wars I and II, army enlistment campaigns appealed to people's sense of duty, and nearly half of all army posters focused on the theme of patriotism. Post-World War II, however, with no war to fight, recruitment campaigns presented the military as a pathway to secure employment, attracting volunteers in numbers that exceeded expectations.

Q What can be inferred from the talk?

(a) Public patriotism continued to grow after World War II ended.

(b) The army's recruiting efforts effectively tapped into public sentiment.

(c) Posters were the least effective recruitment strategy.

(d) Army posters have not changed much since World War II.

60

An artificial neural network is a computational model based on biological neural networks. Much like the human brain, an artificial neural network is able to analyze complex relationships and patterns in data, and most importantly, it is capable of learning from its past performance. Artificial neural networks are particularly useful in investment analysis, where they are used to compare stock-trading patterns and determine what makes financial transactions successful. Although they display incredible powers of prediction when it comes to selecting stocks, they rely on humans to input data and track real world events that could affect the market.

Q What can be inferred about artificial neural networks from the lecture?

(a) They were designed to map the human brain.

(b) They become more effective at making predictions with experience.

(c) Their ability to predict is independent of human input.

(d) Their stock picks are no more reliable than random picks.

Answer Keys

서울대 최신기출 · 1

Listening Comprehension

1 (a) **2** (b) **3** (a) **4** (b) **5** (b) **6** (d) **7** (b) **8** (c) **9** (c) **10** (a)
11 (a) **12** (b) **13** (a) **14** (c) **15** (a) **16** (d) **17** (a) **18** (a) **19** (b) **20** (c)
21 (d) **22** (c) **23** (b) **24** (a) **25** (d) **26** (a) **27** (a) **28** (b) **29** (b) **30** (d)
31 (b) **32** (b) **33** (a) **34** (b) **35** (c) **36** (b) **37** (b) **38** (b) **39** (c) **40** (c)
41 (d) **42** (d) **43** (a) **44** (c) **45** (d) **46** (a) **47** (b) **48** (d) **49** (d) **50** (b)
51 (a) **52** (a) **53** (b) **54** (d) **55** (a) **56** (c) **57** (b) **58** (c) **59** (d) **60** (c)

Grammar

1 (c) **2** (c) **3** (c) **4** (b) **5** (c) **6** (b) **7** (c) **8** (a) **9** (b) **10** (b)
11 (b) **12** (b) **13** (d) **14** (d) **15** (b) **16** (b) **17** (c) **18** (a) **19** (b) **20** (d)
21 (d) **22** (d) **23** (d) **24** (c) **25** (d) **26** (b) **27** (c) **28** (a) **29** (d) **30** (c)
31 (c) **32** (a) **33** (c) **34** (b) **35** (d) **36** (a) **37** (d) **38** (c) **39** (a) **40** (c)
41 (d) **42** (a) **43** (c) **44** (c) **45** (a) **46** (d) **47** (a) **48** (b) **49** (c) **50** (b)

Vocabulary

1 (c) **2** (c) **3** (b) **4** (b) **5** (c) **6** (c) **7** (b) **8** (c) **9** (c) **10** (d)
11 (d) **12** (b) **13** (c) **14** (d) **15** (c) **16** (a) **17** (b) **18** (d) **19** (c) **20** (a)
21 (b) **22** (d) **23** (c) **24** (d) **25** (a) **26** (b) **27** (b) **28** (d) **29** (d) **30** (d)
31 (b) **32** (a) **33** (d) **34** (b) **35** (b) **36** (c) **37** (b) **38** (b) **39** (a) **40** (b)
41 (a) **42** (a) **43** (b) **44** (a) **45** (b) **46** (a) **47** (c) **48** (b) **49** (c) **50** (b)

Reading Comprehension

1 (a) **2** (b) **3** (c) **4** (b) **5** (c) **6** (b) **7** (d) **8** (b) **9** (c) **10** (a)
11 (d) **12** (c) **13** (a) **14** (c) **15** (a) **16** (c) **17** (b) **18** (a) **19** (a) **20** (c)
21 (a) **22** (b) **23** (d) **24** (b) **25** (d) **26** (b) **27** (a) **28** (d) **29** (b) **30** (b)
31 (d) **32** (a) **33** (a) **34** (d) **35** (d) **36** (c) **37** (a) **38** (c) **39** (c) **40** (b)

Listening Comprehension

1 (c)	**2** (b)	**3** (b)	**4** (b)	**5** (a)	**6** (b)	**7** (c)	**8** (d)	**9** (b)	**10** (b)
11 (d)	**12** (b)	**13** (c)	**14** (b)	**15** (c)	**16** (a)	**17** (c)	**18** (d)	**19** (b)	**20** (b)
21 (a)	**22** (c)	**23** (d)	**24** (c)	**25** (b)	**26** (b)	**27** (d)	**28** (a)	**29** (a)	**30** (a)
31 (d)	**32** (a)	**33** (b)	**34** (a)	**35** (a)	**36** (a)	**37** (a)	**38** (d)	**39** (b)	**40** (d)
41 (d)	**42** (b)	**43** (a)	**44** (a)	**45** (b)	**46** (b)	**47** (c)	**48** (c)	**49** (c)	**50** (b)
51 (b)	**52** (b)	**53** (b)	**54** (d)	**55** (b)	**56** (a)	**57** (a)	**58** (d)	**59** (d)	**60** (a)

Grammar

1 (c)	**2** (b)	**3** (d)	**4** (d)	**5** (c)	**6** (c)	**7** (a)	**8** (d)	**9** (d)	**10** (a)
11 (c)	**12** (b)	**13** (a)	**14** (d)	**15** (c)	**16** (b)	**17** (c)	**18** (d)	**19** (b)	**20** (d)
21 (b)	**22** (a)	**23** (b)	**24** (d)	**25** (b)	**26** (c)	**27** (a)	**28** (c)	**29** (a)	**30** (d)
31 (d)	**32** (a)	**33** (d)	**34** (a)	**35** (d)	**36** (a)	**37** (a)	**38** (a)	**39** (a)	**40** (a)
41 (c)	**42** (b)	**43** (c)	**44** (b)	**45** (b)	**46** (b)	**47** (d)	**48** (b)	**49** (a)	**50** (b)

Vocabulary

1 (b)	**2** (b)	**3** (c)	**4** (d)	**5** (b)	**6** (b)	**7** (c)	**8** (b)	**9** (a)	**10** (c)
11 (b)	**12** (b)	**13** (b)	**14** (b)	**15** (a)	**16** (a)	**17** (c)	**18** (c)	**19** (a)	**20** (d)
21 (d)	**22** (c)	**23** (a)	**24** (d)	**25** (a)	**26** (a)	**27** (c)	**28** (d)	**29** (b)	**30** (c)
31 (c)	**32** (d)	**33** (d)	**34** (c)	**35** (b)	**36** (a)	**37** (d)	**38** (b)	**39** (d)	**40** (b)
41 (a)	**42** (c)	**43** (c)	**44** (b)	**45** (d)	**46** (c)	**47** (d)	**48** (a)	**49** (b)	**50** (a)

Reading Comprehension

1 (d)	**2** (b)	**3** (c)	**4** (a)	**5** (d)	**6** (d)	**7** (b)	**8** (b)	**9** (b)	**10** (a)
11 (d)	**12** (b)	**13** (c)	**14** (c)	**15** (c)	**16** (c)	**17** (a)	**18** (a)	**19** (b)	**20** (b)
21 (c)	**22** (d)	**23** (b)	**24** (c)	**25** (c)	**26** (d)	**27** (b)	**28** (c)	**29** (b)	**30** (c)
31 (c)	**32** (c)	**33** (d)	**34** (a)	**35** (b)	**36** (c)	**37** (d)	**38** (c)	**39** (b)	**40** (b)

Answer Keys

서울대 최신기출 · 3

Listening Comprehension

1 (a) **2** (b) **3** (b) **4** (b) **5** (c) **6** (c) **7** (b) **8** (b) **9** (c) **10** (c)
11 (b) **12** (c) **13** (c) **14** (b) **15** (b) **16** (b) **17** (a) **18** (d) **19** (c) **20** (c)
21 (c) **22** (b) **23** (b) **24** (c) **25** (d) **26** (b) **27** (a) **28** (a) **29** (a) **30** (b)
31 (b) **32** (a) **33** (c) **34** (c) **35** (b) **36** (b) **37** (a) **38** (d) **39** (d) **40** (c)
41 (d) **42** (d) **43** (a) **44** (b) **45** (d) **46** (c) **47** (c) **48** (d) **49** (d) **50** (c)
51 (c) **52** (b) **53** (d) **54** (d) **55** (c) **56** (c) **57** (a) **58** (c) **59** (a) **60** (b)

Grammar

1 (c) **2** (a) **3** (c) **4** (b) **5** (b) **6** (d) **7** (b) **8** (b) **9** (d) **10** (a)
11 (b) **12** (d) **13** (d) **14** (b) **15** (d) **16** (a) **17** (c) **18** (d) **19** (a) **20** (a)
21 (b) **22** (a) **23** (d) **24** (d) **25** (c) **26** (a) **27** (c) **28** (c) **29** (a) **30** (a)
31 (c) **32** (d) **33** (c) **34** (c) **35** (c) **36** (d) **37** (b) **38** (a) **39** (a) **40** (a)
41 (c) **42** (d) **43** (d) **44** (c) **45** (b) **46** (a) **47** (d) **48** (c) **49** (b) **50** (b)

Vocabulary

1 (b) **2** (a) **3** (c) **4** (b) **5** (a) **6** (a) **7** (d) **8** (b) **9** (c) **10** (b)
11 (a) **12** (a) **13** (b) **14** (b) **15** (a) **16** (a) **17** (a) **18** (c) **19** (d) **20** (d)
21 (c) **22** (b) **23** (c) **24** (d) **25** (a) **26** (c) **27** (c) **28** (b) **29** (d) **30** (b)
31 (b) **32** (a) **33** (b) **34** (d) **35** (a) **36** (d) **37** (a) **38** (c) **39** (a) **40** (a)
41 (a) **42** (a) **43** (a) **44** (b) **45** (c) **46** (a) **47** (d) **48** (d) **49** (b) **50** (a)

Reading Comprehension

1 (b) **2** (d) **3** (b) **4** (c) **5** (c) **6** (c) **7** (d) **8** (a) **9** (d) **10** (c)
11 (b) **12** (c) **13** (c) **14** (d) **15** (a) **16** (a) **17** (c) **18** (b) **19** (d) **20** (d)
21 (a) **22** (c) **23** (b) **24** (d) **25** (c) **26** (d) **27** (c) **28** (b) **29** (b) **30** (a)
31 (a) **32** (d) **33** (d) **34** (b) **35** (b) **36** (d) **37** (a) **38** (c) **39** (c) **40** (b)

서울대 최신기출 · 4

Listening Comprehension

1 (d)	**2** (c)	**3** (b)	**4** (b)	**5** (c)	**6** (b)	**7** (d)	**8** (b)	**9** (a)	**10** (a)
11 (c)	**12** (b)	**13** (c)	**14** (b)	**15** (d)	**16** (d)	**17** (b)	**18** (b)	**19** (c)	**20** (d)
21 (a)	**22** (b)	**23** (d)	**24** (b)	**25** (c)	**26** (c)	**27** (a)	**28** (d)	**29** (a)	**30** (b)
31 (c)	**32** (c)	**33** (c)	**34** (a)	**35** (c)	**36** (b)	**37** (d)	**38** (d)	**39** (c)	**40** (b)
41 (c)	**42** (d)	**43** (b)	**44** (a)	**45** (c)	**46** (d)	**47** (c)	**48** (a)	**49** (a)	**50** (a)
51 (b)	**52** (a)	**53** (b)	**54** (d)	**55** (d)	**56** (c)	**57** (d)	**58** (b)	**59** (d)	**60** (b)

Grammar

1 (c)	**2** (c)	**3** (b)	**4** (b)	**5** (a)	**6** (a)	**7** (d)	**8** (a)	**9** (b)	**10** (a)
11 (a)	**12** (c)	**13** (b)	**14** (b)	**15** (d)	**16** (d)	**17** (d)	**18** (c)	**19** (b)	**20** (a)
21 (b)	**22** (d)	**23** (b)	**24** (d)	**25** (a)	**26** (d)	**27** (a)	**28** (b)	**29** (b)	**30** (b)
31 (a)	**32** (d)	**33** (c)	**34** (d)	**35** (d)	**36** (b)	**37** (c)	**38** (a)	**39** (b)	**40** (a)
41 (c)	**42** (a)	**43** (d)	**44** (b)	**45** (a)	**46** (c)	**47** (d)	**48** (a)	**49** (b)	**50** (a)

Vocabulary

1 (c)	**2** (d)	**3** (a)	**4** (c)	**5** (a)	**6** (a)	**7** (a)	**8** (b)	**9** (b)	**10** (b)
11 (b)	**12** (c)	**13** (a)	**14** (b)	**15** (a)	**16** (d)	**17** (a)	**18** (c)	**19** (d)	**20** (c)
21 (b)	**22** (c)	**23** (a)	**24** (a)	**25** (b)	**26** (c)	**27** (a)	**28** (b)	**29** (a)	**30** (a)
31 (a)	**32** (c)	**33** (a)	**34** (d)	**35** (b)	**36** (d)	**37** (b)	**38** (b)	**39** (b)	**40** (b)
41 (d)	**42** (c)	**43** (b)	**44** (b)	**45** (d)	**46** (a)	**47** (b)	**48** (b)	**49** (a)	**50** (a)

Reading Comprehension

1 (c)	**2** (d)	**3** (a)	**4** (c)	**5** (b)	**6** (c)	**7** (b)	**8** (b)	**9** (b)	**10** (d)
11 (b)	**12** (b)	**13** (c)	**14** (b)	**15** (c)	**16** (b)	**17** (d)	**18** (a)	**19** (d)	**20** (b)
21 (a)	**22** (b)	**23** (d)	**24** (b)	**25** (d)	**26** (c)	**27** (d)	**28** (b)	**29** (c)	**30** (a)
31 (d)	**32** (c)	**33** (c)	**34** (d)	**35** (d)	**36** (b)	**37** (c)	**38** (b)	**39** (b)	**40** (a)

Answer Keys

서울대 최신기출 · 5

Listening Comprehension

1 (c)	2 (a)	3 (d)	4 (d)	5 (a)	6 (c)	7 (b)	8 (c)	9 (b)	10 (b)
11 (b)	12 (b)	13 (a)	14 (c)	15 (c)	16 (b)	17 (b)	18 (d)	19 (c)	20 (a)
21 (a)	22 (c)	23 (a)	24 (c)	25 (a)	26 (c)	27 (d)	28 (a)	29 (a)	30 (c)
31 (b)	32 (d)	33 (d)	34 (b)	35 (c)	36 (b)	37 (b)	38 (d)	39 (c)	40 (a)
41 (d)	42 (c)	43 (b)	44 (c)	45 (a)	46 (d)	47 (b)	48 (d)	49 (c)	50 (b)
51 (b)	52 (b)	53 (a)	54 (b)	55 (a)	56 (b)	57 (a)	58 (a)	59 (c)	60 (c)

Grammar

1 (a)	2 (a)	3 (b)	4 (a)	5 (c)	6 (d)	7 (a)	8 (b)	9 (b)	10 (c)
11 (c)	12 (c)	13 (b)	14 (b)	15 (d)	16 (c)	17 (a)	18 (b)	19 (a)	20 (a)
21 (b)	22 (a)	23 (c)	24 (d)	25 (b)	26 (d)	27 (d)	28 (c)	29 (b)	30 (c)
31 (b)	32 (a)	33 (c)	34 (d)	35 (a)	36 (d)	37 (b)	38 (b)	39 (c)	40 (a)
41 (a)	42 (b)	43 (d)	44 (d)	45 (c)	46 (c)	47 (c)	48 (b)	49 (a)	50 (d)

Vocabulary

1 (c)	2 (c)	3 (a)	4 (d)	5 (d)	6 (d)	7 (d)	8 (b)	9 (c)	10 (b)
11 (d)	12 (a)	13 (a)	14 (b)	15 (b)	16 (d)	17 (c)	18 (d)	19 (a)	20 (a)
21 (d)	22 (c)	23 (c)	24 (a)	25 (b)	26 (a)	27 (b)	28 (d)	29 (b)	30 (b)
31 (d)	32 (b)	33 (b)	34 (b)	35 (a)	36 (b)	37 (a)	38 (c)	39 (a)	40 (d)
41 (c)	42 (d)	43 (b)	44 (c)	45 (c)	46 (b)	47 (c)	48 (a)	49 (c)	50 (b)

Reading Comprehension

1 (b)	2 (a)	3 (c)	4 (a)	5 (b)	6 (d)	7 (d)	8 (d)	9 (c)	10 (c)
11 (b)	12 (a)	13 (b)	14 (b)	15 (d)	16 (a)	17 (b)	18 (a)	19 (a)	20 (a)
21 (b)	22 (a)	23 (b)	24 (d)	25 (c)	26 (b)	27 (b)	28 (c)	29 (b)	30 (c)
31 (b)	32 (c)	33 (c)	34 (a)	35 (b)	36 (a)	37 (c)	38 (c)	39 (c)	40 (c)

서울대 최신기출 · 6

Listening Comprehension

1 (a)	**2** (c)	**3** (d)	**4** (c)	**5** (c)	**6** (b)	**7** (a)	**8** (a)	**9** (c)	**10** (d)
11 (d)	**12** (a)	**13** (c)	**14** (a)	**15** (a)	**16** (c)	**17** (a)	**18** (c)	**19** (c)	**20** (b)
21 (c)	**22** (b)	**23** (a)	**24** (b)	**25** (d)	**26** (c)	**27** (c)	**28** (c)	**29** (d)	**30** (a)
31 (d)	**32** (a)	**33** (a)	**34** (d)	**35** (b)	**36** (d)	**37** (d)	**38** (c)	**39** (d)	**40** (b)
41 (c)	**42** (b)	**43** (c)	**44** (d)	**45** (d)	**46** (d)	**47** (d)	**48** (b)	**49** (c)	**50** (d)
51 (c)	**52** (a)	**53** (d)	**54** (b)	**55** (d)	**56** (d)	**57** (c)	**58** (a)	**59** (b)	**60** (b)

Grammar

1 (d)	**2** (a)	**3** (c)	**4** (c)	**5** (d)	**6** (a)	**7** (d)	**8** (c)	**9** (b)	**10** (c)
11 (d)	**12** (c)	**13** (a)	**14** (c)	**15** (c)	**16** (a)	**17** (b)	**18** (b)	**19** (c)	**20** (c)
21 (d)	**22** (c)	**23** (a)	**24** (b)	**25** (b)	**26** (a)	**27** (a)	**28** (b)	**29** (b)	**30** (d)
31 (c)	**32** (a)	**33** (d)	**34** (b)	**35** (b)	**36** (d)	**37** (c)	**38** (c)	**39** (a)	**40** (a)
41 (d)	**42** (d)	**43** (c)	**44** (b)	**45** (c)	**46** (b)	**47** (c)	**48** (c)	**49** (c)	**50** (b)

Vocabulary

1 (b)	**2** (c)	**3** (b)	**4** (d)	**5** (d)	**6** (c)	**7** (a)	**8** (d)	**9** (a)	**10** (a)
11 (b)	**12** (d)	**13** (b)	**14** (c)	**15** (d)	**16** (a)	**17** (d)	**18** (c)	**19** (d)	**20** (b)
21 (b)	**22** (d)	**23** (c)	**24** (d)	**25** (a)	**26** (d)	**27** (b)	**28** (b)	**29** (a)	**30** (b)
31 (a)	**32** (a)	**33** (c)	**34** (a)	**35** (c)	**36** (b)	**37** (b)	**38** (c)	**39** (c)	**40** (c)
41 (c)	**42** (c)	**43** (c)	**44** (a)	**45** (b)	**46** (c)	**47** (d)	**48** (b)	**49** (b)	**50** (b)

Reading Comprehension

1 (c)	**2** (d)	**3** (c)	**4** (a)	**5** (c)	**6** (a)	**7** (b)	**8** (c)	**9** (a)	**10** (a)
11 (c)	**12** (b)	**13** (c)	**14** (c)	**15** (b)	**16** (b)	**17** (c)	**18** (d)	**19** (b)	**20** (a)
21 (d)	**22** (d)	**23** (c)	**24** (b)	**25** (d)	**26** (b)	**27** (c)	**28** (c)	**29** (b)	**30** (a)
31 (b)	**32** (d)	**33** (c)	**34** (d)	**35** (a)	**36** (d)	**37** (d)	**38** (c)	**39** (b)	**40** (c)

TEPS 등급표

등급	점수	영역	능력검정기준(Description)
1+급 Level 1+	901~990	전반	외국인으로서 최상급 수준의 의사소통 능력 교양 있는 원어민에 버금가는 정도로 의사소통이 가능하고 전문분야 업무에 대처할 수 있음 (Native Level of Communicative Competence)
1급 Level 1	801~900	전반	외국인으로서 거의 최상급 수준의 의사소통 능력 단기간 집중 교육을 받으면 대부분의 의사소통이 가능하고 전문분야 업무에 별 무리 없이 대처할 수 있음 (Near-Native Level of Communicative Competence)
2+급 Level 2+	701~800	전반	외국인으로서 상급 수준의 의사소통 능력 단기간 집중 교육을 받으면 일반분야 업무를 큰 어려움 없이 수행할 수 있음 (Advanced Level of Communicative Competence)
2급 Level 2	601~700	전반	외국인으로서 중상급 수준의 의사소통 능력 중장기간 집중 교육을 받으면 일반분야 업무를 큰 어려움 없이 수행할 수 있음 (High Intermediate Level of Communicative Competence)
3+급 Level 3+	501~600	전반	외국인으로서 중급 수준의 의사소통 능력 중장기간 집중 교육을 받으면 한정된 분야의 업무를 큰 어려움 없이 수행할 수 있음 (Mid Intermediate Level of Communicative Competence)
3급 Level 3	401~500	전반	외국인으로서 중하급 수준의 의사소통 능력 중장기간 집중 교육을 받으면 한정된 분야의 업무를 다소 미흡하지만 큰 지장 없이 수행할 수 있음 (Low Intermediate Level of Communicative Competence)
4+급 Level 4+	301~400	전반	외국인으로서 하급 수준의 의사소통 능력 장기간의 집중 교육을 받으면 한정된 분야의 업무를 대체로 어렵게 수행할 수 있음 (Novice Level of Communicative Competence)
4급 Level 4	201~300		
5+급 Level 5+	101~200	전반	외국인으로서 최하급 수준의 의사소통 능력 단편적인 지식만을 갖추고 있어 의사소통이 거의 불가능함 (Near-Zero Level of Communicative Competence)
5급 Level 5	10~100		

앞면(Side1)

TEPS

Test of English Proficiency
developed by
Seoul National University

수험번호 Registration No.	
성명 Name 한글	
한자	

문제지번호 Test Booklet No.	감독관확인란

청해 Listening Comprehension

1	a b c d	26	a b c d	51	a b c d
2	a b c d	27	a b c d	52	a b c d
3	a b c d	28	a b c d	53	a b c d
4	a b c d	29	a b c d	54	a b c d
5	a b c d	30	a b c d	55	a b c d
6	a b c d	31	a b c d	56	a b c d
7	a b c d	32	a b c d	57	a b c d
8	a b c d	33	a b c d	58	a b c d
9	a b c d	34	a b c d	59	a b c d
10	a b c d	35	a b c d	60	a b c d
11	a b c d	36	a b c d		
12	a b c d	37	a b c d		
13	a b c d	38	a b c d		
14	a b c d	39	a b c d		
15	a b c d	40	a b c d		
16	a b c d	41	a b c d		
17	a b c d	42	a b c d		
18	a b c d	43	a b c d		
19	a b c d	44	a b c d		
20	a b c d	45	a b c d		
21	a b c d	46	a b c d		
22	a b c d	47	a b c d		
23	a b c d	48	a b c d		
24	a b c d	49	a b c d		
25	a b c d	50	a b c d		

문법 Grammar

1	a b c d	26	a b c d
2	a b c d	27	a b c d
3	a b c d	28	a b c d
4	a b c d	29	a b c d
5	a b c d	30	a b c d
6	a b c d	31	a b c d
7	a b c d	32	a b c d
8	a b c d	33	a b c d
9	a b c d	34	a b c d
10	a b c d	35	a b c d
11	a b c d	36	a b c d
12	a b c d	37	a b c d
13	a b c d	38	a b c d
14	a b c d	39	a b c d
15	a b c d	40	a b c d
16	a b c d	41	a b c d
17	a b c d	42	a b c d
18	a b c d	43	a b c d
19	a b c d	44	a b c d
20	a b c d	45	a b c d
21	a b c d	46	a b c d
22	a b c d	47	a b c d
23	a b c d	48	a b c d
24	a b c d	49	a b c d
25	a b c d	50	a b c d

어휘 Vocabulary

1	a b c d	26	a b c d
2	a b c d	27	a b c d
3	a b c d	28	a b c d
4	a b c d	29	a b c d
5	a b c d	30	a b c d
6	a b c d	31	a b c d
7	a b c d	32	a b c d
8	a b c d	33	a b c d
9	a b c d	34	a b c d
10	a b c d	35	a b c d
11	a b c d	36	a b c d
12	a b c d	37	a b c d
13	a b c d	38	a b c d
14	a b c d	39	a b c d
15	a b c d	40	a b c d
16	a b c d	41	a b c d
17	a b c d	42	a b c d
18	a b c d	43	a b c d
19	a b c d	44	a b c d
20	a b c d	45	a b c d
21	a b c d	46	a b c d
22	a b c d	47	a b c d
23	a b c d	48	a b c d
24	a b c d	49	a b c d
25	a b c d	50	a b c d

독해 Reading Comprehension

1	a b c d	26	a b c d
2	a b c d	27	a b c d
3	a b c d	28	a b c d
4	a b c d	29	a b c d
5	a b c d	30	a b c d
6	a b c d	31	a b c d
7	a b c d	32	a b c d
8	a b c d	33	a b c d
9	a b c d	34	a b c d
10	a b c d	35	a b c d
11	a b c d	36	a b c d
12	a b c d	37	a b c d
13	a b c d	38	a b c d
14	a b c d	39	a b c d
15	a b c d	40	a b c d
16	a b c d		
17	a b c d		
18	a b c d		
19	a b c d		
20	a b c d		
21	a b c d		
22	a b c d		
23	a b c d		
24	a b c d		
25	a b c d		

주민등록번호 National ID No.

고사실란 Room No.

수험번호 Registration No.

비밀번호 Password

좌석번호 Seat No.

A B C D E / 1 2 3 4 5 6 7

서 약	본인은 필기구 및 기재오류와 답안지 훼손으로 인한 책임을 지고, 부정행위 처리규정을 준수할 것을 서약합니다.	

답안작성시 유의사항

1. 답안 작성은 반드시 **컴퓨터용 싸인펜**을 사용해야 합니다.
2. 답안을 정정할 경우 수정테이프(수정액 불가)를 사용해야 합니다.
3. 본 답안지는 컴퓨터로 처리되므로 훼손해서는 안되며, 답안지 하단의 타이밍마크(❙❙❙)를 찢거나, 낙서 등으로 인한 훼손시 불이익이 발생할 수 있습니다.
4. 답안은 문항당 정답을 1개만 골라 ▮와 같이 정확히 기재해야 하며, 필기구 오류나 본인의 부주의로 잘못 표기한 경우에는 당 관리위원회의 OMR판독기의 판독결과에 따르며, 그 결과는 본인이 책임집니다.
   Good ▮ Bad
5. 감독관의 확인이 없는 답안지는 무효처리됩니다.

TEPS

Test of English Proficiency
developed by
Seoul National University

성명	영문	
	서명	

응시일자 : 20 년 월 일

<부정행위 및 규정위반 처리규정>

1. 모든 부정행위 및 규정위반 적발 및 이에 대한 조치는 TEPS관리위원회의 처리규정에 따라 이루어집니다.

2. 부정행위 및 규정위반 행위는 현장 적발 뿐만 아니라 사후에도 적발될 수 있으며 모두 동일한 조치가 취해집니다.

3. 부정행위 적발 시 당해 성적은 무효화되며 사안에 따라 최대 5년까지 TEPS관리위원회에서 주관하는 모든 시험의 응시자격이 제한됩니다.

4. 문제지 이외에 메모를 하는 행위와 시험 문제의 일부 또는 전부를 유출하거나 공개하는 경우 부정행위로 처리됩니다.

5. 각 파트별 시간을 준수하지 않거나, 시험 종료 후 답안 작성을 계속할 경우 규정위반으로 처리됩니다.

성 명 (성 · 이름순으로 기재)

EX H O N G G I L D O N G

A B C D E F G H I J K L M N O P Q R S T U V W X Y Z

단체구분

학생	일반
▯	▯

질 문 란

1. 귀하의 TEPS 응시목적은?
   - ⓐ 입사지원 ⓑ 인사정책
   - ⓒ 개인실력측정 ⓓ 입시
   - ⓔ 국가고시 지원 ⓕ 기타

2. 귀하의 영어권 체류 경험은?
   - ⓐ 없다 ⓑ 6개월 미만
   - ⓒ 6개월 이상 1년 미만 ⓓ 1년 이상 3년 미만
   - ⓔ 3년 이상 5년 미만 ⓕ 5년 이상

3. 귀하께서 응시하고 계신 고사장에 대한 만족도는?
   - ⓐ 0점 ⓑ 1점
   - ⓒ 2점 ⓓ 3점
   - ⓔ 4점 ⓕ 5점

4. 최근 2년내 TEPS 응시횟수는?
   - ⓐ 없다 ⓑ 1회
   - ⓒ 2회 ⓓ 3회
   - ⓔ 4회 ⓕ 5회 이상

학력 / 전공 / 직업

학력	재학	졸업	전공	직업
초등학교	▯	▯	인문학 ▯	공무원 ▯
중학교	▯	▯	사회과학 · 법학 ▯	고시준비 ▯
고등학교	▯	▯	경제학 · 경영학 ▯	교사 ▯
전문대학	▯	▯	자연과학 ▯	군인 ▯
대학교	▯	▯	의학 · 약학 · 간호학 ▯	의료인 ▯
대학원	▯	▯	공학 ▯	자영업 ▯
			교육학 ▯	학생 ▯
			음악 · 미술 · 체육 ▯	회사원 ▯
			기타 ▯	무직 ▯
				기타 ▯

직종 / 직책

직종	직종	직책
고위임직원 ▯	무역 ▯	임원 ▯
전문직(과학,공학) ▯	외환 ▯	부장 ▯
전문직(교육) ▯	자금 ▯	차장 ▯
전문직(법률,회계,금융) ▯	공무 ▯	과장 ▯
기술직 ▯	업무 ▯	대리 ▯
영업 ▯	품질관리 ▯	계장 ▯
홍보 ▯	전산 ▯	사원 ▯
총무 ▯	행정직 ▯	인턴 ▯
인사 ▯	생산관리 ▯	기타 ▯
경리 ▯	서비스 ▯	
기획 ▯	기타 ▯	
구매 ▯		

앞면(Side1)

TEPS

Test of English Proficiency
developed by
Seoul National University

수험번호 Registration No.	
성명 Name 한글	
성명 Name 한자	

문제지번호 Test Booklet No.	감독관확인란

청해 Listening Comprehension (1–60, a b c d)

문법 Grammar (1–50, a b c d)

어휘 Vocabulary (1–50, a b c d)

독해 Reading Comprehension (1–40, a b c d)

주민등록번호 National ID No.

고사실란 Room No.

수험번호 Registration No.

비밀번호 Password

좌석번호 Seat No.

서약	본인은 필기구 및 기재오류와 답안지 훼손으로 인한 책임을 지고, 부정행위 처리규정을 준수할 것을 서약합니다.	

답안작성시 유의사항

1. 답안 작성은 반드시 **컴퓨터용 싸인펜**을 사용해야 합니다.
2. 답안을 정정할 경우 수정테이프(수정액 불가)를 사용해야 합니다.
3. 본 답안지는 컴퓨터로 처리되므로 훼손해서는 안되며, 답안지 하단의 타이밍마크(▌▌▌)를 찢거나, 낙서 등으로 인한 훼손시 불이익이 발생할 수 있습니다.
4. 답안은 문항당 정답을 1개만 골라 ▌와 같이 정확히 기재해야 하며, 필기구 오류나 본인의 부주의로 잘못 표기한 경우에는 당 관리위원회의 OMR판독기의 판독결과에 따르며, 그 결과는 본인이 책임집니다.

   Good ▌ Bad

5. 감독관의 확인이 없는 답안지는 무효처리됩니다.

Test of English Proficiency
developed by
Seoul National University

성명	
영문	
서명	

응시일자 : 20 년 월 일

<부정행위 및 규정위반 처리규정>

1. 모든 부정행위 및 규정위반 적발 및 이에 대한 조치는 TEPS관리위원회의 처리규정에 따라 이루어집니다.

2. 부정행위 및 규정위반 행위는 현장 적발 뿐만 아니라 사후에도 적발될 수 있으며 모두 동일한 조치가 취해 집니다.

3. 부정행위 적발 시 당해 성적은 무효화되며 사안에 따라 최대 5년까지 TEPS관리위원회에서 주관하는 모든 시험의 응시자격이 제한됩니다.

4. 문제지 이외에 메모를 하는 행위와 시험 문제의 일부 또는 전부를 유출하거나 공개하는 경우 부정행위로 처리됩니다.

5. 각 파트별 시간을 준수하지 않거나, 시험 종료 후 답안 작성을 계속할 경우 규정위반으로 처리됩니다.

성 명 (성·이름순으로 기재)

EX	H	O	N	G		G	I	L		D	O	N	G							
A	A	A	A	A	A	A	A	A	A	A	A	A	A	A	A	A	A	A	A	A
B	B	B	B	B	B	B	B	B	B	B	B	B	B	B	B	B	B	B	B	B
C	C	C	C	C	C	C	C	C	C	C	C	C	C	C	C	C	C	C	C	C
D	D	D	D	D	D	D	D	D	D	D	D	D	D	D	D	D	D	D	D	D
E	E	E	E	E	E	E	E	E	E	E	E	E	E	E	E	E	E	E	E	E
F	F	F	F	F	F	F	F	F	F	F	F	F	F	F	F	F	F	F	F	F
G	G	G	G	G	G	G	G	G	G	G	G	G	G	G	G	G	G	G	G	G
H	H	H	H	H	H	H	H	H	H	H	H	H	H	H	H	H	H	H	H	H
I	I	I	I	I	I	I	I	I	I	I	I	I	I	I	I	I	I	I	I	I
J	J	J	J	J	J	J	J	J	J	J	J	J	J	J	J	J	J	J	J	J
K	K	K	K	K	K	K	K	K	K	K	K	K	K	K	K	K	K	K	K	K
L	L	L	L	L	L	L	L	L	L	L	L	L	L	L	L	L	L	L	L	L
M	M	M	M	M	M	M	M	M	M	M	M	M	M	M	M	M	M	M	M	M
N	N	N	N	N	N	N	N	N	N	N	N	N	N	N	N	N	N	N	N	N
O	O	O	O	O	O	O	O	O	O	O	O	O	O	O	O	O	O	O	O	O
P	P	P	P	P	P	P	P	P	P	P	P	P	P	P	P	P	P	P	P	P
Q	Q	Q	Q	Q	Q	Q	Q	Q	Q	Q	Q	Q	Q	Q	Q	Q	Q	Q	Q	Q
R	R	R	R	R	R	R	R	R	R	R	R	R	R	R	R	R	R	R	R	R
S	S	S	S	S	S	S	S	S	S	S	S	S	S	S	S	S	S	S	S	S
T	T	T	T	T	T	T	T	T	T	T	T	T	T	T	T	T	T	T	T	T
U	U	U	U	U	U	U	U	U	U	U	U	U	U	U	U	U	U	U	U	U
V	V	V	V	V	V	V	V	V	V	V	V	V	V	V	V	V	V	V	V	V
W	W	W	W	W	W	W	W	W	W	W	W	W	W	W	W	W	W	W	W	W
X	X	X	X	X	X	X	X	X	X	X	X	X	X	X	X	X	X	X	X	X
Y	Y	Y	Y	Y	Y	Y	Y	Y	Y	Y	Y	Y	Y	Y	Y	Y	Y	Y	Y	Y
Z	Z	Z	Z	Z	Z	Z	Z	Z	Z	Z	Z	Z	Z	Z	Z	Z	Z	Z	Z	Z

단 체 구 분

학생	일반
⬯	⬯

질 문 란

1. 귀하의 TEPS 응시목적은?
   - ⓐ 입사지원 ⓑ 인사정책
   - ⓒ 개인실력측정 ⓓ 입시
   - ⓔ 국가고시 지원 ⓕ 기타

2. 귀하의 영어권 체류 경험은?
   - ⓐ 없다 ⓑ 6개월 미만
   - ⓒ 6개월 이상 1년 미만 ⓓ 1년 이상 3년 미만
   - ⓔ 3년 이상 5년 미만 ⓕ 5년 이상

3. 귀하께서 응시하고 계신 고사장에 대한 만족도는?
   - ⓐ 0점 ⓑ 1점
   - ⓒ 2점 ⓓ 3점
   - ⓔ 4점 ⓕ 5점

4. 최근 2년내 TEPS 응시횟수는?
   - ⓐ 없다 ⓑ 1회
   - ⓒ 2회 ⓓ 3회
   - ⓔ 4회 ⓕ 5회 이상

학력	재학	졸업	전공	직업
초등학교	⬯	⬯	인문학 ⬯	공무원 ⬯
중학교	⬯	⬯	사회과학·법학 ⬯	고시준비 ⬯
고등학교	⬯	⬯	경제학·경영학 ⬯	교사 ⬯
전문대학	⬯	⬯	자연과학 ⬯	군인 ⬯
대학교	⬯	⬯	의학·약학·간호학 ⬯	의료인 ⬯
대학원	⬯	⬯	공학 ⬯	자영업 ⬯
			교육학 ⬯	학생 ⬯
			음악·미술·체육 ⬯	회사원 ⬯
			기타 ⬯	무직 ⬯
				기타 ⬯

직종		직책
고위임직원 ⬯	무역 ⬯	임원 ⬯
전문직(과학.공학) ⬯	외환 ⬯	부장 ⬯
전문직(교육) ⬯	자금 ⬯	차장 ⬯
전문직(법률.회계.금융) ⬯	공무 ⬯	과장 ⬯
기술직 ⬯	업무 ⬯	대리 ⬯
영업 ⬯	품질관리 ⬯	계장 ⬯
홍보 ⬯	전산 ⬯	사원 ⬯
총무 ⬯	행정직 ⬯	인턴 ⬯
인사 ⬯	생산관리 ⬯	기타 ⬯
경리 ⬯	서비스 ⬯	
기획 ⬯	기타 ⬯	
구매 ⬯		

앞면(Side1)

TEPS

Test of English Proficiency
developed by
Seoul National University

수험번호 Registration No.	
성명 Name 한글	
성명 Name 한자	

문제지번호 Test Booklet No.	감독관확인란

청해 Listening Comprehension

1–60: ⓐ ⓑ ⓒ ⓓ

문법 Grammar

1–50: ⓐ ⓑ ⓒ ⓓ

어휘 Vocabulary

1–50: ⓐ ⓑ ⓒ ⓓ

독해 Reading Comprehension

1–40: ⓐ ⓑ ⓒ ⓓ

주민등록번호 National ID No.

고사실란 Room No.

수험번호 Registration No.

비밀번호 Password

좌석번호 Seat No.

A B C D E / 1 2 3 4 5 6 7

서약	본인은 필기구 및 기재오류와 답안지 훼손으로 인한 책임을 지고, 부정행위 처리규정을 준수할 것을 서약합니다.	

답안작성시 유의사항

1. 답안 작성은 반드시 **컴퓨터용 싸인펜**을 사용해야 합니다.
2. 답안을 정정할 경우 수정테이프(수정액 불가)를 사용해야 합니다.
3. 본 답안지는 컴퓨터로 처리되므로 훼손해서는 안되며, 답안지 하단의 타이밍마크(|||)를 찢거나, 낙서 등으로 인한 훼손시 불이익이 발생할 수 있습니다.
4. 답안은 문항당 정답을 1개만 골라 ▮와 같이 정확히 기재해야 하며, 필기구 오류나 본인의 부주의로 잘못 표기한 경우에는 당 관리위원회의 OMR판독기의 판독결과에 따르며, 그 결과는 본인이 책임집니다.

   Good ▮ Bad
5. 감독관의 확인이 없는 답안지는 무효처리됩니다.

뒷면(Side2)

TEPS

Test of English Proficiency
developed by
Seoul National University

성명	영문	
	서명	

응시일자 : 20 년 월 일

<부정행위 및 규정위반 처리규정>

1. 모든 부정행위 및 규정위반 적발 및 이에 대한 조치는 TEPS관리위원회의 처리규정에 따라 이루어집니다.

2. 부정행위 및 규정위반 행위는 현장 적발 뿐만 아니라 사후에도 적발될 수 있으며 모두 동일한 조치가 취해집니다.

3. 부정행위 적발 시 당해 성적은 무효화되며 사안에 따라 최대 5년까지 TEPS관리위원회에서 주관하는 모든 시험의 응시자격이 제한됩니다.

4. 문제지 이외에 메모를 하는 행위와 시험 문제의 일부 또는 전부를 유출하거나 공개하는 경우 부정행위로 처리됩니다.

5. 각 파트별 시간을 준수하지 않거나, 시험 종료 후 답안 작성을 계속할 경우 규정위반으로 처리됩니다.

성 명 (성 · 이름순으로 기재)

EX H O N G G I L D O N G

A B C D E F G H I J K L M N O P Q R S T U V W X Y Z

단체구분

학생	일반
⬯	⬯

질 문 란

1. 귀하의 TEPS 응시목적은?
ⓐ 입사지원 ⓑ 인사정책
ⓒ 개인실력측정 ⓓ 입시
ⓔ 국가고시 지원 ⓕ 기타

2. 귀하의 영어권 체류 경험은?
ⓐ 없다 ⓑ 6개월 미만
ⓒ 6개월 이상 1년 미만 ⓓ 1년 이상 3년 미만
ⓔ 3년 이상 5년 미만 ⓕ 5년 이상

3. 귀하께서 응시하고 계신 고사장에 대한 만족도는?
ⓐ 0점 ⓑ 1점
ⓒ 2점 ⓓ 3점
ⓔ 4점 ⓕ 5점

4. 최근 2년내 TEPS 응시횟수는?
ⓐ 없다 ⓑ 1회
ⓒ 2회 ⓓ 3회
ⓔ 4회 ⓕ 5회 이상

학력	재학	졸업	전공	직업
초등학교	⬯	⬯	인문학 ⬯	공무원 ⬯
중학교	⬯	⬯	사회과학 · 법학 ⬯	고시준비 ⬯
고등학교	⬯	⬯	경제학 · 경영학 ⬯	교사 ⬯
전문대학	⬯	⬯	자연과학 ⬯	군인 ⬯
대학교	⬯	⬯	의학 · 약학 · 간호학 ⬯	의료인 ⬯
대학원	⬯	⬯	공학 ⬯	자영업 ⬯
			교육학 ⬯	학생 ⬯
			음악 · 미술 · 체육 ⬯	회사원 ⬯
			기타 ⬯	무직 ⬯
				기타 ⬯

직종		직책
고위임직원 ⬯	무역 ⬯	임원 ⬯
전문직(과학,공학) ⬯	외환 ⬯	부장 ⬯
전문직(교육) ⬯	자금 ⬯	차장 ⬯
전문직(법률,회계,금융) ⬯	공무 ⬯	과장 ⬯
기술직 ⬯	업무 ⬯	대리 ⬯
영업 ⬯	품질관리 ⬯	계장 ⬯
홍보 ⬯	전산 ⬯	사원 ⬯
총무 ⬯	행정직 ⬯	인턴 ⬯
인사 ⬯	생산관리 ⬯	기타 ⬯
경리 ⬯	서비스 ⬯	
기획 ⬯	기타 ⬯	
구매 ⬯		

앞면(Side1)

TEPS

Test of English Proficiency
developed by
Seoul National University

수험번호 Registration No.	
성명 Name 한글	
성명 Name 한자	

문 제 지 번 호 Test Booklet No.	감독관확인란

청 해 Listening Comprehension

1–60 ⓐ ⓑ ⓒ ⓓ

문 법 Grammar

1–50 ⓐ ⓑ ⓒ ⓓ

어 휘 Vocabulary

1–50 ⓐ ⓑ ⓒ ⓓ

독 해 Reading Comprehension

1–40 ⓐ ⓑ ⓒ ⓓ

주 민 등 록 번 호 National ID No.

고사실란 Room No.

수 험 번 호 Registration No.

비밀번호 Password

좌석번호 Seat No.

A B C D E / 1 2 3 4 5 6 7

서 약	본인은 필기구 및 기재오류와 답안지 훼손으로 인한 책임을 지고, 부정행위 처리규정을 준수할 것을 서약합니다.	

답안작성시 유의사항

1. 답안 작성은 반드시 **컴퓨터용 싸인펜**을 사용해야 합니다.
2. 답안을 정정할 경우 수정테이프(수정액 불가)를 사용해야 합니다.
3. 본 답안지는 컴퓨터로 처리되므로 훼손해서는 안되며, 답안지 하단의 타이밍마크(┃┃┃)를 찢거나, 낙서 등으로 인한 훼손시 불이익이 발생할 수 있습니다.
4. 답안은 문항당 정답을 1개만 골라 ● 와 같이 정확히 기재해야 하며, 필기구 오류나 본인의 부주의로 잘못 표기한 경우에는 당 관리위원회의 OMR판독기의 판독결과에 따르며, 그 결과는 본인이 책임집니다.
   Good ● Bad
5. 감독관의 확인이 없는 답안지는 무효처리됩니다.

뒷면(Side2)

TEPS

Test of English Proficiency
developed by
Seoul National University

성명	영문	
	서명	

응시일자 : 20 년 월 일

<부정행위 및 규정위반 처리규정>

1. 모든 부정행위 및 규정위반 적발 및 이에 대한 조치는 TEPS관리위원회의 처리규정에 따라 이루어집니다.

2. 부정행위 및 규정위반 행위는 현장 적발 뿐만 아니라 사후에도 적발될 수 있으며 모두 동일한 조치가 취해집니다.

3. 부정행위 적발 시 당해 성적은 무효화되며 사안에 따라 최대 5년까지 TEPS관리위원회에서 주관하는 모든 시험의 응시자격이 제한됩니다.

4. 문제지 이외에 메모를 하는 행위와 시험 문제의 일부 또는 전부를 유출하거나 공개하는 경우 부정행위로 처리됩니다.

5. 각 파트별 시간을 준수하지 않거나, 시험 종료 후 답안 작성을 계속할 경우 규정위반으로 처리됩니다.

성 명 (성 · 이름순으로 기재)

EX	H	O	N	G		G	I	L		D	O	N	G							
A	A	A	A	A	A	A	A	A	A	A	A	A	A	A	A	A	A	A	A	A
B	B	B	B	B	B	B	B	B	B	B	B	B	B	B	B	B	B	B	B	B
C	C	C	C	C	C	C	C	C	C	C	C	C	C	C	C	C	C	C	C	C
D	D	D	D	D	D	D	D	D	D	D	D	D	D	D	D	D	D	D	D	D
E	E	E	E	E	E	E	E	E	E	E	E	E	E	E	E	E	E	E	E	E
F	F	F	F	F	F	F	F	F	F	F	F	F	F	F	F	F	F	F	F	F
G	G	G	G	G	G	G	G	G	G	G	G	G	G	G	G	G	G	G	G	G
H	H	H	H	H	H	H	H	H	H	H	H	H	H	H	H	H	H	H	H	H
I	I	I	I	I	I	I	I	I	I	I	I	I	I	I	I	I	I	I	I	I
J	J	J	J	J	J	J	J	J	J	J	J	J	J	J	J	J	J	J	J	J
K	K	K	K	K	K	K	K	K	K	K	K	K	K	K	K	K	K	K	K	K
L	L	L	L	L	L	L	L	L	L	L	L	L	L	L	L	L	L	L	L	L
M	M	M	M	M	M	M	M	M	M	M	M	M	M	M	M	M	M	M	M	M
N	N	N	N	N	N	N	N	N	N	N	N	N	N	N	N	N	N	N	N	N
O	O	O	O	O	O	O	O	O	O	O	O	O	O	O	O	O	O	O	O	O
P	P	P	P	P	P	P	P	P	P	P	P	P	P	P	P	P	P	P	P	P
Q	Q	Q	Q	Q	Q	Q	Q	Q	Q	Q	Q	Q	Q	Q	Q	Q	Q	Q	Q	Q
R	R	R	R	R	R	R	R	R	R	R	R	R	R	R	R	R	R	R	R	R
S	S	S	S	S	S	S	S	S	S	S	S	S	S	S	S	S	S	S	S	S
T	T	T	T	T	T	T	T	T	T	T	T	T	T	T	T	T	T	T	T	T
U	U	U	U	U	U	U	U	U	U	U	U	U	U	U	U	U	U	U	U	U
V	V	V	V	V	V	V	V	V	V	V	V	V	V	V	V	V	V	V	V	V
W	W	W	W	W	W	W	W	W	W	W	W	W	W	W	W	W	W	W	W	W
X	X	X	X	X	X	X	X	X	X	X	X	X	X	X	X	X	X	X	X	X
Y	Y	Y	Y	Y	Y	Y	Y	Y	Y	Y	Y	Y	Y	Y	Y	Y	Y	Y	Y	Y
Z	Z	Z	Z	Z	Z	Z	Z	Z	Z	Z	Z	Z	Z	Z	Z	Z	Z	Z	Z	Z

단체구분

학생	일반
( )	( )

질 문 란

1. 귀하의 TEPS 응시목적은?
ⓐ 입사지원 ⓑ 인사정책
ⓒ 개인실력측정 ⓓ 입시
ⓔ 국가고시 지원 ⓕ 기타

2. 귀하의 영어권 체류 경험은?
ⓐ 없다 ⓑ 6개월 미만
ⓒ 6개월 이상 1년 미만 ⓓ 1년 이상 3년 미만
ⓔ 3년 이상 5년 미만 ⓕ 5년 이상

3. 귀하께서 응시하고 계신 고사장에 대한 만족도는?
ⓐ 0점 ⓑ 1점
ⓒ 2점 ⓓ 3점
ⓔ 4점 ⓕ 5점

4. 최근 2년내 TEPS 응시횟수는?
ⓐ 없다 ⓑ 1회
ⓒ 2회 ⓓ 3회
ⓔ 4회 ⓕ 5회 이상

학력	재학	졸업	전공	직업
초등학교	( )	( )	인문학 ( )	공무원 ( )
중학교	( )	( )	사회과학 · 법학 ( )	고시준비 ( )
고등학교	( )	( )	경제학 · 경영학 ( )	교사 ( )
전문대학	( )	( )	자연과학 ( )	군인 ( )
대학교	( )	( )	의학 · 약학 · 간호학 ( )	의료인 ( )
대학원	( )	( )	공학 ( )	자영업 ( )
			교육학 ( )	학생 ( )
			음악 · 미술 · 체육 ( )	회사원 ( )
			기타 ( )	무직 ( )
				기타 ( )

직종		직책
고위임직원 ( )	무역 ( )	임원 ( )
전문직(과학.공학) ( )	외환 ( )	부장 ( )
전문직(교육) ( )	자금 ( )	차장 ( )
전문직(법률.회계.금융) ( )	공무 ( )	과장 ( )
기술직 ( )	업무 ( )	대리 ( )
영업 ( )	품질관리 ( )	계장 ( )
홍보 ( )	전산 ( )	사원 ( )
총무 ( )	행정직 ( )	인턴 ( )
인사 ( )	생산관리 ( )	기타 ( )
경리 ( )	서비스 ( )	
기획 ( )	기타 ( )	
구매 ( )		

앞면(Side1)

TEPS

Test of English Proficiency
developed by
Seoul National University

수험번호 Registration No.		
성명 Name	한글	
	한자	

문제지번호 Test Booklet No.

감독관확인란

청해 Listening Comprehension

No.					No.					No.				
1	a	b	c	d	26	a	b	c	d	51	a	b	c	d
2	a	b	c	d	27	a	b	c	d	52	a	b	c	d
3	a	b	c	d	28	a	b	c	d	53	a	b	c	d
4	a	b	c	d	29	a	b	c	d	54	a	b	c	d
5	a	b	c	d	30	a	b	c	d	55	a	b	c	d
6	a	b	c	d	31	a	b	c	d	56	a	b	c	d
7	a	b	c	d	32	a	b	c	d	57	a	b	c	d
8	a	b	c	d	33	a	b	c	d	58	a	b	c	d
9	a	b	c	d	34	a	b	c	d	59	a	b	c	d
10	a	b	c	d	35	a	b	c	d	60	a	b	c	d
11	a	b	c	d	36	a	b	c	d					
12	a	b	c	d	37	a	b	c	d					
13	a	b	c	d	38	a	b	c	d					
14	a	b	c	d	39	a	b	c	d					
15	a	b	c	d	40	a	b	c	d					
16	a	b	c	d	41	a	b	c	d					
17	a	b	c	d	42	a	b	c	d					
18	a	b	c	d	43	a	b	c	d					
19	a	b	c	d	44	a	b	c	d					
20	a	b	c	d	45	a	b	c	d					
21	a	b	c	d	46	a	b	c	d					
22	a	b	c	d	47	a	b	c	d					
23	a	b	c	d	48	a	b	c	d					
24	a	b	c	d	49	a	b	c	d					
25	a	b	c	d	50	a	b	c	d					

문법 Grammar

No.					No.				
1	a	b	c	d	26	a	b	c	d
2	a	b	c	d	27	a	b	c	d
3	a	b	c	d	28	a	b	c	d
4	a	b	c	d	29	a	b	c	d
5	a	b	c	d	30	a	b	c	d
6	a	b	c	d	31	a	b	c	d
7	a	b	c	d	32	a	b	c	d
8	a	b	c	d	33	a	b	c	d
9	a	b	c	d	34	a	b	c	d
10	a	b	c	d	35	a	b	c	d
11	a	b	c	d	36	a	b	c	d
12	a	b	c	d	37	a	b	c	d
13	a	b	c	d	38	a	b	c	d
14	a	b	c	d	39	a	b	c	d
15	a	b	c	d	40	a	b	c	d
16	a	b	c	d	41	a	b	c	d
17	a	b	c	d	42	a	b	c	d
18	a	b	c	d	43	a	b	c	d
19	a	b	c	d	44	a	b	c	d
20	a	b	c	d	45	a	b	c	d
21	a	b	c	d	46	a	b	c	d
22	a	b	c	d	47	a	b	c	d
23	a	b	c	d	48	a	b	c	d
24	a	b	c	d	49	a	b	c	d
25	a	b	c	d	50	a	b	c	d

어휘 Vocabulary

No.					No.				
1	a	b	c	d	26	a	b	c	d
2	a	b	c	d	27	a	b	c	d
3	a	b	c	d	28	a	b	c	d
4	a	b	c	d	29	a	b	c	d
5	a	b	c	d	30	a	b	c	d
6	a	b	c	d	31	a	b	c	d
7	a	b	c	d	32	a	b	c	d
8	a	b	c	d	33	a	b	c	d
9	a	b	c	d	34	a	b	c	d
10	a	b	c	d	35	a	b	c	d
11	a	b	c	d	36	a	b	c	d
12	a	b	c	d	37	a	b	c	d
13	a	b	c	d	38	a	b	c	d
14	a	b	c	d	39	a	b	c	d
15	a	b	c	d	40	a	b	c	d
16	a	b	c	d	41	a	b	c	d
17	a	b	c	d	42	a	b	c	d
18	a	b	c	d	43	a	b	c	d
19	a	b	c	d	44	a	b	c	d
20	a	b	c	d	45	a	b	c	d
21	a	b	c	d	46	a	b	c	d
22	a	b	c	d	47	a	b	c	d
23	a	b	c	d	48	a	b	c	d
24	a	b	c	d	49	a	b	c	d
25	a	b	c	d	50	a	b	c	d

독해 Reading Comprehension

No.					No.				
1	a	b	c	d	26	a	b	c	d
2	a	b	c	d	27	a	b	c	d
3	a	b	c	d	28	a	b	c	d
4	a	b	c	d	29	a	b	c	d
5	a	b	c	d	30	a	b	c	d
6	a	b	c	d	31	a	b	c	d
7	a	b	c	d	32	a	b	c	d
8	a	b	c	d	33	a	b	c	d
9	a	b	c	d	34	a	b	c	d
10	a	b	c	d	35	a	b	c	d
11	a	b	c	d	36	a	b	c	d
12	a	b	c	d	37	a	b	c	d
13	a	b	c	d	38	a	b	c	d
14	a	b	c	d	39	a	b	c	d
15	a	b	c	d	40	a	b	c	d
16	a	b	c	d					
17	a	b	c	d					
18	a	b	c	d					
19	a	b	c	d					
20	a	b	c	d					
21	a	b	c	d					
22	a	b	c	d					
23	a	b	c	d					
24	a	b	c	d					
25	a	b	c	d					

주민등록번호 National ID No.

						–							
0	0	0	0	0	0			0	0	0	0	0	0
1	1	1	1	1	1		1	1	1	1	1	1	1
2	2		2	2	2		2	2	2	2	2	2	2
3	3		3	3	3		3	3	3	3	3	3	3
4	4		4		4		4	4	4	4	4	4	4
5	5		5		5	–	5	5	5	5	5	5	5
6	6		6		6		6	6	6	6	6	6	6
7	7		7		7		7	7	7	7	7	7	7
8	8		8		8		8	8	8	8	8	8	8
9	9		9		9		9	9	9	9	9	9	9

고사실란 Room No.

0	0
1	1
2	2
3	3
4	4
5	5
	6
	7
	8
	9

수험번호 Registration No.

0	0	0	0	0	0	0
1	1	1	1	1	1	1
2	2	2	2	2	2	2
3	3	3	3	3	3	3
4	4	4	4	4	4	4
5	5	5	5	5	5	5
6	6	6	6	6	6	6
7	7	7	7	7	7	7
8	8	8	8	8	8	8
9	9	9	9	9	9	9

비밀번호 Password

0	0	0	0
1	1	1	1
2	2	2	2
3	3	3	3
4	4	4	4
5	5	5	5
6	6	6	6
7	7	7	7
8	8	8	8
9	9	9	9

좌석번호 Seat No.

A	1
B	2
C	3
D	4
E	5
	6
	7

서 약	본인은 필기구 및 기재오류와 답안지 훼손으로 인한 책임을 지고, 부정행위 처리규정을 준수할 것을 서약합니다.	

답안작성시 유의사항

1. 답안 작성은 반드시 **컴퓨터용 싸인펜**을 사용해야 합니다.
2. 답안을 정정할 경우 수정테이프(수정액 불가)를 사용해야 합니다.
3. 본 답안지는 컴퓨터로 처리되므로 훼손해서는 안되며, 답안지 하단의 타이밍마크(|||)를 찢거나, 낙서 등으로 인한 훼손시 불이익이 발생할 수 있습니다.
4. 답안은 문항당 정답을 1개만 골라 ▮와 같이 정확히 기재해야 하며, 필기구 오류나 본인의 부주의로 잘못 표기한 경우에는 당 관리위원회의 OMR판독기의 판독결과에 따르며, 그 결과는 본인이 책임집니다.

Good ▮ Bad

5. 감독관의 확인이 없는 답안지는 무효처리됩니다.

뒷면(Side2)

TEPS

Test of English Proficiency
developed by
Seoul National University

성명	영문	
	서명	

응시일자 : 20　　년　　월　　일

<부정행위 및 규정위반 처리규정>

1. 모든 부정행위 및 규정위반 적발 및 이에 대한 조치는 TEPS관리위원회의 처리규정에 따라 이루어집니다.

2. 부정행위 및 규정위반 행위는 현장 적발 뿐만 아니라 사후에도 적발될 수 있으며 모두 동일한 조치가 취해 집니다.

3. 부정행위 적발 시 당해 성적은 무효화되며 사안에 따라 최대 5년까지 TEPS관리위원회에서 주관하는 모든 시험의 응시자격이 제한됩니다.

4. 문제지 이외에 메모를 하는 행위와 시험 문제의 일부 또는 전부를 유출하거나 공개하는 경우 부정행위로 처리됩니다.

5. 각 파트별 시간을 준수하지 않거나, 시험 종료 후 답안 작성을 계속할 경우 규정위반으로 처리됩니다.

성　명 (성 · 이름순으로 기재)

EX H O N G　G I L　D O N G

A
B
C
D
E
F
G
H
I
J
K
L
M
N
O
P
Q
R
S
T
U
V
W
X
Y
Z

단체구분

학생	일반
○	○

질 문 란

1. 귀하의 TEPS 응시목적은?
ⓐ 입사지원　ⓑ 인사정책
ⓒ 개인실력측정　ⓓ 입시
ⓔ 국가고시 지원　ⓕ 기타

2. 귀하의 영어권 체류 경험은?
ⓐ 없다　ⓑ 6개월 미만
ⓒ 6개월 이상 1년 미만　ⓓ 1년 이상 3년 미만
ⓔ 3년 이상 5년 미만　ⓕ 5년 이상

3. 귀하께서 응시하고 계신 고사장에 대한 만족도는?
ⓐ 0점　ⓑ 1점
ⓒ 2점　ⓓ 3점
ⓔ 4점　ⓕ 5점

4. 최근 2년내 TEPS 응시횟수는?
ⓐ 없다　ⓑ 1회
ⓒ 2회　ⓓ 3회
ⓔ 4회　ⓕ 5회 이상

학력	재학	졸업	전공	직업
초등학교	○	○	인문학 ○	공무원 ○
중학교	○	○	사회과학 · 법학 ○	고시준비 ○
고등학교	○	○	경제학 · 경영학 ○	교사 ○
전문대학	○	○	자연과학 ○	군인 ○
대학교	○	○	의학 · 약학 · 간호학 ○	의료인 ○
대학원	○	○	공학 ○	자영업 ○
			교육학 ○	학생 ○
			음악 · 미술 · 체육 ○	회사원 ○
			기타 ○	무직 ○
				기타 ○

직종		직책
고위임직원 ○	무역 ○	임원 ○
전문직(과학,공학) ○	외환 ○	부장 ○
전문직(교육) ○	자금 ○	차장 ○
전문직(법률,회계,금융) ○	공무 ○	과장 ○
기술직 ○	업무 ○	대리 ○
영업 ○	품질관리 ○	계장 ○
홍보 ○	전산 ○	사원 ○
총무 ○	행정직 ○	인턴 ○
인사 ○	생산관리 ○	기타 ○
경리 ○	서비스 ○	
기획 ○	기타 ○	
구매 ○		

앞면(Side1)

TEPS

Test of English Proficiency
developed by
Seoul National University

수험번호 Registration No.	
성명 Name 한글	
성명 Name 한자	

문 제 지 번 호 Test Booklet No.	감독관확인란

청 해 Listening Comprehension

No.					No.					No.				
1	a	b	c	d	26	a	b	c	d	51	a	b	c	d
2	a	b	c	d	27	a	b	c	d	52	a	b	c	d
3	a	b	c	d	28	a	b	c	d	53	a	b	c	d
4	a	b	c	d	29	a	b	c	d	54	a	b	c	d
5	a	b	c	d	30	a	b	c	d	55	a	b	c	d
6	a	b	c	d	31	a	b	c	d	56	a	b	c	d
7	a	b	c	d	32	a	b	c	d	57	a	b	c	d
8	a	b	c	d	33	a	b	c	d	58	a	b	c	d
9	a	b	c	d	34	a	b	c	d	59	a	b	c	d
10	a	b	c	d	35	a	b	c	d	60	a	b	c	d
11	a	b	c	d	36	a	b	c	d					
12	a	b	c	d	37	a	b	c	d					
13	a	b	c	d	38	a	b	c	d					
14	a	b	c	d	39	a	b	c	d					
15	a	b	c	d	40	a	b	c	d					
16	a	b	c	d	41	a	b	c	d					
17	a	b	c	d	42	a	b	c	d					
18	a	b	c	d	43	a	b	c	d					
19	a	b	c	d	44	a	b	c	d					
20	a	b	c	d	45	a	b	c	d					
21	a	b	c	d	46	a	b	c	d					
22	a	b	c	d	47	a	b	c	d					
23	a	b	c	d	48	a	b	c	d					
24	a	b	c	d	49	a	b	c	d					
25	a	b	c	d	50	a	b	c	d					

문 법 Grammar

No.					No.				
1	a	b	c	d	26	a	b	c	d
2	a	b	c	d	27	a	b	c	d
3	a	b	c	d	28	a	b	c	d
4	a	b	c	d	29	a	b	c	d
5	a	b	c	d	30	a	b	c	d
6	a	b	c	d	31	a	b	c	d
7	a	b	c	d	32	a	b	c	d
8	a	b	c	d	33	a	b	c	d
9	a	b	c	d	34	a	b	c	d
10	a	b	c	d	35	a	b	c	d
11	a	b	c	d	36	a	b	c	d
12	a	b	c	d	37	a	b	c	d
13	a	b	c	d	38	a	b	c	d
14	a	b	c	d	39	a	b	c	d
15	a	b	c	d	40	a	b	c	d
16	a	b	c	d	41	a	b	c	d
17	a	b	c	d	42	a	b	c	d
18	a	b	c	d	43	a	b	c	d
19	a	b	c	d	44	a	b	c	d
20	a	b	c	d	45	a	b	c	d
21	a	b	c	d	46	a	b	c	d
22	a	b	c	d	47	a	b	c	d
23	a	b	c	d	48	a	b	c	d
24	a	b	c	d	49	a	b	c	d
25	a	b	c	d	50	a	b	c	d

어 휘 Vocabulary

No.					No.				
1	a	b	c	d	26	a	b	c	d
2	a	b	c	d	27	a	b	c	d
3	a	b	c	d	28	a	b	c	d
4	a	b	c	d	29	a	b	c	d
5	a	b	c	d	30	a	b	c	d
6	a	b	c	d	31	a	b	c	d
7	a	b	c	d	32	a	b	c	d
8	a	b	c	d	33	a	b	c	d
9	a	b	c	d	34	a	b	c	d
10	a	b	c	d	35	a	b	c	d
11	a	b	c	d	36	a	b	c	d
12	a	b	c	d	37	a	b	c	d
13	a	b	c	d	38	a	b	c	d
14	a	b	c	d	39	a	b	c	d
15	a	b	c	d	40	a	b	c	d
16	a	b	c	d	41	a	b	c	d
17	a	b	c	d	42	a	b	c	d
18	a	b	c	d	43	a	b	c	d
19	a	b	c	d	44	a	b	c	d
20	a	b	c	d	45	a	b	c	d
21	a	b	c	d	46	a	b	c	d
22	a	b	c	d	47	a	b	c	d
23	a	b	c	d	48	a	b	c	d
24	a	b	c	d	49	a	b	c	d
25	a	b	c	d	50	a	b	c	d

독 해 Reading Comprehension

No.					No.				
1	a	b	c	d	26	a	b	c	d
2	a	b	c	d	27	a	b	c	d
3	a	b	c	d	28	a	b	c	d
4	a	b	c	d	29	a	b	c	d
5	a	b	c	d	30	a	b	c	d
6	a	b	c	d	31	a	b	c	d
7	a	b	c	d	32	a	b	c	d
8	a	b	c	d	33	a	b	c	d
9	a	b	c	d	34	a	b	c	d
10	a	b	c	d	35	a	b	c	d
11	a	b	c	d	36	a	b	c	d
12	a	b	c	d	37	a	b	c	d
13	a	b	c	d	38	a	b	c	d
14	a	b	c	d	39	a	b	c	d
15	a	b	c	d	40	a	b	c	d
16	a	b	c	d					
17	a	b	c	d					
18	a	b	c	d					
19	a	b	c	d					
20	a	b	c	d					
21	a	b	c	d					
22	a	b	c	d					
23	a	b	c	d					
24	a	b	c	d					
25	a	b	c	d					

주 민 등 록 번 호 National ID No.

						–							
0	0	0	0	0	0			0	0	0	0	0	0
1	1	1	1	1	1		1	1	1	1	1	1	1
2	2		2	2	2		2	2	2	2	2	2	2
3	3		3	3	3		3	3	3	3	3	3	3
4	4		4		4	–	4	4	4	4	4	4	4
5	5		5		5		5	5	5	5	5	5	5
6	6		6		6		6	6	6	6	6	6	6
7	7		7		7		7	7	7	7	7	7	7
8	8		8		8		8	8	8	8	8	8	8
9	9		9		9		9	9	9	9	9	9	9

고사실란 Room No.

0	0
1	1
2	2
3	3
4	4
5	5
	6
	7
	8
	9

수 험 번 호 Registration No.

0	0	0	0	0	0	0
1	1	1	1	1	1	1
2	2	2	2	2	2	2
3	3	3	3	3	3	3
4	4	4	4	4	4	4
5	5	5	5	5	5	5
6	6	6	6	6	6	6
7	7	7	7	7	7	7
8	8	8	8	8	8	8
9	9	9	9	9	9	9

비밀번호 Password

0	0	0	0
1	1	1	1
2	2	2	2
3	3	3	3
4	4	4	4
5	5	5	5
6	6	6	6
7	7	7	7
8	8	8	8
9	9	9	9

좌석번호 Seat No.

A	1
B	2
C	3
D	4
E	5
	6
	7

서 약 **본인은 필기구 및 기재오류와 답안지 훼손으로 인한 책임을 지고, 부정행위 처리규정을 준수할 것을 서약합니다.**

답안작성시 유의사항

1. 답안 작성은 반드시 **컴퓨터용 싸인펜**을 사용해야 합니다.
2. 답안을 정정할 경우 수정테이프(수정액 불가)를 사용해야 합니다.
3. 본 답안지는 컴퓨터로 처리되므로 훼손해서는 안되며, 답안지 하단의 타이밍마크(|||)를 찢거나, 낙서 등으로 인한 훼손시 불이익이 발생할 수 있습니다.
4. 답안은 문항당 정답을 1개만 골라 ▮와 같이 정확히 기재해야 하며, 필기구 오류나 본인의 부주의로 잘못 표기한 경우에는 당 관리위원회의 OMR판독기의 판독결과에 따르며, 그 결과는 본인이 책임집니다.
   Good ▮ Bad
5. 감독관의 확인이 없는 답안지는 무효처리됩니다.

뒷면(Side2)

TEPS

Test of English Proficiency
developed by
Seoul National University

성명	영문	
	서명	

응시일자 : 20 년 월 일

<부정행위 및 규정위반 처리규정>

1. 모든 부정행위 및 규정위반 적발 및 이에 대한 조치는 TEPS관리위원회의 처리규정에 따라 이루어집니다.
2. 부정행위 및 규정위반 행위는 현장 적발 뿐만 아니라 사후에도 적발될 수 있으며 모두 동일한 조치가 취해집니다.
3. 부정행위 적발 시 당해 성적은 무효화되며 사안에 따라 최대 5년까지 TEPS관리위원회에서 주관하는 모든 시험의 응시자격이 제한됩니다.
4. 문제지 이외에 메모를 하는 행위와 시험 문제의 일부 또는 전부를 유출하거나 공개하는 경우 부정행위로 처리됩니다.
5. 각 파트별 시간을 준수하지 않거나, 시험 종료 후 답안 작성을 계속할 경우 규정위반으로 처리됩니다.

성 명 (성·이름순으로 기재)

EX	H	O	N	G		G	I	L		D	O	N	G							
A	A	A	A	A	A	A	A	A	A	A	A	A	A	A	A	A	A	A	A	A
B	B	B	B	B	B	B	B	B	B	B	B	B	B	B	B	B	B	B	B	B
C	C	C	C	C	C	C	C	C	C	C	C	C	C	C	C	C	C	C	C	C
D	D	D	D	D	D	D	D	D	D	D	D	D	D	D	D	D	D	D	D	D
E	E	E	E	E	E	E	E	E	E	E	E	E	E	E	E	E	E	E	E	E
F	F	F	F	F	F	F	F	F	F	F	F	F	F	F	F	F	F	F	F	F
G	G	G	G	G	G	G	G	G	G	G	G	G	G	G	G	G	G	G	G	G
H	H	H	H	H	H	H	H	H	H	H	H	H	H	H	H	H	H	H	H	H
I	I	I	I	I	I	I	I	I	I	I	I	I	I	I	I	I	I	I	I	I
J	J	J	J	J	J	J	J	J	J	J	J	J	J	J	J	J	J	J	J	J
K	K	K	K	K	K	K	K	K	K	K	K	K	K	K	K	K	K	K	K	K
L	L	L	L	L	L	L	L	L	L	L	L	L	L	L	L	L	L	L	L	L
M	M	M	M	M	M	M	M	M	M	M	M	M	M	M	M	M	M	M	M	M
N	N	N	N	N	N	N	N	N	N	N	N	N	N	N	N	N	N	N	N	N
O	O	O	O	O	O	O	O	O	O	O	O	O	O	O	O	O	O	O	O	O
P	P	P	P	P	P	P	P	P	P	P	P	P	P	P	P	P	P	P	P	P
Q	Q	Q	Q	Q	Q	Q	Q	Q	Q	Q	Q	Q	Q	Q	Q	Q	Q	Q	Q	Q
R	R	R	R	R	R	R	R	R	R	R	R	R	R	R	R	R	R	R	R	R
S	S	S	S	S	S	S	S	S	S	S	S	S	S	S	S	S	S	S	S	S
T	T	T	T	T	T	T	T	T	T	T	T	T	T	T	T	T	T	T	T	T
U	U	U	U	U	U	U	U	U	U	U	U	U	U	U	U	U	U	U	U	U
V	V	V	V	V	V	V	V	V	V	V	V	V	V	V	V	V	V	V	V	V
W	W	W	W	W	W	W	W	W	W	W	W	W	W	W	W	W	W	W	W	W
X	X	X	X	X	X	X	X	X	X	X	X	X	X	X	X	X	X	X	X	X
Y	Y	Y	Y	Y	Y	Y	Y	Y	Y	Y	Y	Y	Y	Y	Y	Y	Y	Y	Y	Y
Z	Z	Z	Z	Z	Z	Z	Z	Z	Z	Z	Z	Z	Z	Z	Z	Z	Z	Z	Z	Z

단체구분

학생	일반
○	○

질 문 란

1. 귀하의 TEPS 응시목적은?
   a 입사지원 b 인사정책
   c 개인실력측정 d 입시
   e 국가고시 지원 f 기타

2. 귀하의 영어권 체류 경험은?
   a 없다 b 6개월 미만
   c 6개월 이상 1년 미만 d 1년 이상 3년 미만
   e 3년 이상 5년 미만 f 5년 이상

3. 귀하께서 응시하고 계신 고사장에 대한 만족도는?
   a 0점 b 1점
   c 2점 d 3점
   e 4점 f 5점

4. 최근 2년내 TEPS 응시횟수는?
   a 없다 b 1회
   c 2회 d 3회
   e 4회 f 5회 이상

학력	재학	졸업	전공	직업
초등학교	○	○	인문학 ○	공무원 ○
중학교	○	○	사회과학·법학 ○	고시준비 ○
고등학교	○	○	경제학·경영학 ○	교사 ○
전문대학	○	○	자연과학 ○	군인 ○
대학교	○	○	의학·약학·간호학 ○	의료인 ○
대학원	○	○	공학 ○	자영업 ○
			교육학 ○	학생 ○
			음악·미술·체육 ○	회사원 ○
			기타 ○	무직 ○
				기타 ○

직종		직책
고위임직원 ○	무역 ○	임원 ○
전문직(과학.공학) ○	외환 ○	부장 ○
전문직(교육) ○	자금 ○	차장 ○
전문직(법률.회계.금융) ○	공무 ○	과장 ○
기술직 ○	업무 ○	대리 ○
영업 ○	품질관리 ○	계장 ○
홍보 ○	전산 ○	사원 ○
총무 ○	행정직 ○	인턴 ○
인사 ○	생산관리 ○	기타 ○
경리 ○	서비스 ○	
기획 ○	기타 ○	
구매 ○		